DEALS
DANGER
DESTINY

JOHN LaCASSE
WITH BARBARA KINDNESS

Mechanicsburg, PA USA

Published by Sunbury Press, Inc.
Mechanicsburg, Pennsylvania

www.sunburypress.com

Copyright © 2023 by John LaCasse.
Cover Copyright © 2023 by Sunbury Press, Inc.

Sunbury Press supports copyright. Copyright fuels creativity, encourages diverse voices, promotes free speech, and creates a vibrant culture. Thank you for buying an authorized edition of this book and for complying with copyright laws by not reproducing, scanning, or distributing any part of it in any form without permission. You are supporting writers and allowing Sunbury Press to continue to publish books for every reader. For information contact Sunbury Press, Inc., Subsidiary Rights Dept., PO Box 548, Boiling Springs, PA 17007 USA or legal@sunburypress.com.

For information about special discounts for bulk purchases, please contact Sunbury Press Orders Dept. at (855) 338-8359 or orders@sunburypress.com.

To request one of our authors for speaking engagements or book signings, please contact Sunbury Press Publicity Dept. at publicity@sunburypress.com.

FIRST SUNBURY PRESS EDITION: July 2023

Set in Adobe Garamond | Interior design by Crystal Devine | Cover by Lawrence Knorr | Edited by Lawrence Knorr | Photos by Christine Burgoyne and Charles Loomis.

Publisher's Cataloging-in-Publication Data
Names: LaCasse, John, author.
Title: Deals danger destiny / John LaCasse with Barbara Kindness.
Description: First trade paperback edition. | Mechanicsburg, PA : Sunbury Press, 2023.
Summary: John LaCasse ricochets through life, making deals and dodging traps from bad guys as he threads the needle between business fact and fantasy. Then after spending 17 years questioning the worth of faculty, he earns his own Ph.D., becoming a Fourth Dimension research junkie in Paris, where he manages to manifest the most important theologian in history.
Identifiers: ISBN : 979-8-88819-106-4 (softcover) | ISBN : 979-8-88819-107-1 (ePub).
Subjects: BIOGRAPHY & AUTOBIOGRAPHY / Personal Memoirs | BIOGRAPHY & AUTOBIOGRAPHY / Business | EDUCATION / Teaching / Methods & Strategies.

Product of the United States of America
0 1 1 2 3 5 8 13 21 34 55

For the Love of Books!

Dedicated to the memory of

My two boys

John LaCasse 1964–2012

Jeff LaCasse 1968–1989

Their brothers

Bob LaCasse

Erik LaCasse

And their remarkable mothers

Carol LaCasse and Karen LaCasse

INTRODUCTION

Sometimes we don't have the stamina to say or write what we feel. Most of our choices are our own. It takes time. It just takes time to step into the arena of growing up and maturing to middle age and old with a manifesto in hand. *This is what I did, and this is what I think.* Then there's the problem of the ordinary. Was my life ordinary?

This story meets those concerns straightaway. Nothing ordinary here—nothing!

The first part of the story is about how a young man had to react his way through life. No education. Just a talent for rhetoric that he could monetize into a lifestyle beyond the reach of most. And, yet, when reaching for justice, someone is there to kill you.

Then the confusion and depression that money and power can be a terminal disease. That to fight for power, there is an uneasy association with humanity. Then a shift to curiosity and education. Reaching the highest rung in the academy. To take the experience and lay it on the academic table for students to learn from its authenticity.

And finally, to walk into the light before you get lost in a self-induced death. To walk away from it all and learn the value of random acts of kindness from people who see you as opposed to look at you.

Finally, to win, again, for all the right reasons.

John

So an interviewer asks, "How in the world did you two hook up to write such an intrinsic piece of literature when you seem to be totally opposite in your own personal way of thinking, acting, feeling?"

Well, first off, this is John's story, not mine. It is true that I've had to get inside his head and heart to understand his motives and ways of expressing his mood, whatever it might be. But my main goal was to be sure that the reader throughout the book saw the changes that were happening—sometimes sudden and dramatic, sometimes requiring careful analysis; that they could relate to the emotion of the moment, be it anger, disappointment, fear, resignation, sorrow.

John is the most amazing, complex, genuine person I've ever known, and yes, if you were to use an animal illustration to portray us, you'd probably show the fierce lion in a drawing his dad did, but next to it, you'd have a calm coyote reaching out to stroke the fur of his companion.

He is so well-read and coherent in his thought processes that I know readers will seize the opportunity to enhance their own knowledge of transcendental thinking.

This has been the most educational, heartwarming experience of my lifetime and a constant source of joy and amazement for me. How lucky I feel that John and I met, and, of course, I have my own opinion of how this came about!

Barbara

FOREWORD

Sometimes I sit and do nothing. Sometimes I listen to nothing. Carlo Rovelli, author of *The Order of Time*, says that's listening to time. At some point in time, this becomes a reflection instead of something in the moment. As ordinary people, we inhabit time like fish inhabit water. We know it's there like we know gravity is there. We don't know where—but it's there. The problem is that we are inclined to squander it—time, I mean—until we're out of it.

In the last few months, I realized that the *out-of-time* thing is exactly where I'm positioning myself. And I asked myself, how can that be if I view myself as *scientifically aware, artistically inclined, and energetically centered*? How does someone with those mental credentials run out of time? There is probably some psychological reason grounded in Freud or Fiedler that discusses how we use available resources from higher orders. How we take what God et al. (and so on . . .) give us for granted. If I look at my cat, and she looks back at me, the question becomes: *Are we collectively squandering time?*

For the last ten years, as my cat Guy Noir Bug Detective (whom I call kitty) sits on the windowsill looking back at me, we have had this kind of secret discussion about what I'm doing with my time. I know she thinks I'm wasting it. She says, *Look at me. I have, at best, a tenth amount of your time, and yet you sit there staring at me, listening to nothing—listening to time.*

She says *I wish I could have your time.* I know she is saying that. I know she understands that. I know from research her brain is 95 percent like mine. I know she can hear me and other things up to 38,000 Hz. And somewhere in that 38,000 Hz, she's listening to my brain waste time. So, on this day, I lean in and change my head angle 35 degrees down and 20 degrees to the right. Our eyes lock into position. I give her the old wave-particle double-slit look and utter in the synapse of my silence, *Well, my dear kitty, no more; another book is in the queue.*

What makes my cat and me similar is that some people believe I've lived multiple lives, like the nine lives of the cat. Shiah Sarkowsky (in the foreword of my *Fight for the Quantum*) wrote that I've lived *ten* lives. Laura Loomis (a businesswoman on top of her game) wrote that I "live more lives than anybody she knows."

I don't see it that way necessarily—the multiple lives idea. Conceptually, it establishes a frame for who I am, but, more importantly, it says how I operate in the quintessence of the universe. I react.

I have three previous books in print: *Fight for the Quantum: Essays on Spirituality and Science, After Your Children Die: Finding Yourself in the Fourth Dimension,* and *International Baccalaureate: The Effects of Transcendental Teaching Styles.*

Typically, writers who are finished writing books are also finished reading them. Going back to read previously written books can be stressful because, as *The Order of Time* reports, we do not grasp the actuality of time. Things change. They change enough that what the writer finds in the old book is embarrassingly outdated. Even if the writer is Cicero, Aristotle or Plato, things change. The best approach may be that codices (books) have a useful life and should be given society as their own moment in time.

This could become more expansive when books are bestsellers. It is easier to imagine your bestsellers in categories like Most Copies Sold to Friends and Relatives, Most Popular Bookstore Free Giveaway, or Employee Book-of-the-Month Published by Company Owner. In my imagination, I can see this book becoming a movie. In fact, one of the stories in the book has already been considered for a movie. I suppose *considered for a movie* is some distance from the packed-house multiplex. Regardless, seeing me on the screen as a McCann Erickson A-lister off the Hollywood walk of fame would be fun.

So now, with my strategic position clear, and Hollywood in the queue, I must decide how to punctuate a stream of consciousness and turn that into a book. Like almost all my species, I tend to convert music into reflections. My active times were around the sounds of Al Green, Roberta Flack, Don McLean, Jackson Browne, The O'Jays, and the queen of the last quartile of the 20th century, Helen Reddy. I enjoyed their music, and their lift helped me stay on top of my game. Today, I shall add Elizabeth Gilbert to that list. Not a singer, but a hell of a writer.

It will be fun to watch my cat synthesize my trying to be the writer-alpha-male version of Roberta Flack channeling bestselling author Elizabeth Gilbert as I hum Helen Reddy's anthem from 1971, *I Am Woman*.

In my personal mid-century, there was Gloria Steinem who drew the woman's line in the sand, and it was Helen Reddy who made it real. A decade and a half later, Elizabeth Gilbert took those prospects to a new level as she walked out of one life and into another in *Eat Pray Love*. I should be so lucky that I might be a reflection of, or the male perspective of, Elizabeth Gilbert. In my case, the man who walks from one life into another, and another, and another, who makes decisions on the fly, reinvents himself as situations appear, who views life as his reaction instead of his plan. Maybe the doppelganger, aka Elizabeth Gilbert.

In the social construct of *Bear Cave*, is it possible for a man to model himself after a woman? My position is foursquare behind that notion. Gender is not the criteria for modeling behavior. So, I don't need to become Che Guevara motorcycling down the spine of South America to become a revolutionary, or Christopher Hitchens deciding that God is not great, to write a book. I can be *Myself* reflecting on the multiplex of genders who influenced my life in collective countries and sometimes furious circumstances.

I get to revisualize that I am sitting in Seattle's Four Seasons Hotel atrium across the table from Adriana Salinas. Her brother Carlos, the President of Mexico, couldn't make it. Her husband, Manuel, is still asleep upstairs. Her security detail is all fidgety because they notice I am driving a GMC Sierra 4x4 pickup with no armor, and Adriana wants to ride to the PACCAR Corporate Yacht in my truck. She was about to buy it. I was representing the owner. My truck was stacked with case upon case of champagne. It was explosively dangerous based on capped $Co2$ alone. Then the truck situation is neutralized because Adriana's husband Manuel wakes up, decides he will be late for breakfast, so he has the hotel manager find us in the lobby and invite us to the main dining room for breakfast before we leave. We all file to the dining room like *why those people are being escorted to their table dilettantes.*

From his room, Adriana's husband is concerned about bad form because he is the host and is unclear about protocol. By now, we are at the table (a big round table) surrounded by many men at many tables dressed in black suits with wires in their ears and bulges in their coats. I'm starting to imagine "Chapo" Joaquin Guzman has laced the other tables with his men, just in case yachts are not the reason for this meeting.

Manuel Ricardo Perez is up, showered, dressed, and on his way down. Adriana greets him. Then Manuel walks around the table, touching each of us on one shoulder while leaning into the other. It was a scene lifted straight out of *The Godfather*. Then he sits down and stares at his water. My eyes keep darting around, looking for a baseball bat. Simultaneously, the hotel kitchen staff are rolling out carts of breakfast orders, dozens of them—stacks of them. Manuel, not wanting to offend anyone, ordered everything on the Four Seasons Olympic Hotel breakfast menu—*everything*—and had the whole shebang rolled out for us to decide which entree we might like. Sort of his apology for being late for breakfast.

Or, in the owner's bunker of Harrah's in Las Vegas as Celine Dion walks in for a conversation with the chairman. And she carries herself in a way that does not notice the transparent glass floor with nude women swimming under the conference table.

Or, while I'm standing on the dock and Sam Belzberg walks his wife down the ramp to see the astoundingly impressive mega yacht he just purchased, and she refuses to step on board. "It's ugly," she says. Sam turns to me and says, "*Sell it*," and they walk back to their car.

Or, his brother William (Bill) Belzberg, when I'm about to approach a Chinese delegation about an automotive joint venture in Detroit, Bill asks, *"How big is this deal?"* I say, *"All in about three billion."* He picks up the phone and calls Drexel Burnham's Fred Joseph. *"He's here,"* Bill says.

"Three billion, he tells me." Bill puts down the phone. *"Okay, John, you have a three-billion-dollar flag. We get first count money. Good luck."*

Before this center hump of my life's standard distribution curve, there was a beginning to my reactive day-to-day. My ramping up on the curve, so to say. The curve on the ark of life is consistent for everyone. Nobody gets to skate on the inevitable ending. There may be some preferred outcomes along the way; however, when our life fades to black, the equation could not be more balanced between all organic structures in the universe, including our own predisposition toward being saved by a deity who remains elusive except in our imagination. In Big Sky Country Montana, however, there's not much worry about the downside of the distribution curve.

I grew up in the West, Montana—western Montana. There's a difference in that state between East and West, like in many states. Sometimes the demarcation has to do with geography. Sometimes it's politics based on the tension between higher education and agrarian pockets of organic tradition. Splitting the difference between those two are the worker bee families who don't come from education or agrarian backgrounds but rather from a mix of society's understanding of what socially constructed people should be in their arena. In my case, that meant I had a mother who early in life became responsible for her family, therefore morphed into a self-taught worker in bookkeeping and office management; and a father who left home as a young man, went around the world three times as a merchant seaman, coming back to his hometown base for a career in the U.S. Forest Service as a draftsman cartographer, based solely on his natural talent.

My father was seventeen years older than my mother, and as a seasoned world traveler, more travel was nowhere in his wheelhouse. When they married, my mother had been nowhere besides the soda fountain at the Florence Hotel on Higgins Avenue. Occasionally, she would approach my dad about travel with a specific destination in mind. His response was always the same: "There's nothing about that that a copy of *National Geographic* and a good bowel movement won't cure." That repeated litany evolved into tension, eventually causing my mother to travel alone or take me with her while my father spent his idle time in the mountains of Idaho and Montana.

Dad was familiar with being outside. Up until he was twenty years old, his family spent time working a gold mine in a place called Cedar Creek, close to the northern Montana-Idaho border. The family had a placer mine operation that used a water dredge to run the creek for gold. By today's environmental standards, it probably had to be the most glaringly invasive mining method possible. But, at the turn of the century, environmental concerns were minimal. The Industrial Age was in full swing.

In ordinary people's relative terms, mine created enough wealth within the family to support everyone, including nieces and nephews, by completing their higher education and supporting my grandmother after my grandfather's untimely death. The family owned a ranch outside Missoula in a grass valley called "Frenchtown." My grandfather sold the ranch to a man who fell ill soon after the transaction, so my grandfather agreed to work the ranch in the new owner's absence until he recovered and could return to the payment schedule. In that process, my grandfather managed to kill himself with arsenic trying to exterminate gophers working the ranch as unwanted interlopers.

His death threw the family into a cocked hat, especially my dad, who, when my grandfather died, was somewhere on the streets of Shanghai with his Chinese Merchant Marine buddy Fuyang. They were waiting for a cargo load on the *President Jefferson* back to the United States. Word got to my dad in China that his father was dead. On that overwhelming news, he and Fuyang decided to drink and reminisce about their ancestors and, maybe descendants, by barhopping around Shanghai's Hengshan Road district.

It was New Year's Eve, 1924. Right after midnight, Fuyang decides to get in a pissing match with some stink-eye lookers at the bar, who don't like the looks of Fuyang's friend. One guy flashes a knife. Fuyang makes a pass with his arm at the blade fighter. He misses, and the knife does a long, clean entry into Fuyang's neck—straight down his torso into his lung. My dad sees Fuyang—at this moment, his only friend in the world—hit the deck, and he accelerates into full John Wick. When Dad could shoulder his buddy back to the ship, Fuyang was dead.

Growing up, I watched and listened to my dad tell this story, usually over breakfast at home on Saturday mornings. There were changes now and then, however, as he punctuated the key events. I would watch him transcend his own presence at the table back to Hengshan Road. He would flinch in jerks sometimes as he recalled the moments, like he was living it in real-time, again and again. I never doubted the script. It just wasn't his style to invent his way through the death story of his best friend in China. For his remaining eighty years, he never took a drink or went out on New Year's Eve. And on those New Year's nights, he wouldn't speak of Fuyang. He would sit quietly, but with purpose, on a Stagger-Back Morris chair in the fireplace room of the main house and look out the window toward the reach of the Bitterroot Mountains of west-central Montana.

Juxtaposed with my dad was my mom. All theater and arts. The mountains, not so much. So, in their search for parity, I got equal amounts of both. A Winchester Model 70, 270 on my shoulder, with season tickets to the opera in my pocket. When I traveled with my mother, we went east. Chicago, Ann Arbor, and Detroit, mostly. Her family lived there. Those trips were exciting for a kid who would get trapped between rail cars because he couldn't push the doors open. I had my first Club Sandwich at the Conrad Hilton Hotel on the Loop in Chicago.

It was right after the Second World War. We traveled on troop trains, my mom and me. The Milwaukee Road Olympian. The family arranged for me to wear a scaled-down United States Army Officer Uniform on the troop trains. Can you just imagine what a time that was? As the story goes, the train took a jerk, and I flew forward to hit my head and place a cut above my right eyebrow. I was lucky. But I got luckier. Dozens of GI first-aid kits were at the ready. Men returning home from France and Germany stood over this miniature Army officer, applying Band-Aid upon Band-Aid. Everyone wanted a piece of the kid.

In the winter, the trains would stop east of the Rockies because there was too much snow on the tracks. We would need to wait for these big road grader-like things to remove the snow. These stops got everyone off the train for snow fights. Usually, the Army against the Marines or Navy. I became the mascot for the Army guys. I remember the snow. It was so high!

In Michigan, Mom's family owned the White Swan Laundry in Ann Arbor. They had the contract for the medical school at the University of Michigan. My days were spent in laundry carts being pushed by workers from washer to dryer to truck. The whole process was big and scary, but the smell of fresh, clean cotton sheets was everywhere. In the evenings, nobody knew what to do with me. Not like my dad back in Montana, who had me polishing rifle stocks before I could walk.

PART ONE

THE JOURNEY BEGINS
OR
PREAMBLE TO A PERSONA

"I shall stride across the 20th Century breaking down doors with my shoulder, sweeping women away in my arms, and earning fortunes only to squander them promptly in dissipation" (The Count of Monte Cristo)

My image of me on my way to High School.

That changed around 9:30 A.M. on Day One after a football player upperclassman hit me on purpose with a full body slam into the hallway lockers. Then, he stepped back, laughing with his collective upperclassmen as the lockers crashed to the floor, taking me with them. I began clawing and fighting to get out from underneath the steel, but one of the doors had opened on the way down, so my head was jammed inside. I was in a jam (literally)—desperately needing to recover whatever pride I had left and distance myself from a culture that did not match my previous experience.

In raw nature with my dad, the mountain environment was our colleague—our contemporary. There was civility in the upper-middle-class society of Michigan, where my mom was from. Now, in high school, I find myself in an eleemosynary enterprise whose components operate beyond the power of my experience. Inside the ramparts of a Catholic high school, where I was to receive a top-tier Jesuit education.

The school was Loyola High School (for boys) and was an academic companion to Sacred Heart Academy (for girls) across the street. The schools were on the north side of town. The north side of town was socially constructed of Northern Pacific Railroad workers; all were considered outliers to the academics who lived on the south side surrounding the University of Montana at Missoula. The city was bifurcated like many agrarian populations. Academics and professionals on the south side of (*A River Runs through It*) Clark Fork and members of the labor community north of the river. There was no crossover apart from city government. I lived on the south side, about four blocks from the university campus. Loyola High was on the north side, closer to the railroad. So, my first day of school was a full course run-in with the boys who live on the north side. I was immediately branded as an *academic pussy* from the south side. Social history suggested that label would stick. South-side men were pussies, and north-side men were rough-and-ready guys.

My dad and mom were visibly uneasy after my Day-One story. They searched each other for advice. Wanted me to be careful. *Stay away from these lesser-than-occasional scholars spending their time in the grass-laced fields of white chalk.*

I stayed in school and remained strategically clear of the north-side boys. I ran with the lesser-than-crowd who made up the speech and debate team and the radio club. I became an extemporaneous speaker on the speech team. To that team's credit, in 2016, for the 30th year in a row, Loyola Speech and Debate ran the table—believed to be the most back-to-back wins in high school speech and debate history. (www.daily missoulian.com) In football, there isn't much on record, except recently, the athletic director was minstrelsy placed on leave. (www.reddit.com)

By the end of my sophomore year, I had gathered enough confidence to contrive a plan to get even. I was going to publicly *drop a dime on this guy* for the schoolyard bully that he was. *South-side pussy* notwithstanding.

This was not a reflection about high school socially constructed discrimination. That kind of analysis was not in my academic wheelhouse, but it did not change how I felt. In retrospect, this was the enigma of social bearing in a young man. I was raised in diverse circumstances, loved by both parents, exposed to a variety of circumstances, and I thought that was normal. If I could skin a deer, shoot a bear, come home to sit through *The Marriage of Figaro*, then go back and spend all night trying to stay warm inside the carcass of an elk, I could sure-as-hell take this guy down without the need to make him a trophy hanging upside down in my garage.

He was bigger than me and stronger than me, so this was going to be David and Goliath, and I had no plans to change the outcome.

Among my speech/debate and radio club buds were some savvy guys. These were young men who knew how to calculate time in process. The geometry of movement. Harmonic frequency as it relates to confusion. We planned.

And this is how it went. At 11:45 A.M., the bell rang. We started filing out of class toward the lunchroom attached to the gymnasium. We had to walk across an open pavement common area separating the buildings. It was a simple walk, and the order was usually the same. Athletes first, setting them up for the best seats. The Lesser-Than next for the rickety seats. Except on this day, I walked faster because I wanted to get comingled in amongst the football players so I could present myself at their table while there was still an open seat in front of my target. Like all primates might change in order was recognized quickly. *What's that guy doing up here?* was the question. I kept pace anyway.

The lunchroom doubled as a conference center, so the tables were arranged like rifle companies on a parade ground. Perfect. The chairs addressed each position in exquisite geometry. Social order was stacking in the usual way. Football team first, speech and debate and radio club last. Undefined humanities mingling in the center. The students filed past the kitchen opening, presented their trays for food, and walked to a table. I broke ranks and began slow walking to gauge my intercept with my target. Dragonflies are the best at this intercept process. The Department of Defense has been studying them for years, trying to recreate Dragon skill for Close Combat Missile Systems, an intercept using geometry instead of tracking. We humans are kind of hit-and-miss at this stuff, but Dragonflies are perfect every time.

Evolutionary biology provides humans with stereotypic vision. Like big cats as opposed to deer or antelope that have good peripheral vision but lousy focus until they can triangulate on the sound. Got to be why they have big ears. So, in this case, we have two cats: one staring at his tray and the other gauging the geometry of an intercept.

As brain science would have it, we arrived at the same table at the same time, juxtaposed to each other in a face-off. His face delivered a twisted smile. The kind you would see from any bully in the 1950s Hot Rod high school movie. *Why are you here?* his glance told me. I sat down. He sat down. Our eyes were locked like close combat missile systems. In between us was a large bowl of mixed whipped honey and peanut butter. I reached forward and palmed the bowl in my right hand. He was watching me—specifically my hand. I raised my arm and, in one fluid motion, shoved the gooey mixture into his face with all the force I could develop.

He reacted by pushing away from the table, and I stood up. There was a great deal of movement everywhere as people began to react. I grabbed the bottom of the table and lifted it as hard as I could. I managed to stack the table directly on his chest as he rocked backwards. I scissored my leg over the top of the table, taking my chair with me. The din of noise in the room was ramping up in orders of magnitude. My radio club and speech debate pals were clapping and shouting. The football team was milling in stunned amazement. I took a swing with my chair, and then another swing, and then another swing. Two lunchroom proctors and a priest pulled me off and hustled me out of the room.

I was thrown out of high school that very afternoon.

2

The bowl of whipped honey and peanut butter set me for a narrative life of didactic intention, sometimes seen as borrowed skill. A way of Being that kept me close to the edge. That place where fewer people go but wish they had. Thinking fast, as thinking slow plays catch-up. But thinking fast is an acquired skill.

I got a graphic example of that a few years later while I was scuba diving in the Caribbean. There was a woman from New York who taught me how *thinking fast can be mighty crucial*. I was in Tobago, the farthest-most point before the northern tip of South America. That's around five thousand miles (about twice the width of the United States) from the West Coast of the USA—a place that advertised the longest, whitest sand beaches in the world. What I also found was the largest and most obnoxious sand fleas in the world. Faced with that itchy reality, I ditched the beaches for more scuba diving.

Already a diver, I wasn't interested in the show-and-tell newbie tourist scuba diving. What I was after was some serious adventure with local dive contractors who would take me without tourists once I could shoehorn my way into their confidence. The solution turned out to be a barter relationship between myself and the contractors. I had flown in all my personal gear, tanks regulators, and gauges.

I noticed my new Caribbean commercial dive contractors were more interested in my gear than they were in me. As I learned, having dive gear shipped into the country was laced with heavy tariffs. I became an easy and less-expensive option if I would be willing to leave my gear in their country, avoiding the price and tax. So, I agreed to leave my gear in exchange for access, and that began the relationship.

Every morning I would make my way to the waterfront dive shack staging area, where dive masters and instructors held quick lessons for hotel/resort guests. Always the same routine—how to clear a mask, shoulder tanks, read gauges, and be serious about not drowning on their watch. What I witnessed was two groups of people bullshitting each other to either get fees or go diving. Money was always there; capacity to dive was incidental.

My deal with the contractors: I got to go on the boat—no cost—as a stand-alone outlier. Not a tourist, but not a dive master either. I would help without helping. The weekends were chock-a-block with hotel people. Families from everywhere looking for the white sand beaches found the sand fleas too, and started looking for options.

Midweek was different. Lighter loads, deeper water. Midweek people were seasoned in the ways of gauges, tanks, and proper weights. In scuba, there is a buoyancy thing that is caused by the wetsuit. These zip-in bodysuits are a quarter-inch or less neoprene that, if left to their own devices, add buoyancy to the diver. Varying amounts of lead weights are belted on for compensation.

The weight belts must be secure but come off quickly in case someone needs to float instead of sink. Most tourist divers work in shallow water plus or minus thirty feet (or one atmosphere). Every thirty feet of depth doubles the atmospheric pressure, which is 29.92 inches of mercury on the earth's surface. A diver can quickly ascent from thirty feet without worry of an embolism. Below that, it gets dicey or impossible.

If a diver gets panicky—which happens—the dive master swims under that person and unhooks the weights, leaving the new diver to immediately rise to the surface for some fresh air and reflection.

On warmer days, we simply used women's panty hose. Remarkable how they kept away coral scratches while providing warmth. The best part was watching men work their way into the things as the women laughed and took pictures.

So, that was how we were day-to-day in Tobago. Lots of color and coral. Seeing forever underwater. Small fish, game fish, and sharks all in the same frame. Took your breath away to break under the surface. It was a *pow* of marine wildlife. TMI everywhere! Scary.

After a while, this abundant routine became normal. Every day was a 10 on a "10" scale. Savvy travel divers, interesting conversations, more nature than one could take with standard cognitive ability. Sensing this, one contractor diver suggested. *"Why don't we go poach some Conch?"*

Now, that was illegal. I was not sure what the jails were like in Trindad/Tobago, but they could not be good. On the other hand, a slice of raw conch dipped in lime juice and chased with a Heineken lager was to die for. The way I rationalized this was these guys know what they're doing, have lived here their entire life, know the local ropes—probably to spiff the police—the reward was worth the risk.

So, that evening we sniffed around for some takers. A couple of men. A couple of women. A few master divers and me. Early in the morning, we collectively moved one of the open boats into position, loaded stacks of gear, mesh, canvas bags, sling spears, and gloves. We were off to gather a conch feast suitable for a first-century Roman Basilica. The morning was bright, the sun dancing on the water; we were in the concentration of the flow. Important things became peripheral.

On the site, the nets and bags went over first. We tossed a sea anchor to hold us to windward and slow down our drift. Half of us stayed in the boat, and the others went down with gloves and nets on sling spears. The hunt for conch began. I was part of the *stay-in-the-boat* team. Me, a couple of diver locals, and the woman from New York. She held herself as powerful—easy to like. Easy to look at, but *Do not cross the line*. This woman knew her shit. No discussion.

As the morning went on, the boat floorboards were one conch after another. Sideways. Stacked. Positioned for transport. We did good—very good.

One of the local divers turned his head, craned his neck, squinted his eyes, put his hand to his forehead. *BLOWEEBLE,* he shouted! Everyone knew from his tone he was scared. On the horizon, we could see the crashing bow wave of a very fast boat. The waves were parting on equal sides—a bone in his nose, so to say. Coming straight at us. If it was the Trinidad and Tobago Police Service (TTPS), we could be out of time and out of options. We began tossing conch over the side. The divers below saw them coming down and knew right away we were in trouble.

The fast boat was coming closer but at flank speed—a white hull with a light on the yard flashing. I looked at the woman from New York. We were both tossing conch as fast as we could. We were going to lose that race. Not enough time.

She stood looking over the bow. She took a step up to the thwart plank forward. She quickly began stepping and pulling out of her clothes. Then she was naked. She began pumping her torso and swinging a blue-and-white bra with her right hand. The fast white hull with the flashing light dove into a complete stop. With their engines at idle, diesel smoke drifting along the surface, the men of the TTPS gathered forward and looked at the woman from New York. They looked at her and sent her cat calls. They whistled. She smiled and smiled. I was watching the tight muscles down her back and along her butt. She was in some sort of dynamic tension. She was a da Vinci.

The men of the TTPS turned away, brought their throttles forward, and headed back to the horizon. Ah, yes. Thinking fast can pay off.

3

There was no doubt that fear distorts reality. People who chronically reside in fear lose vision. Nobody taught me that; it was an observation. Just in terms of social order, how much fun was it to listen to someone discuss fear in their context—"I'm afraid of this." "I'm afraid of that." "I mustn't do that . . . I won't; I won't."

Unless the speaker has a basket of comorbidities, fear was overrated. Some people discuss healthy fear. Like that guy has a healthy fear of whatever the situation might be, and I suppose, taken in context, there's some validity there. A person should have a healthy fear of driving on the wrong side of the road. Everyone should have a healthy fear of drinking a gallon of Jack Daniels in one sitting. But those fears do not distort your life. I suppose I could have worried about getting pummeled at the lunchroom table in high school. What if I had missed pushing the whipped honey and peanut butter into his face and had gone prostrate on the table like the fool he imagined?

Being risk-averse was not being fearful. So, then the obvious question, was it good sense to get myself tossed out of high school? Well, in retrospect, it was just dandy. Just imagine how interest applies to both these frames. *(One) I went to high school, graduated, and went to college. (Two) I went to high school, got thrown out. Went to college and got thrown out several more times.*

When I finally (age 59) did get serious about college, I remained defiant. I was never dismissed academically. GPAs were 3.6 to 3.9. What

I did wrong was tell my instructors that they were "incompetent dilettantes sucking on the academic tit."

When I began an Education Administration internship for The George Washington University, I found my assigned middle school had been cooking the books for three generations. They expected a twenty-one-year-old graduate student. I was a fifty-nine-year-old captain of industry. They let me go; *get out alive* was more accurate. Finally, a recruiter asked the question: Do you understand who has the power here, Mr. LaCasse?

I was dismissed form Heriot-Watt University in Edinburgh, Scotland; the University of Maryland University College; and The George Washington University in D.C.'s Foggy Bottom—finally taking degrees from University of Phocnix, Benedictine University in Chicago, Northcentral University in San Diego, and was a *walk-on* at Harvard University, in Cambridge. I'm sure Harvard took me off the street because I passed a timed blind and cited test on English philosopher and historian Thomas Carlyle. The recruiters had to look up my answers.

My dad bought my way back into Loyola so I could be instructed outside the wire and walk in the graduation ceremony. It was important to my dad and mom that I graduate with a certain amount of dignity, if not academic worth. The day I graduated, one of the priests handed me my diploma cover and said, "You better look inside here to make sure there's something there."

He was snarky with that remark. I didn't have much use for him then, and I still don't. It was becoming clear that I had an attitude. I spent too much time in the woods dealing with real situations to put up with contrived regulations leading to fabricated discipline. I enrolled in the University of Montana, where I majored in shooting pool and drinking beer. I still have my take-down inlayed cue leaning against my wall. The beer has long since passed, so to say.

I stayed at the University of Montana long enough to flunk out and begin my life in whatever I could do. I picked my final University of Montana grades out of the mailbox, keeping them away from my parents so I could avoid the drama. I was telling myself I didn't care, but I did. I rushed into a marriage, so it would appear I wanted that all along. I didn't. The marriage lasted through three children, then divorce. Two more marriages followed and two more divorces.

Leaving the University of Montana and now married, I went to work at the Anaconda company lumber mill. I worked the green chain and the elephant blocks. Learned how to chew tobacco and spit on lumber. Learned how not to get my fingers removed in a chop saw. Learned how to stand inside the teepee burner when it was 54° below zero, and one day was invited to go fishing with my fellow-workers.

I wasn't one of them, and they knew it, but they also had a sense about me that none of my teachers ever had. I was one of them—but I wasn't. I knew how to walk on both sides of the line—management and labor—and that got their attention. These men drove big Detroit iron, ate out of steel lunch buckets, and worked with no more than three fingers per hand. As they let me into the club, I could sense their protection, their willingness to keep me but with a guarded refrain: *"If you're smart, Johnny, you won't stay. If you stick around here, you will end up like us, and we will end up calling you flypaper, Johnny. You need to leave here, kid. You just do."*

One afternoon, after days of -50° temperatures, I left the mill. The next morning, I cleaned up, put on my high school graduation suit, and drove downtown. It was so cold people had to keep their cars running in town, or the cars would freeze up and not run. I walked to the JCPenney Company, the first place I saw, and asked the first person I saw if they might have a job. The person I asked turned and pointed up to the mezzanine. She said, "They're interviewing up there."

I walked upstairs. There were two men standing in what appeared to be an important office. One was the store manager, and the other was the regional manager. They were talking about a management trainee position in either Spokane, Washington, or Ogden, Utah. I was standing there in a fresh Hickey Freeman suit. They offered me the job and asked what city I wanted. I reached into my pocket and put a quarter on the table. I said, "Let's toss for it. Heads, it's Spokane; tails, it's Ogden." The regional manager picked up the coin and flipped it onto the carpet.

I left for Ogden, Utah, the following day.

I was on my way.

4

A live-at-home college dropout/flunkout who majored in playing pool and drinking beer and was now leaping into independent life saying, "I was on my way," was almost laughable. What does *on my way* mean when there was no track record beyond staying alive next to a campfire somewhere down range of the Montour Ranger Station?

On the other hand, maybe surviving in the wilderness isn't bad training after all. I did spend a little time at the pool table looking at people sliding their quarter under the cushion and thinking what they would do if I said you must build a fire using a flint, crawl inside this dead elk carcass, and stay warm until sometime tomorrow morning when you will make four trips walking out of here with a frame pack and one hundred pounds of meat on your back.

My relatively new wife, Carol, had I noticed, was probably walking silently like a deer in the headlights. My command decision to leave the state and go south into Mormon country as a $300-per-month trainee could have used a little conversation in advance. But that's not how I operated. What was good for me was good for everyone. A manly approach that worked well in the nuclear family unit three hundred thousand years earlier.

As an only child, I was a prince and privileged. But my privilege did not come from unlimited wealth. It simply came from love, exposure, and freedom. Collective worry was put aside when my eighth-grade teacher, Sister Mary Ludwina, leaned into my mother at graduation and told her not to worry because *Someday, John will find himself.* Of course, she was right. She just forgot to mention *when.*

The car was packed, and my mom and dad were on the front porch. Carol's parents did not see us off because her dad, Chester, was free with his personal dislike for me. I was taking his daughter away, and more importantly, I wasn't a seasoned professional moving into my new office building in northern Utah.

In the last moments on the front yard, my dad reached out and put his arms around me. He pulled me into his chest, and he began to quietly cry. At the time, I was nervous—and a little embarrassed for my mountain man dad. Now, I understand. Today, I reflect on my own moments with my own children, and I easily cry. Sometimes it's music; sometimes, it's a lucid memory; but always, it's authentic. I can feel that man like it was today—and maybe it is—as he put all his faith and hope and love into what was arguably flawed and leaving home, as it turns out, forever.

It was Joseph Smith who ended up at Promontory Point to declare *This is the place* as he felt he was on the West Coast. The Great Salt Lake is a big place, and I can understand how he mistook Promontory Point for the ocean. The Mormon (Saints) settlers coming west were not having a particularly enjoyable time of it. I suppose seeing any broad expanse of water was a relief. None of this confusion speaks well for the follow-on of the angel Moroni, ancient warrior turned angel, who was responsible for getting the golden plates to Smith in western New York; so he could translate the sacred word, reverse-engineer the migration of western civilization, and establish his church. The plates went back to Moroni when Smith was finished. So, there was no evidence to examine.

It does point to the fallibility of the human condition where we, as abstract thinkers, tend to live in our minds. Whether it was the Transubstantiation of the host to the body of Christ in the Roman Catholic Church, or the Spiritualism of the Coyote in Native American culture, or Georges LeMaitre SJ's "Big Bang" in Cosmology, Terence McKenna, of the famous Trialogues between himself, Ralph Abraham, and Rupert Sheldrake, branded such beliefs as the height of credulity, saying, *if you believe that, you will believe anything*.

I was coming into Utah as a Gentile in the eyes of the LDS church. But there are elevated levels of tolerance among Christians, so I was one to be converted rather than discarded. The pending reality: religious comings and goings for me ended in the lunchroom of Loyola High School.

Retail clerks in Utah have a way of being mostly women. In northern Utah, they are mature women. Their families are grown. They belong to religious clubs designed around the want-not-waste-not patterns of the Mormon Relief Societies, random organizations of Mormon *Saints* who provide piece goods for members. Not to be trifled, there are over seven million of these Relief Society women in one hundred and eighty-eight countries.

My eye-opening experience with knowing the local culture was in foundations and garments. Mormons are consecrated (made official) in a Mormon Temple and, going forward, elect to wear a "marked" undergarment that establishes their fidelity to their religion. Commonly called garments on the street.

I was coming from Montana, where there was underwear and union suits. With that the extent of my background in foundations, this man came in and asked me for some garments. Since he did not ask for underwear, I figured he wanted a union suit. He gave me his size; I went to stock and brought back two union suits. The plastic packages were trimmed in yellow. He remarked that he noticed the color change as the packages were usually blue. Thinking on my feet *(Note to young readers: Do not bullshit your way through a fact-set)*, I told him that was revised packaging; the new color was yellow. He smiled and left the store.

The next morning at F.W. Woolworth coffee time, I heard the Hail to the Chief whistling coming from the mezzanine. Mr. Patrick stopped at my position. Did his precision turn. Looked at me. He opened with his standard pre-attack. "Do you like it here?" He was in midnight blue with a silver tie. His shoes were black. He brought around a yellow plastic package union suit.

"Do you know what this is?"

"Yes, sir, it is a union suit."

He moved in toward me like an International Space Station (ISS) docking until he was on my nose. He said, "Mormons do not wear union suits. They wear garments," and he produced a blue plastic package.

"These are *garments*."

He placed the package on my head. Did a precision turn and walked out to coffee.

The female clerks thought I was being harassed. Mr. Patrick thought I was being trained. I intuitively knew I could walk both sides of that line. I began to analyze the environment during these (on the way to coffee) training meetings. These were in the times before change could be made at the cash register. There were pneumatic (air) tubes running through the store. At each transaction, a beer can-size brass cylinder was opened, and the money to be changed was placed inside. Then immediately whisked along the tube up to the business office where the change would be made, and the container returned. So, it was like the opening scenes in a space movie when there was an endless parade of tiny spaceships rocketing around the exoplanet.

These pneumatic tubes were popular during the American Civil War—1863. Our store was still using them. So, Mr. Patrick's precision bravado was constantly being interrupted by these small brass cylinders whizzing and snapping over his head, along his sides, or both. And each time one passed, he would blink, like an eagle or hawk trying to triangulate the sound of a field mouse. Mr. Patrick was nearsighted. His correction left him with thick glasses, but his vanity kept them off his face, and all this precision marching and precision turning was about maintaining his bearing inside a limited focal range. As his sentences were short, he was not harassing; he was making short-shift remarks and using right-angle turns to keep his bearing. He was the one in trouble.

The way he compensated was by dominating the environment through quick, powerful appearances. He could see enough to function but not enough to be completely comfortable. For example, he invited all management trainees and their managers to dinner at a local upscale steak house. The invitation came down about a week in advance. There was a great deal of buzz about the event. About three days out, he let it be known that he watched new people at dinner. His philosophy was men who eat fast advance fast.

So, we arrived at the restaurant. The meal was classic—drinks, steak, potato, and salad. We ordered drinks and tried to remember if we were supposed to down these things fast or slow. Fast won, and we began to hiccup at the table. Now, the food. We knew this was fast. We instantly became a table of burping chipmunk cheeks and greasy chins. The meal was over in minutes. Mr. Patrick said he must leave early, was sorry, and he was gone with a driver.

The Patrick management process was enigmatic. When you saw him, you saw full bravado in quick time. When you did not see him, he was behind closed doors with task lights and thick glasses.

▲ ▲ ▲

Part of the seasoning process at the JCPenney Company was (maybe still is) to move trainees from department to department. One of my assignments was piece goods and draperies. That was on the third floor and the domain of women in the Relief Society. Everything I did was new, so every day became an adventure. What was happening to me without realizing it was, I was moving from autocracy to autocracy. From Top-down Catholic to Top-down Mormon.

In every society where top-down power prevails, rules of conduct become dogma. Inside these constraints, people find ways to beat the system. Some of those are tragic—like the pedophilia of the celibate behind closed doors.

However, along the Mormon Wasatch, it is, and was, unique social engineering for pre-marital tactility when sex is not sex but is still sex but not sex. Current constructs find their way to TikTok messages around a practice called "soaking," an approach where the male inserts his penis into his female counterpart's vagina and lies silently with no movement that would effect a climactic ejaculation or any other associated synapse to nerve stimulation that would end up meeting the definition of sex. Certainly in my Pantheon of Best in Class rule beaters.

As I roll this activity backward in my JCPenney mind, I realize that *soaking* had been an ongoing experimental process. Modern social media has no corner on creative sex.

In piece goods, we had the authority to buy fabric in hundreds of linear feet of counter space, including drapery, to accommodate the Relief Society's need for material. For me, that meant learning how to manage hundreds of bolts of fabric to the cutting tables and help customers run pins in the crinoline, select bric-a-brac, place the pins on the rail in such a way that the pleated tops did not roll forward, and do this seamlessly while in the store or in the home. I became surprisingly good at that, and store management decided that I should begin teaching classes in fabric recognition and evaluation of patterns. Drapery installation was ad hoc as required. That was all dandy because Mr. Patrick kept spinning me new suits. His reward for about everything.

In biological science, learned habits become habitual and are demonstrated to place an effect on characteristics among species. The habituation of women undressing for men covers thousands of years. On the other hand, when men undress for women, the police arrive. So, there is a socially understood difference.

I came face-to-face with these timeless truths while on a ladder in the master bedroom of a customer's house. The husband (man) was at work. The wife (woman) was chatting with me from her position in a corner lounge chair. As we continued chatting and I kept pinning crinoline, she moved from the chair to the bed. And then, through a series of interesting evolutions, began removing her clothes. I was frozen on the ladder. I looked at her as I tried to do the double duty of observing a supine naked woman while pinning crinoline. Nothing was mentioned of this in the company manual. I rested my hands on the top of the ladder and let the drapery fall across my arms. Then I took a step down. The scene changed.

"No, no," she said, "stay on the ladder. I just want to enjoy you looking at me." So I think, *Is this a kind of diorama of pornogra*phy? I am stuck in an ex officio sexual encounter. This was her house, and she got to call the shots.

Then she changed her requirements. "It will be okay if you touch me as long as you close your eyes."

The remarkable part of this mid-morning exercise was that true to the playbook of rule-beating flutter, none of this seemed like infidelity.

6

At some point, even a titillating routine becomes simply routine. The evolution of the human condition within the confines of those three retail stores on Washington Boulevard became more remarkable by the day. Whether the trainees were mounting women in the elevators or making visitations to the third-floor property room for group sex—taken in context—by masturbating in front of store window mannequins that were undressed with only imaginary animation. People playing in gray zones when sex isn't sex because the participants were made of papier-mâché.

So, there were two things in constant play. One was to stay ahead of the management curve related to advancing within the organization. The other was to be as creative as possible without breaching the morally binding customs of celibacy by developing a relationship with one or more papier-mâché mannequins or simply exposing oneself in the property room in front of this motionless audience. All the stockrooms were open season for anyone who could get their clothes on and off as rapidly as possible.

One day, midweek, I was in the lunchroom and noticed a dog-eared copy of *Yachting* magazine. The magazine slid across the table to me, almost as if we were communicating. Inside were big yachts, some revolving around stories, others around brokerages, and still more around cruising all over the world. At that moment, the magazine had more appeal to me than the metronome existence I had in this brick three-story retail complex teaching sewing with an erection or stacking shirts and underwear.

That night, I wrote a letter to Richard Bertram and Company in Miami because they were the magazine's largest advertiser. The letter was my longhand shot-in-the-dark application for a job as a yacht broker. I sent the letter to Miami the following day and spent the rest of the week dreaming about soft breezes, teal blue water, and palm trees.

The following Friday, I got a call from Miami. I'm listening with my brain in a kind of too-young "No Shit" posture. On the line was Kirby Brooks, the sales manager for Richard Bertram Yachts. They liked my letter—at least enough to invite me to Florida for a sit-down interview. When the conversation ended, I put down the receiver and spent another two weeks gazing in various dressing room mirrors, speculating on my look. The tickets came, I took some off-work time, and I found my way to an Eastern Airlines Lockheed Constellation to Miami with a backpack and much excitement.

Kirby Brooks and I were to meet by my arrival gate inside the Eastern Airlines terminal. He said there was a cigarette machine next to a water fountain, and we would meet there. On landing, passengers had to de-plane down a stairway and onto the tarmac and concrete ramp, so my first exposure to Florida was as if I had been covered with a hot, wet wool blanket. The heat and humidity were stifling. Now I was re-examining my decision as I walked toward the terminal.

I found my way to the cigarette machine and the water fountain. The whole place smelled moldy. I had the pack across one shoulder and a dressed fatigue cap over my eyes. There was a man standing there. He was tall, had gray hair, looked distinguished. He was on one side of the vending machine, and I on the other. We stood for a while, fidgeting and looking at the crowd and each other. He approached me and asked if I might be John? My answer saw him visibly shaken. They forgot to ask how old I was, and from their perspective, I was too young to be a yacht broker. In some ways, I didn't care. Of course, I was serious, but the whole affair was kind of a lark anyway. A put-my-toe-in-the-water kind of deal on their nickel. From Kirby Brooks's perspective, this was serious business, and he had made a big mistake. His organization operated in tens of millions of dollars among captains of industry. That expectation rested on solid maturity, maybe even gray hair.

So, as we walked out of the terminal toward his car, he was in a constant state of apology. He kept telling me he was sorry for the inconvenience, for the time, for the mistake. What I remember most about that conversation was not his apology but rather his convertible car, the humidity, and the heat. My shirt resembled a hose fight. As we drove, I saw water distillers and coolers on the buildings. Window air-conditioning units everywhere. It was like I had just arrived at the Eleventh Commandment: **Thou shalt live in artificial air.** The situation got better because his convertible began providing a kind of convection oven environment where I could cook and dry off at the same time.

As we drove, he began to unpack my history and some from the University of Montana surfaced. As a student, I worked part-time for KXLL, an NBC affiliate. I did a jazz show with a guy named George Page. He was black—rare in Montana—and knew a hell-of-a-lot about the music. We evolved into a good team popular among the eight thousand students on campus.

Also, my major at the University of Montana was journalism, radio and television production management. Kirby and I did not discuss my grades or my spending more time holding a pool cue at the bar than in class. I think if I ever get a forearm tattoo, it will be in the letter "F," which could be projected as my recurring assessment of the Phi Beta Kappa Academy, "Fuck you and the horse you rode in on!"

My J-School news united our conversation because Brooks was a former radio guy and had industry connections. His question to me: Would I be interested in working in radio and television until I grow up—or, that's what it sounded like. I think it was in that moment when my life became reactionary, because the next word out of my mouth was, *"Sure."*

We meandered along the intercoastal highway toward the Coral Gables Yacht Club for dinner. The building was stucco—white with light orange/yellow trim. Inside were random rattan chairs and green. None of this stuff resonated with my Rocky Mountain West. Kirby told me he had a relationship with the barrister board of the Bahamas Broadcasting Commission. He felt he might "pull in a marker" for me at ZNS (ZedNS) Nassau. That was an affiliate of the British Broadcasting

System, commonly referenced as the BBC. For me, getting a job with the BBC was "POW! A big fallback win for me. It put me in an interesting foreign environment—a legitimate new adventure—so why not take a run at it. The following day Kirby and I were on a flight to Nassau New Providence, British Virgin Islands (BVI). I met with the chairman of the barrister board, a decidedly short interview, and was offered a job.

A couple of signals these first two days got past me. One: when Kirby Brooks said he could call in a "marker" for me. Two: when my job interview lasted about five minutes. I would be working broadcast music and local news, handling live broadcasts in the sound studio, reading the news from London (London Calling), and starting a campaign to cure the outer island people of rickets. I would have a car, a staff, a house with a pool, including a maid.

It was all too good to be true in any ordinary slice of sensibility. And it was; however, I was taking the whole affair at face value, just as presented.

I gave my notice to the JCPenney Company, and we left for the British Virgin Islands. The only official complication was Charlie, our dog. He was a Manchester Terrier—very British. Still, regardless of his background, there was a six-months quarantine on pets coming into the BVI. But, when Charlie's pet carrier cleared the gate in Nassau, this tall man was standing there waiting. The customs agent looked at Charlie, then the tall guy. Some sort of signal happened between them, and Charlie was free and clear in the country. The tall guy was Rusty Bethel. He was the manager of ZNS (ZedNS) Nassau and a local personality of some consequence. Today, streets and buildings bear his name on New Providence Island. Rusty was a combination of bluster and influence. He was John Wayne tall and Christopher Walken smart.

This was the first time I was seeing the leverage of political power in action. It was centered on our dog, but it was the opening round in my course of progress. We were driven to our house in the ZNS van. A white-painted concrete block house shiny clean like a new penny. There was the pool, the maid, and a view. Our maid was Cynthia. She was young and out of the way. Like a cat, always within the distance but never in your face. We exchanged a brief hello then Rusty and I left to get a car. We drove to the British Leyland (MG) Dealership, and Rusty handed me the keys to a new Convertible MG Sports Car. It was red with all fabric in tan. New and paid for by the Broadcast Commission.

There were only seven miles of paved road on the island, so the car was status, not utility. Then off to the station, with me driving the shiny new MG on the wrong side of the road. The ZNS van stopped in front of me, and I got my first lesson on how to drive in the British Virgin Islands. On the left—"ON THE LEFT!" Rusty said. *"Stay left, or get left."*

When we arrived at the station, my walk-in moment felt like a "shave tail" pilot walking into a seasoned Fighter Pilot Convention. The staff was stunned by my age. The chief engineer took me aside quickly and invited me to go fishing—soon. All the key people were white, and all the not-so-key people were black. It didn't occur to me that was unusual or race-based discrimination. I had no experience with black people beyond George Page and our jazz show at the University of Montana.

The station was big with a big-studio kind of feel. ZNS was the voice of government news and entertainment for 185,000 Bahamians between Florida and Cuba. So, it had the look and feel of an official British icon. I would start the next day.

Back at the house and pool and maid and view, Carol and I sat the evening away in stunned amazement. We did try the pool later that night, and the water agitation brought dozens of lizard-like creatures to the pool edges. I had a hell-of-a-time convincing Carol it would be ok. I don't think she ever went in the pool again.

I opened the main console in the morning, introducing myself to all of the Bahamians and telling them I was going to be providing important information regarding food and diet. For some reason, these people who lived in the sun were suffering from a Vitamin D deficiency. They were on a solid diet of chicken and fish, and we were to turn that toward Vitamin "C" any way we could.

My turn at across-the-Atlantic news (London Calling) was at a large Hallicrafters Model S-4B receiver. The kind with a black crackle frame with a dim-lit faded yellow/tan dial flanked by two large bakelite knobs; "Tuning" and "Band Spread."

The whole affair was Amplitude Modulation (AM) on a long wire antenna direct from London. So, with the skill of a safecracker, we were to tune the receiver and play the news. There was the *Weeeee... Ooooooo... Weeeee... Oooo...* tuning to null, and then this voice would arrive. The sound was nothing short of, maybe, hearing Winston Churchill tell us to fight on from the basement of our homes. *To never, never give up!* At the frequency null, we would hear *This is London Calling, This is London Calling,* repeated several times. At that moment, the entire British Empire was on the frequency all over the planet. It was an amazing goose bump kind of experience.

Every Sunday, groups of non-denominational Christian singers would come to the station for a live religious broadcast. Handling them was part of my job. And they did need to be handled. To many, the whole radio thing was magic. That made me some kind of a walk-on Wizard. And I was white, so the authority layering was expected. We had a great deal of fun. I was way too familiar with everyone because I didn't know any better. That would be discussed later behind soundproof glass.

The Chief Engineer's fishing trip happened within days and was an early-morning affair in an open boat. We would fish off Paradise Island—a sand pile then, not the A-List resort it is today. We were on the Opening Day of the All-Bahamas Big Game tournament. A big deal in the Empire. Even the Queen got involved with a special award plaque—HMS Seal and all.

So, off we went. The engineer told me about the importance of the tournament and handed me a Heineken beer off fresh ice. It was going to be a lovely day indeed. His name was Kim. Didn't fit his appearance. He looked like a tan Mustela weasel—but with a smile. He always spoke sideways, like he was expecting the wind to carry his voice back to the conversation. Kim had entered us both in the tournament. "Just in case," he said.

As we drifted, we spoke of the broadcast industry and our position in the politics of the BVI. He was curious how I came to the job, *being so young and all.* I didn't have a good answer. I guess because I was so *young and all.* Then Kim got a strike on his line. The fish broke the water and streaked across the surface like a hydroplane. "It's a barracuda," he shouted.

Long sweeps at flank speed. The fish was using every physical resource to shake the hook. The fight kept on and on. Kim was excited, I think, for the sheer pleasure of the competition. Sort of a quick-time Hemingway experience. While this was underway, I grabbed a short pole with some sort of thing on the line and dropped it over that side and let it fall. Kim was in Hog Heaven. And the barracuda would make every effort to kill him when he finally saw the inside of this boat.

Me, on the other hand, I was feeling a tug on my line! My rig was light tackle. Kim's was wire and heavy line. Big gold reel. Large rod ferrules and guides. Kim was in for the duration, no matter what. I was trying to figure out how to work my gear. Then my tug got powerful and about jerked the rod out of my hands. Now both Kim and I were in a fight. It would make a great beer commercial. Maybe Budweiser at the Gold Cup or something.

Eventually, the barracuda was in the boat, and we fishermen were standing on thwart seats. I'd never seen such a set of snapping razor teeth. But, my rod was bending in half, and it was all I could do to hang on. Kim saw the problem and started hitting the barracuda with a billy club. The boat was being towed by my fish. I got some kind of epiphany about fly fishing in Montana and started to let my fish run. Kim agreed and shouted, "Not too much strain—that's light tackle!"

The contest went on. Kim killed the barracuda and cracked a beer. I felt like I should be strapped in a chair—deckhands with gaffs on both sides. When we finally landed my fish, it was an Atlantic goliath grouper. Big for light tackle—way big! Kim said, "We're going to shore. I think we have a prize here!"

He was right. I won the tournament. The rules allowed for the tackle to weigh in the final tally. I came in at ten to one and first overall. I was to get the HMS plaque from London. Kim and I are, by now, buds, and both *in the bag*, as it were. He is teaching me shanties from the Royal Marines as I ply him with my version of "The Eddystone Light." In a matter of hours, I was barely an adult in cultural lockstep with Nassau, New Providence, BVI.

Kim and I stayed close. He would vector off potential missteps as I walked my line between labor and management. Soon after we arrived in Nassau, Carol's mother began having serious health issues in Montana. Carol flew home to be with her mom. That left me with a house, a pool, a view, a maid, and a red sports car. Cynthia was always out of the way, but around. She cleaned and ironed nonstop. She ironed everything, including my underwear.

I came home for lunch one afternoon, made sandwiches, including one for Cynthia, and asked her to join me. "Oh no," she said and went into the bathroom to eat her bag lunch. She told me she could not sit at the same table with a white person. I was flat fucking stunned. "You must be kidding," I said.

A few days go by, and I said I would like to drive her home. Holy shit, that scared her. *"No, no, no!"* she said. So I dropped the idea and maintained my distance. No lunch, no ride home, no nothing except ironed underwear.

About a week later, I'm home making sandwiches. I move to the table. Cynthia walks in, puts her lunch bag on the table, and sits down. No words. She just sits down and looks at me. I don't know how long we stared at each other, but it was a long time. Then she opens with, "I want you to talk to my dad." I suppose I was anticipating *I want you to come to the bedroom with me;* however, this was a start.

Well, no luck there. What she wanted was a serious sit-down with her father. And, I could drive her home. So, I'm thinking, maybe if he approves of me? Maybe that's how this starts.

At day's end, I am as nervous as a whore in church. We get in my red MG convertible and head *over the hill.* In Nassau, *over the hill* was a phrase indicating the poverty line between the haves and have-nots. As we drive, the environment keeps getting worse. Houses are becoming corrugated steel tilt-ups. The road changes to ruts. These are homes, except the streets look more like homeless camps. People walk in the street, and when we approach, they step aside and sort of exhale. Like an over-the-hill Bahamian version of *What the fuck!* There was no way Cynthia was supposed to be in that car with me.

When we get to her house, her brothers and sisters are in front, stopping and looking—staring at this circumstance. We get out and gingerly walk together toward the front door. Her father is at a table inside. He smiles at both of us and motions me to sit. The house was clean—comfortable compared to the environment. He addresses me as *Mister LaCasse*. I'm thinking; *you must be kidding*. He says, "We have a problem." He goes on about how land is being taken from the Bahamian people by big business interests from outside the island. There are promises being made and not kept. Ordinary Bahamians do not have the resources to defend themselves against this situation. And he wants to know if I can help. It's occurring to me that this is not about taking his daughter to the Saturday night dance.

So, I straighten up in my chair and try to address myself to him as a radio journalist—sort of. I ask for more information. He goes on with specifics where subdivision plats are encroaching on lands not part of the developments with no discussions about why. He feels much is at stake, and he sees no way to establish regress. It's quickly apparent this guy has a sophisticated vocabulary, has his shit together, and is giving me the courtesy of treating me as an adult. So I try to reach his expectation.

Cynthia is smiling. Her siblings are now standing with her in a half-moon circle behind their dad. Our conversation continues until I have enough to do some checking on the other side of the hill. We both stand in unison. He thanks me, Cynthia smiles, the rest of the family giggles, and I go to my car. As I turn the ignition, there is a small crowd gathered. There is music; the people are undulating up and down at the knee and clapping. It was an unexpected benchmark moment in my life.

Enter Che Guevara / Fidel Castro / Meyer Lansky

The next morning, I approach Rusty Bethel about my meeting the evening before. Rusty tells me the barrister board has some thoughts about the situation. I'm stunned to hear the station management is already on top of the story. Rusty then tells me my format is changing to accommodate what's going on. My local news broadcast will be designed to calm things down. I'm thinking, *Calm things down? The land is being conscripted from Bahamian citizens. What's to be calm about?*

My revelation began slipping into focus as the world was learning about the revolution in Cuba. About Fidel Castro's overthrow of Batista and about his wandering revolutionary right-hand man, Che Guevara. Castro and Guevara wanted American business interests out of Cuba.

That included organized crime, which, before 1959, was managed by Meyer Lansky, deported from the USA ten years before, and now the developer of the National Crime Syndicate. He had been running the operation from Cuba with multiple casinos and planning the largest hotel ever to support his properties. But, the Cuban Revolution dogma had no room for American organized crime. Lansky was moving the National Crime Syndicate into the Bahamas.

It seems the top two percent of *Bay Street Bandits*—the main businessman nomenclature in Nassau—were somewhere between understandable greed and racketeering. The National Organized Crime Syndicate had a nice money ring to it. What I had been missing was deals were being cut everywhere, and the radio station, with a little abuse of power through graft, was to be the calming effect on the upended population.

Rusty was arranging for me to spin a story about how the new Bahamian economy will benefit everyone and across-the-board cooperation will be the key to success. My day is split between station management manipulation and Cynthia's take on how her people are being shanked by Bay Street. And I do not have enough experience to know how to manage the play. If I stay on the air with the contrived bullshit coming from downtown, I will not be able to justify who I want to be, if nothing else, based on the impact on Cynthia's father. And, if I don't, I am out of a job.

I can't decide whether to hedge my bets or work on both sides. This becomes the first crisis where maturity would have come in handy. I was stuck in a classic labor/management struggle that rested on color lines, economic stations, and leveraged power. I was from a fundamental family in Montana wherein the facts were sacrosanct, even though I was personally as drifty as a *willow in the wind*.

So, I make a dilettante command decision. I walk into the studio for my board shift, turn up the right mic pot, and tell 185,000 Bahamians that their land is being stolen from them by crooked business interests in the United States. Rusty Bethel kicked open the studio door, red-faced and shouting. He fired me on the spot.

I was smart enough not to mention organized crime, but the organized crime syndicate was smart enough to recognize my target. The *Nassau Guardian* newspaper ran an editorial branding me *The Yankee from Over the Hill.* A not-to-be-trusted carpetbagger from over the hill. The word was out that I was a Conchy Joe who had a sit-down with the other side. Bay Street was pissed. But so was the over-the-hill crowd. With my broadcast still resonating with their anger, they started marching in the streets and burning cars. I was going to be their Che Guevara.

The Bahamas Barrister Commission Board held a quick meeting. The decision that came from the Chair: *LaCasse must be sequestered away from public view before this thing spins out of control more than it already has.* That same day the Commission staff find me an outlier apartment, authorize full-time security, and make it clear, *if you show up marching down Bay Street, you will turn to vapor.*

My apartment was on the third floor. There was razor wire at my front door. A one-eyed guy standing watch. I couldn't decide if I was scared or heroic. Very much alone, I confabulated dozens of outcomes. None were very good. Through deduction, I calculated that if they were going to kill me, they would have already done so. Or, at least, wait until they could gauge the impact. So, I figured I had some time. They provided food, but it was a prison atmosphere. No talk. Very abrupt. I was getting scared.

About a week and a half in, I am up early shaving. I'm nude. I hear a scream—a loud scream. It sounds like a woman. I run into the living room and out on my deck. As I step onto my deck, a man drops onto my shoulders from above. We both fall down, except I ricochet into the wall, and this guy does a kind of unintentional high-bar grab, loses his grip, and falls one floor, vectors off another rail, and does a crashing fighter plane flat spin to the street below. That would be three stories. He's not dead. He crawls into the surrounding brush. By then, people are darting out onto their decks to see what happened. The Royal Bahamas Police Force barracks troops are arriving. A busload of them. In the Bahamas, the police do not carry guns. So, if the dispatcher suspects a capital crime, the scene gets thirty-six officers from the police barracks until the scene commander decides to unlock the armory—or not.

What we learned was the building climber/robber was a Haitian. He scaled the building, entered the apartment above mine, and while robbing the place, the occupant woke up. She was a local doctor. She screamed, and the guy hit her on the head with a hammer. Scared, he started coming down the decks, mine being first. He and I did this awkward dance that put him in the parking lot. The doctor was not dead—but barely alive.

As this is unfolding, I am becoming a witness for the Crown. The tension is becoming apparent. Radio Broadcaster champions black Bahamian loan owners' cause will be their revolutionary leader soon—against—Radio Broadcaster becomes a witness for the Crown against a Black Man. The stroke of good luck was that I now represented the tension between the two sides, and nobody wins if I'm dead. For the moment, Bay Street is positioned better if I'm alive to testify. The Over the Hill gang believes I will stay their course and say, *"I cannot identify the alleged assailant"* at the hearing. The Barrister Board saw the benefits of having me testify against the Haitian, and they figured I would be a witness for the Crown based on my truth-telling over the air. And they were right. The situation was obvious—on its face, on my shoulders, and on my deck.

But now the bigger problem. No matter what I decide, the outcome will produce marching in the streets, more burning cars, and maybe major property damage. So what to do? The only sure thing was to make me go away. Kill me or make me disappear—forever. Bay Street money knew I would have enough tags back in the States to cause way more trouble than the National Crime Syndicate was willing to tolerate in an already dicey situation. No need to be thrown out of two or three countries in succession. They also knew that if my presence went away, so would my—albeit hypothetical—disruptive power. All news to me at this point.

Within seventy-two hours after the building scaling and attack, the Chairman of the Barrister Board arranges to meet me incognito for a drive on the seven miles of paved road. At this point, I am reliving every gangster movie ever produced. *Wise guys get the crime boss's surreptitious nod to eliminate the troublemaker.* Somehow it's always in the salt marsh with a 45 ACP to the back of his head.

Cynthia's father doesn't know where I'm locked in; I can't call anyone. So this is going to require some cosmic stroke of incredible luck.

The car is long and black with two men in the back. I'm in front with the Barrister Board Chair. He's driving. Windows down, lots of air. We get on the road, and I am trying to decide what would happen if I grabbed the steering wheel and forced the car into a sideways drift. Could I jump and escape? I keep calculating how the guys in the back are packing pistols. Maybe a belt holster. They're in suits, so most likely have shoulder holsters. Maybe I could grab one on his draw and force him to shoot the other. Then kick over the driver and ride out the crash. At least I would have a chance.

Finally, we roll to a stop. The car is idling, and the worst possible outcome is at hand. My time has come. The Chair of the Bahamas Broadcast Barrister Board turns to my face. He gives me simple instructions. "We are going to give you a one-way ticket to the city of your choice in the United States. You will agree to never return to this island again."

That night I am driven to the Nassau International Airport and escorted aboard a connecting flight to Salt Lake City.

As the situation in the Bahamas became increasingly worse, London sent a Scotland Yard team to investigate. Over time the playing field began to change. Among the powerful politicians, Sir Lynden Pindling, locally known as "Black Moses," became an active target of U.S. drug enforcement agencies, and Kirby Brooks committed suicide. It took until 1995 for Scotland Yard to unravel the connections to organized crime.

In 1986 the United States Department of Justice published Abstract NCJ Number 103849.

Casinos and Banking - Organized Crime in the Bahamas
Journal Deviant Behavior Volume: 7 Issue: 4 Dated: (1986)
Pages: 301-312
Author(s)
A A Block;
F R Scarpitti
Date Published 1986
Length 12 pages

Annotation

This paper traces the development of complex symbiotic relationships among gambling casinos, offshore banks, and professional criminals and shows how American organized crime interests penetrated the Bahamas by using gambling and banking to gain a firm foothold.

Abstract

In numerous contemporary cases, professional criminals from the United States and elsewhere are known to utilize both casinos and financial institutions to launder money and to hide large amounts of illicitly acquired money. Long before recent revelations of such activities became known in the Caribbean and the United States, developers in the Bahamas had started the process of bringing casinos and banks together to serve underworld interests.

7

As I arrive back in Utah, it's occurring to me that I am unemployed with no residential address. Carol is still in Montana with her mom. I get off the plane with one pair of pants, a shirt, underwear, socks, a pair of tennis shoes, and some pound sterling in my pocket from the Bank of Nova Scotia. Some old JCPenney buddies pick me up at Salt Lake Airport and listen to me relive my adventure on the way back to Ogden. I'm riding in a station wagon with three golf/work buddies who are trying to straddle my story as my words seduce them into an adventure of privilege, plunder, and corruption. And, of course, organized crime. As we ride, a cosmic bolt strikes my brain. *In a moment of time, I've become demonstratively ahead of these guys in orders of magnitude.* I have become a gallant man. The gentleman of the convention—my outsized importance in this rolling piece of chrome and steel on Interstate 15. It is my sunniest hour. The best of times without the worst of times.

Now, back in the USA, Jane Fonda and Donald Sutherland are spooling up to piss-off half of the United States population with *Hanoi Jane*. Ken Burns calls it "A Disrespectful Loyalty" in Episode 9 of PBS's "The Vietnam War." With all that yet to come, when I got back, the insurgency in Vietnam was still under the radar for most Americans; however, in Ogden, Utah, there were one thousand one hundred and thirty-nine acres supporting the U.S. Army Defense Supply / Utah General Depot / Defense Distribution Depot Ogden (DDDO). The Army was hiring. I gave the JCPenney Company a few moments' thought. Then was off to the Army.

I was hired as Labor Grade 1 (LG-1) warehouseman. At the same time, I found an apartment in a converted military barracks close to the DDDO. No car, but I could walk to work. I was still coming down from my first ride in a long black car. I don't think it was PTSD, but I did a few rounds of night sweats as the weeks went by.

Soon it would be 1972 when Jane Fonda would go on the air to admonish the U.S. Government for continuing the war in Vietnam. She would go beyond the temper point of many Americans. But, in the actual government, there were concerns well before Jane tried to make her case. On May 20, 1966, then-Congressman Gerald R. Ford gave a press release of his speech on the floor of the House of Representatives. He identified a Black Market in Vietnam. He said that the Vietcong was getting more of its supplies from the black market and other South Vietnam sources than through the famous Ho Chi Minh Trail.

The black market involved radio receivers, drugs, food stocks, and seeds. What I was about to find out was that the black market also involved military supplies, with American trucks delivering military supplies into the wrong hands. The American stevedoring operators virtually encouraged pilferage. The tragedy here was that two-thirds of Vietnam's commercial import dollars came from United States Aid funds. (USAID). At that time, we were delivering fifty tons of military supplies per day into Danang Harbor. And that distribution curve was accelerating.

So, I'm not here to absolve Jane Fonda or Donald Sutherland. And I am not going to affirm or deny USAID's involvement, but this is how I remember when some USAID supplies were designed to kill or injure when opened inside the confines of the Vietnamese black market. Our government was stuck between the devil and the deep blue sea. President Johnson was proposing that he would come to Congress with a debt refinancing scheme that would cost Americans added millions of dollars each year as he poured billions of dollars into government-owned mortgages and other financial assets at the Federal National Mortgage Association (Fannie Mae) and sell those shares to private banking interests. While doing that, he was also aware, as was Congress, that the budget for the war was being gerrymandered into black-market activities not seen since the Second World War. And my new job was to help package that material so we could ship it off to South Vietnam and sell it to the Vietcong up the Ho Chi Minh Trail. The whole affair was comedic.

On reflection, it compares to a circumstance that happened to a friend's daughter in San Francisco. Two men were planning to break into her house. They established a ruse by putting a twelve-year-old boy knocking at the door so the situation would appear benign. When she opened the door to the boy, the two men appeared, forcing an entrance with weapons. She maintained the conditioned social construct of not allowing her dog to bite someone—holding back her angry, barking dog as one of the bandits is pistol-whipping her. That's what we were doing in Vietnam. We continued bringing supplies to be pistol-whipped by the Army of the Republic of Vietnam (ARVN)—our allies—so they could establish a black market with the Vietcong. And, of course, the Vietcong were buying the USAID supplies with American dollars.

▲ ▲ ▲

So, I'm in this giant warehouse wearing an apron and carrying a claw hammer in the loop on my specially designed warehouseman pants. There are wooden pallets stacked thirty feet high in every direction. There is a center line where bigger things roll in through enormous hangar doors.

My supervisor was old compared to me. Black bib overalls with pockets of Beech-Nut chewing tobacco. A couple of flat Carpenters pencils with white chalk snap line sprinkled here and there. He began my orientation by explaining the cultural relationship between what is ordered and what is provided. For example, he said the ARVN will order a Fire Engine. Our catalog description will be to provide a classification 10-B: C large dry chemical container, bracket-mounted on brass wheels, with harness mounts forward for a dog. Maybe a goat.

I quickly learned that a claw hammer will pound nails and staples; however, it will also pry splitting wood, split fiberboard, and manage most small demolition tasks. I expect every Grainger catalog hammer in existence was somewhere in that warehouse. There seemed to be a rank-and-file system between framing hammers and claw hammers. The people who carried framing hammers didn't do much clawing; they were sort of the drivers of the nails. Behind them were lesser-than people who clawed at framing hammer mistakes. Then there were the pry bar people who took on the role of hammer supervisors when the entire pound, claw, strap miscalculation needed to start again.

Many of the supplies were nonstandard-size custom materials that required creative packing. Men walked with wooden slats and strip tape to create a pallet configuration that would sustain itself while being forked and lifted onto trucks for transport to the shipping ports on the West Coast of the United States.

Lunch breaks were in place with bag lunches, and bathroom breaks were social events in a kind of pentameter dance understood by everyone and abused by opportunity. The lifts were fueled with propane, so there were about 200+ lbs. of carbon monoxide (per unit) deposited in the air each year. That ongoing environmental pollution was feeding our lungs every day. So, oxygen delivered from hemoglobin into our body tissue was reduced. Everyone walking around there was setting up for heart and lung problems and, not least, anoxic brain injury. Maybe that's why our tools were simple.

One morning, two men were standing outside the bunkers in my bay area. They were wearing white hard hats and were reading papers on clipboards and randomly looking around the warehouse as they read. One of them looked at me and asked, "Are you John LaCasse?"

I said, "Yes," and they entered my bay. They said, "We've been reviewing your file. You were in the Army ROTC at the University of Montana. That was an Army officer program with counterinsurgency training. Do you recall that program?"

"Yes, I do," I replied. And then I asked, "Who are you?"

"We are the tactical supervisors for this facility. You are working for the United States Army, except that today we are changing your assignment. Now you are with I Corps United States Marines and advisor to USAID."

"Does that mean I get a raise?"

"No," they answered. "You are now operational under Article 54 of the State Department as a counterinsurgent in the Republic of Vietnam. Someone will contact you shortly and discuss your assignment."

I put down my claw hammer. They smiled, adjusted their hard hats, and walked away.

So, what the fuck is that supposed to mean?! I was thinking.

▲ ▲ ▲

My mind drifts back to the Army ROTC at the University of Montana. We trained in sneaking around and blowing stuff up—with tags, not real explosives. Based on what I learned with tags, I graduated to diamond bits, caps, and forty percent nitroglycerin sticks. Or, put another way, I became officially dangerous.

We put black greasepaint on our faces, operated in small groups, and were assigned objectives without protocols on how to proceed. We were expected to just do it. Like, *show us your stuff.* One time my group was to ambush a squad of seniors on a field maneuver. I decided to do some deer hunting from a quiet stand. I placed my guys whispering in the grass and behind trees close to an obvious marshaling point for our target. When they arrived, we opened with a Browning M2 50 Cal tripod-mount machine gun and a bunch of M-1 rifle fire. The M2-50 was a confidence builder for graduating seniors. It sounded and felt like Real War Equipment. So, we sprayed them with noise and smoke and declared all the seniors dead.

The captain, aka Head Military Figure in Charge (HMFIC), was sort of happy but thought we were a little extreme. I was delighted by the comparison and told my team to clear their weapons. My machine gun guy cranked back the bolt, lost control, spun the barrel, and fired a blank round into my crotch. I went down with the muzzle blast. All the dead seniors stood up. The HMFIC captain walked over. I hurt so fucking bad I couldn't even cry. He smiled and said, "Ok, boys, back to the trucks."

By the time we got into the city, my balls were growing. By the time I got home, I had regulation baseballs growing in my crouch. By the end of the week, they were basketballs.

We continued sneaking, tagging, and occupying targets for the three years I was there. When I wasn't at the bar with a pool cue, I was a dilettante pretend spook for the Army Reserve Officer Training Corps (ROTC).

Now I get to do play for real. But how am I going to do that from a giant warehouse in Ogden, Utah?

▲ ▲ ▲

Within hours, an important-looking dark suit shows up in my bay. He starts to give me the USAID take on down-range problems with a black market at the harbor in Danang and up the trail. He tells me we need to eliminate the black marketers. Then he says our targets are ARVN troops we support. He says this whole operation is black. I say, with a great deal of quiet reserve, "So I am going to start killing South Vietnamese soldiers on behalf of the United States, *yes?*"

He says, "well, yes and no. These are bad actors who have no allegiance to us. They are profiteers—ARVN in name only."

Then he drops the *Black* part. This process will be unnoticed. These people will disappear without damaging our relationship with Ngô inh Diêm, the President of South Vietnam. I am searching the air around me for some conversation on the rules of engagement. Does not happen.

All this sort of plays into the William Westmoreland war package— *we win by attrition.*

The conversation continues. I ask, "What's the play here? What do I do?"

The answer: "You work with us to booby trap USAID supplies."

"So, they explode?"

"No, when they are delivered up the trail, the deliverer gets executed by his Vietcong counterpart."

Now I'm thinking, *I just went through this process—the shoot the messenger part—but my long black car guys decided not to shoot me. What in the hell is going on here!? This is sanctioned Murder Incorporated under the USAID/Hand Shaking/ United States flag?*

He goes on . . .

"At the end of every shift, you will pack one last box with trash off the shop floor. Wood scrap, banding shorts, clips, and sawdust. In other words, you sweep the floor and put all the trash in a packing crate. Then you put one of our special labels on the box. Someone, from USAID will direct the box to I Corps personnel in Danang."

He shows me the *special label*. It looks just like all the other labels. I tell him as much. I ask, "What's special?"

He says, "Look carefully—*very carefully*. Do you see the thumbs on the shaking hands?"

Then I see it. The thumbs are crossed the wrong way. The reverse of what they should be. Not noticeable, but obvious when you do. He tells me these special boxes will be used by I Corps when they suspect a worker is siphoning stuff up the trail. On the ground, the Marines turn away so the bad guys can make off with the box. When the box is opened, several things come into sharp focus. The ARVN guy knows he's been found out. The VC guy knows the ARVN guy is no longer useful. The quick solution is a K-50 round to the back of his ARVN head.

The dark suit finishes with . . . "this transaction is representing a normal casualty of war."

So, I resurrect some JCPenney trainee history and declare to myself, *we go full circle. We do not stop the process with USAID management discipline. We simply kill the perpetrator by casualty of war. No middle management training is required. A simple three-part process. (a) Pack box (b) Deliver box (c) Shoot messenger.*

I prefer not to remember how many DDDO boxes were branded with the special USAID label, but a great many. Without a doubt, a very effective process in its microcosm.

In retrospect, Jane Fonda maybe didn't win on style points, but intellectually she was correct.

Eventually, I get tired of arranging USAID / U.S. Marine Corps assassinations by remote control and move back to Montana. By now, we have three boys and a life running on a hamster wheel. I start selling insurance, and Carol enrolls in the University of Montana School of Sociology. My job becomes the General Agent for Occidental Transamerica. Nice office in the Western Montana National Bank at the business anchor intersection of Higgins and Main in Missoula. We rent a turn-of-the-century Craftsman house—with a yard—from a retired Army Colonel (Edward Cook) near the university campus. We are a textbook-perfect, middle-class American family—except we're not.

Carol immerses herself in social work and brings it home, including students who enjoy the privilege of living on the floor while taking pills in several formats. Carol feels these people require her guidance. I feel we should call the cops.

Our boys seem to remain well-adjusted as we try to play our tension outside the wire. I bury myself in my work and Carol in school. The boys follow in my family tradition by getting acquainted with the forest primeval. However, by taking little time to go into the forest, we have conversations with one another about the future experience. To that end, the boys begin to experiment with the actuality. On a Saturday, I am standing in the front yard looking at the house. I notice smoke coming from the second-floor window. All the obvious emotions jump into play. I run into the house shouting for anyone. I get no response. I run up the stairs continuing to shout everyone's name. Still nothing. I see the smoke coming from a bedroom. I blast my way in. More smoke from the small door opening to the attic. I drop to my knees and crawl inside. The boys are in a circle around a "campfire," they tell me.

I completely unravel. Get them out of the attic like tossing sacks of feed into a half-ton truck. I shout, "GET DOWNSTAIRS!" as I jump over them on my way to get some water. I pivot on the curve of the first landing and come head-to-head with this guy in a tan and black raincoat and a red hardhat dragging a canvas hose. It took me a moment to realize he was a city employee. What helped me was my glance out the window to notice this enormous ladder truck with a sprinkle of neighbors in a kind of surreal *holy shit* panorama. Someone—I don't know who—had called the Fire Department.

That whole affair required some paperwork and a meeting with the homeowner and his insurance agent. Each conversation was so impacted by the drama of what might have been that nobody seemed to care about the official process. It was like everyone simply averted their eyes and declared a kind of played-out fatigue. We did have a firm discussion with the kids about why building a campfire in the attic is a bad idea.

Then, on another day, I'm standing in the backyard. I notice a liquid line of discoloration streaming down the back of the house from a second-floor window. My curiosity brings me upstairs. When I arrive at the bedroom, I notice our son Robert is standing at the window, facing out. His younger brother, Jeff, is standing on a positioned masking tape line saying, "I'm next."

Robert was peeing on the bottom sill of the double-sash window. The house had one bathroom, and that was downstairs. So, the double-sash window upstairs becomes a tailor-made latrine at just the right height for the little boys close enough in age to salute the trough one after the other as a convenience item to avoid going downstairs.

The conversation about how NOT to pee in the window frame was less frantic than the one about the attic campfire. But the socially constructed gerrymandering was priceless. The room with the window was the territory of all three boys. But it was open with no walls. Well-established territory with masking tape on the floor. John Patrick—the oldest—got the end of the room with the window. It never occurred to

Carol or me to make the area around the window a collective common. So, John Patrick, alone, controlled routine access to the window. As his brothers would run downstairs to pee, capitalism was finding its way into John's head by cosmic osmosis. He began selling access to the window. More like barter, but the same process. So, every time the homeostasis of one of his brothers required a void of pee, John collected for access to the window. It was the business equivalent of pay toilets. I was thrilled with this cosmic sign that John would be successful in America.

Eventually, time became a function of reactions instead of stuff. Carol and I get divorced, and she takes up with a faculty member at the University. She had custody of the boys, although the shake-out became both of us. John Patrick came to live with me full-time while Bob and Jeff were in and out as their mother's schedule permitted. That eventually evolved into full-time for dad when Carol got a contract in Alaska.

The boys and I enjoyed the bear cave life men dream about. We had no furniture, so we spread camping and diving gear around to compensate. That included dive gear and an AVON inflatable that mirrored the Special Air Service (SAS). It was solid fun on Puget Sound, in the Olympic Mountains, and in the Cascade Range. The boys grew into everything Recreational Equipment (REI), which we continue with a forever membership at the flagship store. Today, the boat is a Zodiac Futura MK 2. aka Special Operations Command (SOCOM) kind of stuff. The camps are at sea level. The reminiscence remains the same.

As *living the life* continued, I unloaded the insurance business and began working as a private consultant. I opened an office with a couple of other guys and shared a secretary. In the fine tradition of matchmaking, the office secretary had a single friend, Karen, who was looking for a date to the annual Beta Sigma Phi Sweetheart Ball. She was a nurse/EMT from St. Patrick's Hospital in Missoula. She had a little boy, Erik. Karen and I get close, get married, and I adopt Erik. Now we are *four* boys, with dad, in the bear cave, all being managed by our very own EMT.

Our life outside continued as we reconditioned a twenty-seven-foot sailboat we called the *Four West*. We six would stuff ourselves in that boat and work the water on Flathead Lake in west-central Montana. It's the largest body of fresh water west of the Great Lakes—not everyone knows that factoid. We named the boat after the psych ward at St. Patrick's Hospital. And for good reason. Six people plus friends overnighting in a twenty-seven-foot sailboat can generate a certain amount of psychotic behavior.

One day, a lawyer walked into my office. I knew him through a lawyer friend in the same building. He sat down and announced, "John, I am going to run for congress." His name was Max Baucus. He did become a congressman, then became the longest-sitting Senator in the history of the State of Montana; then, under the Obama administration, was appointed the American Ambassador to China. He continues holding sway in global affairs through the Baucus Institute at the University of Montana.

But, on that day, he was Max from Alex's office on the fourth floor. He wanted to know if I would help him—maybe get involved?

Max's family was known for their Republican influence in the Montana ranching community. Max wanted to run against Richard G. Shoup, an enormously popular and successful Republican. I uttered something with a great deal of insight: "You must be kidding. Where do you plan to live when your dad kicks your ass off the ranch?"

That started the *631 Club*—the brainy idea that in order to win against Shoup, Max would need to shake every hand in western Montana before the election, covering some 631 miles and meeting thousands of voters. I told Karen we were going to help Max run against Shoup, to which she uttered, *"you must be kidding!"*

So, with the help of some Democratic National Committee (DNC) professionals and one Eddie Bauer sleeping bag, we started walking and shaking hands. The bag occupant would change every other night. The handshaking was extraordinary. When Max would be invited to a large *Meet and Greet*, I would enter the room or city park site ahead of him and count the people. Then divide that into the time we had. When Max arrived, he would look at me for a hand signal indicating the maximum amount of time he could spend with each person. Then, from time to time, he would check back for the pace. It was a baseball catcher/pitcher signaling exercise of extraordinary precision.

Karen and I went with Max to Washington, D.C. We got into the compression of political power as it was interpreted in the first election cycle of campaign finance reform. Most lobbyists still operated in the old tradition. They would do a kind of hat trick and stuff cash in your suit pocket as their arm came over your shoulder. The AFL-CIO guys were experts at the sight of hand cash deposits.

The Majority Leader was Mike Mansfield (twenty-four years in power). We, of course, knew who he was. We had no idea how powerful he was. Or that beginning that year, Max would eventually best Mansfield to serve thirty-six years. Everyone seemed to understand the possibility but us. We were still trying to find street addresses in the District.

The day we went to see Mansfield, we were also to go with him to a reception at P.J. Donich's house on Embassy Row. We were the chosen ones. Mansfield was the *King Maker*. As the day progressed, we learned that the Senator was known for his pipe-smoking. Always had a pipe in one hand. Even his official Senate portrait has him holding a pipe. What we found, while in his office, was that the pipe was how he signaled his intentions. It was the Mansfield pipe version of Max and me trading hand signals at a campaign *Meet and Greet*.

Every day, every network—plus wire services—would gather in the hall outside his office for the possibility of an audience. Mansfield was soft-spoken and introspective, so vocal crowd management was not a part of his style. We were ushered in and sat before the Senator. He was in his chair holding his pipe. The hall was chockablock with network correspondents. I was watching the Senator. There was about a 220-degree arc to the swing to his pipe stem. There seemed to be several positions that sent meaning to the open door. Nobody was guarding the entrance—no gatekeeper. Yet, the network people seemed to know what to do. It was all about his pipe stem. Each position on the arc had a separate meaning. Like 15 degrees off vertical was CBS. Thirty degrees was NBC. Then he circled back and started using fractional positions like 7 degrees off vertical would be United Press International (UPI).

Nobody got out of line. I could visualize him taking a position on the arc with his pipe and then driving the stem into a black bean bag on his desk. Sort of the Mansfield version of Roman Emperor Hadrian deciding to kill the gladiator.

That afternoon, Karen and I took a walk near our hotel. After the walk, the reality struck home that we were onlookers to a police officer who had been cut in half with multiple shotgun rounds. She was lying open on an entry ramp to another hotel. The coroner had uncovered the body for some official reason. There were flies around her. That is when the District of Columbia began losing its appeal.

We went to P.J. Donich's house that night for the Mansfield reception. The place was sardine-packed. When the Senator arrived, the press of the crowd was so intense that he and his wife were unable to join a reception line. Instead, he lifted his arm above those near him and let them touch his fingers as he motioned his hand over the crowd. It was Emperor Hadrian all over again. Just a different address.

We returned to Montana and continued the campaign, but Karen and I were emotionally done with Washington, D.C. We got through the dirty tricks of campaign protocol, union compromises, railroad leverage, and business uncertainty. We entertained string quartets, rodeo cowboys, and the Sisters of Charity. We took thirty-six hundred pictures of Max shaking hands. We used three in the campaign material. We forgot to buy the 631 Club lapel buttons from a union shop and caught hell for that. But on the final night of the final day, we were about to win, running away. And we did. Max Baucus was beginning his journey to one of the most successful political careers in history. It all began with a young and inexperienced prospect believing that if we shook every hand in the western district of Montana, we would win.

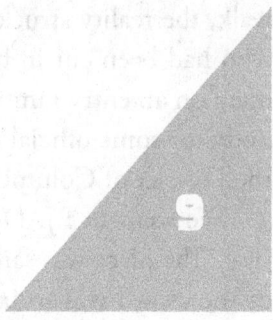

9

Back in Montana, I was sitting at my office desk. To save some money after the campaign, I moved my office location across the hall. That gave me a window that looked out through a façade to cover the fire escape. So, when I looked out the window, it was like looking through a cheese grater. The good news was it was painted blue.

As I sat looking through the blue cheese grater, I could see movement as the cars on Broadway passed below me in front of the oblong holes. In a moment of a lucid dream, I supposed this was a Thomas Young double-slit experiment. Except—at least in construction—it wasn't 1801, and I wasn't a famous physicist.

What I was, in retrospect, was a very unhappy fellow. All the key decisions to date were spun off my wanting to be a yacht broker with Bertram Yachts in Miami. My life was certainly interesting, but not my life as I imagined years before. And I still didn't have the Kirby Brooks required gray hair. On my desk was a copy of *Sea Magazine*. It was the West Coast print media competition to *Yachting Magazine* in the east.

I had been here once before—the spontaneous magazine job hunt. And that almost got me killed in the Bahamas. But, what-the-hell, maybe lightning doesn't strike twice. I opened the magazine and turned to the brokerage section. There was Bertram with a kind of placeholder ad. Next to Bertram was McGinnis Yacht Sales—a multiple-page ad. Big presence on the West Coast. Seattle. So, this time I did not write a letter. I picked up the phone and dialed McGinnis in Seattle. Jim McGinnis answered. I asked if he would consider putting on another broker. He answered with, "Well . . . maybe. Next time you are in Seattle, stop by my office, and we can talk."

Karen was home. The boys were in school. I locked the office, drove home, and told Karen, "I'm driving to Seattle." It was winter. She said, "Maybe you should pack a lunch—take a blanket—a sleeping bag. In case you get stuck on the pass." I take none of that, get in the car, and start driving five hundred miles west.

I get to Seattle late at night, find a motel, and at 8:00 A.M. the next morning, I am standing at the McGinnis Yacht Sales front door as Jim McGinnis comes to work. I introduce myself. He stands there. "Wait, you are the guy who called yesterday!?"

"Yes."

He opens the door, and we go inside. He switches on the lights, and we walk into a room—The Chart Room—to make some coffee. Nautical charts cover all the walls. There are dark walnut-stained bamboo captain's chairs with red upholstery against the walls. A glass-top coffee table in the middle with legs to match the chairs. Jim ground his own coffee beans. All new stuff to me.

Jim says, "I wasn't expecting you this soon." I apologize for not calling.

He adds: "Sometimes people stop by in the morning on their way to work. They like fresh ground coffee."

We both sit down in the bamboo chairs. "So tell me, what brings you here so fast? That was John, right?"

We talk about who I am. About who he is. About the yacht business. The front door opens. This tall guy walks in. Jim says, "Hi, Bill." Jim turns to me and says, "John, I would like you to meet Bill Boeing."

Bill Boeing asks, "Where are you from? John, right, John? You work on Westlake, maybe?"

I answer with, "Missoula, Montana."

He leans back in his chair and says, "Well, I'll be goddamned! Bill Allen sits on our board. He was the president of our company before William and Sampler came along. Allen is from Lolo, you know. I guess nowadays a suburb of Missoula."

I say, "yes, sir!"

Bill Boeing turns to Jim McGinnis and says, "We like people from Montana."

Jim looks at me and half-smiles.

I'm thinking to myself; *I can't believe what just happened. Bill Boeing has just leveraged my hometown into a job.*

We drink coffee, talk about Bill's new boat, and drink more coffee. Bill Boeing stands, "Well, I got to go," walks to the door, and out into the morning sun.

Jim says, "I must wind the clock. I usually wind it on Saturday, but we will be gone, so it gets wound today. Why don't you stop by here after work, and we can go to the Seattle Yacht Club for a drink."

I agree.

10

I left McGinnis Yacht Sales to return at 5:00 P.M. Never having been in Seattle, I still knew I was staying. Or, put another way, *Bill Boeing had just so stated.* As I was getting into my car, a cargo van pulled up alongside me. In the driver's seat was Richard (Dick) Everett from Missoula. This was a kind of cosmic experience because it was Everett who sold me (actually, my mom) my first real boat. A 13-foot fiberglass sloop I sailed on Flathead Lake. *What is he doing here?* I'm thinking.

Well, moms are prone to do this kind of stuff. She and Karen got together on the phone about my trip, and my mother, who knew Everett, called him in Seattle to get a handle on what I'm up to. Everett says to me, "Marie *(my mom)* wants to know what McGinnis Yacht Sales is. Who is Jim McGinnis? Does any of this make sense?"

So, I jump in the van with Everett, and we go to coffee ... like I hadn't had enough coffee. Dick is concerning but interested. He tells me *McGinnis is the real deal. He is the dealer for Hatteras Yachts*—an even bigger deal in Everett's mind. At that time, Hatteras had eclipsed Chris Craft as the most prestigious thing that floats. He closes with, "Furthermore, Dan Blocker (Hoss Cartwright of *Bonanza)* has just ordered a new 72-footer—and one of the fellows on my dock told me that he saw Gene Hackman *(The French Connection)* at the Westin Hotel talking about building a new Trawler!" So, both sides of this conversation were good. My mother would receive a Hollywood report, and I was happier than I was an hour earlier. Dick and I say goodbye, his job done, and my job beginning.

By now, I have about six hours before the meet-up with McGinnis back at his office. What I do next is classic John LaCasse. I drive until I see a real estate office. I walk in and say, "You have five hours to sell me a house."

We find a house on the edge of the bowl-overlook at Northgate. About $33,000, as I recall. A remodel two-story with the kitchen and living room up and bedrooms/bathrooms/utility down. Nice yard. Small garage. I call Karen and tell her *we are moving to Seattle*. The response was dead air. This was moving so fast that I'm not sure if she ever actually hung up the receiver. At 5:00 P.M., I meet McGinnis. He asks what I did the remainder of the day. I smiled, "I bought a house."

Now his office manager, Beverly, is with him. They stare at each other. They stare back at me. They stare back at each other.

Jim says, "Welcome Aboard!"

What he didn't tell me was he had already hired someone. Some guy out of Western Airlines cabin service. So, McGinnis has one available desk with two people jockeying for the position.

We drove to the yacht club for drinks. The place was oozing with tradition. Started in 1892, it was second only to the St. Francis Yacht Club in San Francisco as the oldest on the West Coast. The register had fifty-six pages of rules. The whole place smelled like a rack of unread library books. The patrons at the bar were just as stuffy.

After the yacht club, we drove to a big marina called Shilshole on the west side of the city in a Norwegian suburb called Ballard. I'm learning that Norway and Ballard are doppelgangers of each other. The people eat strange fish. When they dance, they just stand there—nobody moves. The houses in Ballard are paid for. All the cars are used. Most foreign countries try and place their national presence in Washington, D.C. Not Norway! They put their national museum, culture center, and imprint stamp in Ballard. When Norwegian royalty come to the United States, they arrive in Ballard. There are motorcade traffic jams, just like in the District of Columbia. The last time I was caught in one, it was for a Princess from Norway. I was in my truck, in a position to see the national Norway thing underway. Watching the Norwegian crowd is like running the camera in slow motion. They stand and look at each other. Barely move. I bet it's because they are usually frozen in Norway.

Jim drives a Mercedes-Benz 300D. He tells me, "You will need to get a Mercedes as my everyday driver." That I should consider a Yacht Club. That I will be required to wear a white shirt and tie at work. That my shoes will be elk Topsiders. That his parking space is in front of the office—right in front. That McGinnis Yacht Sales is open seven days a week. (When I began working for McGinnis, I worked fifty-four days before my first day off.)

We drive slowly along the face dock of the Shilshole Bay Marina. There are about five hundred boats on the docks. Most of them have a mast. Jim says, "You see those masts, John? Under every one of those masts is a $100,000 sale."

Beverly turned in her seat and told me not to worry. "You will do just fine," she said. And I believed her.

Jim drove us back to my car, and I left for Montana. I drove all night. Karen was ready for the adventure. The kids had no reference point. We unloaded all the big stuff and left Missoula with what would fit in suitcases. When we arrived at our new house, we found there was no kitchen stove. I forgot to notice when I bought the house. What we all missed was the remodeling contractor forgot to vent the roof. We also noticed there was low water pressure, so I began a dig to upgrade the line from the house to the city's mainline in the street. John decided to help me and put the pic through the municipality's line. That got us quickly acquainted with the City of Seattle. Eventually, the ceiling became saturated with moisture and fell into the living room. We vented the roof and drywalled up a new ceiling. We were homeowners, no doubt about that.

On my first day on the job, I was one of two new salesmen. Jim was still avoiding the situation. Like we were two gladiators. Last man standing wins. It was the oddest ritual I had ever encountered. I won and got the desk. I realized the win when the other guy got on the phone and called his mother. He told her *he didn't like the job*.

I quickly sensed Jim McGinnis was the Marquis and office manager Beverly Mosley was the Keeper of the Keys. Jim's only official duty was to—once a week—wind the brass Chelsea clock on the north wall. He had secondary duties like being certain nobody took his parking spot and reminding John Franco—Franco's Bar/Restaurant was below the office—that Jim always sat at the corner table on the outside dock. Jim was the maximization of a self-absorbed attitude. Before yachts, Jim was a Navy fighter pilot. His favorite put-down of young pilots was, "Kid, I've got more time in the top of a loop than you have at the stick." Puffed himself up nonstop. At the Seattle downtown Rotary, Jim McGinnis was known as The Baron of Boats.

But all this puffery did not stop all the captains of industry to play at Jim's call. He was the biggest yachting act in the Pacific Northwest and had a splashy cache. The license plate on his Mercedes-Benz read "BOATS."

Beverly was positioned to manage the puffery while guarding the books. She was a trophy woman, so Jim would parade her on the point. Throwing money to keep her satisfied. Beverly banked every penny as Jim confabulated his station, keeping himself close to the edge. She became the bank. Jim ended up being her walk-around man.

On my first day on the sales floor, I'm addressing my Arrow short sleeve white shirt and tie, my navy blue Dacron and cotton pants, and my new lace-up elk Topsiders. The elk Topsider has got to be the ugliest shoe Topsider ever put on the market. Sort of a light ghee butter yellow/tan. Just awful. Anyway, I'm looking through my McGinnis Yachts inventory book. I look up. Gene Hackman opens the front door.

11

Like many things in my life, when Gene Hackman came through the McGinnis Yacht Sales door, I didn't realize I would be standing in Hackman's house many years later looking at Picasso art treasures while knocking back some Johnny Walker Blue.

Gene Hackman was Hollywood's authentic Actor, Writer, and Yachtsman—in equal shares.

In my arena, he was a long-distance yachtsman. No bling for him. The boat had to be an understated world-class traveler. Small engine, large fuel, and a bazillion miles of range. Hackman was following naval architect Jack Hargrave (One-eyed Jack, we called him). Hargrave was the designer of Hatteras and the developer of the "Long Range Cruiser" concept. So, of course, he found his way to our office. By the time Hackman arrived in Seattle, we had thirteen 58-foot long-range cruisers in the queue and underway from New Bern, North Carolina, to Seattle—five thousand-mile deliveries on the open ocean. Hackman had done his homework—he knew who we were.

McGinnis Yachts had the most experience in the long-range delivery business, with the best captains delivering the boats in showroom condition. And that stood us apart. The other Hatteras retail dealers were flummoxed by the McGinnis long-range delivery quality. If day-to-day Jim McGinnis was Beverly's walk-around man clock-winder, he was also on top of his game in style strategy.

The formula was deceivingly simple. At the beginning of each delivery, we would do a kind of Donald Crowhurst false narrative. Crowhurst was the guy who cooked the logbooks to appear to complete a circumnavigation *without* actually doing so. His ship's logbooks, found after his disappearance, suggest that the stress he was under and associated psychological deterioration may have led to his suicide. *(Donald Crowhurst - Wikipedia)*

Suicide was not in our wheelhouse, but cooking the logbooks was. We would slow-walk the trip by giving the new owner false date reports on trip progress. The boat would arrive two weeks earlier than we were reporting to the owner. We would dock the boat—usually at the Port of Everett or Edmonds—and would detail the boat back to perfect. No salt, no dock marks, no bumper scratches, no spilled fuel stains, no nothing but perfect.

Then we would get underway to Seattle. We put the crew in dress whites standing at parade rest and arranged to have a staggeringly impressive food and drink display on the aft deck. Then, slowly drop the lines of a showroom condition boat on the McGinnis dock to the background music of Aaron Copland's *Fanfare for the Common Man*. Then Jim would step forward and raise his forearm to his brow while saying, "You just can't beat the quality of a Hatteras yacht." Sometimes the new owners would simply start to cry.

Years later, when I moved into Yacht Construction, one of my firm's fellows (Don Martin) came up with an idea to give the new boat life as it came off the shipways at the launch. We played the same music (Aaron Copland's *Fanfare for the Common Man*), but we needed to add magic. A kind of *Transformers* movie approach. So, we would hide someone in the engine room in advance. The sequence was all would be quiet as the owner's wife stepped onto the platform and announced the boat's name while breaking the champagne across the bow. Then we would bring up Copland's *Fanfare*. The boat would start down the shipways like everyone would expect—except, when the hull hit the water, the guy in the engine room would light off (start) the engines.

At that moment, the *Transformers* thing happened. The boat became alive with nobody on the bridge. It transformed into something it wasn't moments before. And once again, people started to cry. *We are a species capable of enough abstraction to anthropomorphize thousands of tons of glass, aluminum, and steel into a living being.*

So, Gene Hackman was also one among us who saw both states of the boat. As a piece of equipment and one that was . . . alive.

I got Hackman as my "up" on the floor. I found that unusual as nobody was in a rush to stand in his light. Eventually, I understood why. High-profile celebrity was common in our Marina Mart office. Just another piece of meat he was in our arena.

We approach each other; he extends a hand. "Hi, I'm Gene Hackman."

We both move to the back window and look over the marina as he begins his interest. I am standing with an A-List actor on a red carpet, anchored by walnut panels, and on one entire twenty-foot wall, an enlarged wallpaper print of three-masted lumber schooners in Blakely Harbor one hundred years earlier. I'm trying to gauge my appearance—even how do I smell. He continues looking out the window like he believes I know what I'm doing.

We move to my desk. We sit. He folds his legs in a relaxed position. His Topsiders are way nicer than mine. I keep my Elks under my desk. I say, "Nice Topsiders."

He looks at his shoes. "Gold Cups," he says. "I think the nameplate on the counter is real gold." I keep my Elks under my desk.

For the next hour, we talk about open ocean passages. He's teaching me about long distance cruising. He doesn't know that. After all, I work for Hatteras Yachts of Jack Hargrave fame, in a walnut-paneled office, in the Pacific Northwest—like almost Alaska.

Finally, he says the opening words. "What do you have . . ."

We end up on a 72-foot Long Range Cruiser (LRC) under construction at Delta Marine on the Duwamish waterway in Seattle. Delta was— and remains—a commercial yard gone recreational. They pioneered the retro crab boat into the yacht market segment. I called as we drove in my new black 240D Mercedes-Benz—yep—and announced *I was on the way with Mr. Gene Hackman*. As we walked in, I got my first taste of celebrity. People looking at you. More and more looking at you. It's like a segment of Nature on NOVA. Onlooking fans like hyenas watching an antelope on the Serengeti—dodging in and out behind trees, extending their necks, and coming tentatively closer on each pass.

Hackman was smiling and nodding. Occasionally a hand wave to small groups. I was looking back, kept turning around, walking backward—and squinting. We got to the boat. The coffee brown Gold Cup Topsiders with the real gold nameplates on each side counter made their way on deck. A couple of Elks on the trail. We are alone on the boat to search and see all day if we like. Hackman was like Mr. Rogers on his Very Best Day in the Neighborhood. No tough guy *French Connection* . . .

We are standing on the bridge. The instrument array was beyond impressive. Hackman seemed to understand everything he touched. What a great lesson this day was becoming for me right out of the box. The ease of experience. The grace of personage. The quality of time. Gene Hackman was teaching me my career in a few hours.

As we stood on the bridge—me to his right—I noticed the compass kept following him. As he would move, so the compass would move. For a moment, I thought, *is this guy Gene Hackman, or is this a deity sent to train me from a galaxy far, far away?*

He noticed I was noticing. He smiled and said, "I have a steel plate in my chest."

After that day, I never saw him again, but the time we did spend was priceless. Years later, I was sitting with Bill Belzberg in Beverly Hills. We were about to leave his house for dinner at a local Italian restaurant. The restaurant was where everyone stood when Mr. Belzberg cleared the door. Bill was consistently among *Fortune*'s Top Ten wealthiest men in the world. He poured me a couple of fingers of Johnny Walker Blue. I opened with, "This is a hell of a house, Bill!"

He said, "Yeah, I got it from Gene Hackman when he went upside-down after his divorce."

I cradled my drink and kept my emotions inside, but I was sad.

12

I sat at my desk reflecting on Gene Hackman. What did I learn? I won my sales desk with aggressive action, but my learning from Hackman was about authenticity. The people coming through that door were successful. I surmised successful people could spot bullshit a mile away. So, I decided that I would learn slowly about boats and front-load my yachting conversations on risk and adventure. I had plenty of that.

Going forward, I never opened a transom hatch or rendered an opinion about the boat in a yacht sale transaction. I left all that to the marine surveyors. All I did was sell the dream. Everyone had a dream. Some were short-sighted, some were silly, some were religious, and some were dangerous. Regardless, the dream was what opened our door. It was never about hull material, horsepower, top hamper, or burn rate.

Sometimes I would subvert the dream. Maybe that was me having a counterinsurgent opinion. I had a history with that.

One afternoon this suit walks in. Announces he is the President of a Savings and Loan. "Going to try living the life," he tells me. He had just left his wife of thirty-four years. "Got an apartment and am on my way," he says.

I ask about his boating experience because his dream seemed to have nothing to do with boats. "None," he reports.

"Ok," I say, "let's do this. You mentioned you have an apartment?"

"Yes."

"Is there a small window in the bathroom?"

"Yes."

"Is there a tub/shower combination?"

"Yes."

"Ok. Great. I want you to go to REI and get a two-burner Coleman stove. Then to a hardware store and get an extension ladder. Your apartment is on which floor of your building?"

"The 2nd floor."

"Excellent! So here is how our boat training works. You get the stuff I just mentioned, as well as a large roll of masking tape. I want you to move into the bathroom with the two-burner gas stove. Move all your bedding into the tub/shower. Hang all your work clothes on the shower rack. Place the extension ladder outside leading to the window. Go into your apartment, turn around, and tape the bathroom door shut. Go back outside and use the ladder to come and go from the bathroom window, the new door to your new apartment. Cook all your meals on the Coleman stove. Use your leisure time at home sitting on the toilet. Then, I want you to come back here to my office in thirty days and let me know how that worked out for you."

▲ ▲ ▲

Sometimes captains of industry are in full command of the situation with a *make no mistake about that* posture. Jack Hargrave called one morning to say that the *Calliope* was coming on the market. The *Calliope* was the longtime yacht of the Kaiser family. That was Henry J. Kaiser, the Kaiser Aluminum icon; Edgar Sr., the son; and Edgar Jr., the firebrand owner of the National Football League (NFL) Denver Broncos, and a bunch of other stuff. Hargrave was a family friend, not the broker. However, we would give Hargrave the courtesy of his position and act accordingly.

So what Hargrave was doing was giving us a heads-up. Armed with that, I decided to call Don Snellman, a Seattle entrepreneur who had just won a $7.5 million lawsuit against IBM for patent infringement. Rumor had it that it was actually $12 million. Who better as a big yacht buyer than a guy with millions of dollars of new money? The problem was that Snellman was not tuned into old money protocol. Hargrave had mentioned that the *Calliope* would come on at $1.1 million when Edgar

Sr. died. That was expected to be not far into the future, but Edgar Jr. did not want to signal to his father or the family that he was going to sell the *Calliope* when Edgar Sr. died.

Snellman didn't care. He just went up against IBM and won; why not Kaiser! I wasn't strong enough to hold him off. Snellman told me to offer Hargrave $900,000 cash—no survey—possession immediately.

I'll call Hargrave—no, wait, I have Jim call Hargrave, and the offer is rejected out-of-hand.

"NO," says Hargrave, and he's disappointed that we are not honoring his request for discretion. So, I have the cat out of the bag. Snellman is telling colleagues he is buying the *Calliope*. Hargrave is telling Jim to fire me. Then, Edgar Jr. hears of the confusion on Westlake Avenue (our office), and he comes back that the price is One Million One—cash—and Snellman cannot take possession until Edgar Sr. dies.

With this, I go to Snellman's office on King Street to see if I can work him up to the terms and the $1.1 million.

King Street was a line of commercial buildings. Substantial, brick, and big. I find that Snellman owns them all, housing his copy machine company. Through the main entrance, the place is dark. One desk—one receptionist—dim lights. I say my name, and from the no-light dim of the obvious private office door, I hear, "Come in!"

The receptionist acknowledges the invitation, and in I go. The room is enormous. No lights. Snellman is sitting at an aircraft carrier-size desk. Next to him is a world globe about four feet in diameter. The globe is illuminated with internal lights. So, the glow in the darkness is a stage for Bela Lugosi by any Dracula measure.

I sit and decide to pitch the deal straightaway. "Mr. Snellman, Mr. Kaiser is willing to sell you the *Calliope* for one million one, but the delivery must be delayed until his father dies."

Snellman continues looking at his globe. He begins to turn it on its axis. He stops it with his index finger. He asks, "What do you know about high power lines?"

I tell him, "Not much."

He says, "I've got to get a new base for my flagpole." Then he looks over the top of his globe and says, "I will take that deal. Tell Kaiser I will give them One Million One and accept the delivery considerations. Tell Kaiser I will give them One Million and **One Dollar.**

I see the humor. Snellman gives me a book as a gift. The author was someone else, but Snellman signed it anyway. I head back to our office.

Beverly sets up a conference between Hargrave, Kaiser, and Jim—except Jim has me take the call because he obviously doesn't want to get in an embarrassing exchange with Hargrave over his slipshod new salesman. I play the counteroffer as presented by Snellman.

There is a long silence then Kaiser asks, "What's the commission?"

I say, "One hundred thousand dollars and ten cents."

Kaiser says, "I'll take the deal."

Jim and I went to the Polynesian Club on the Seattle waterfront and had the bartender set up an unending Mai Tai cocktail chain of rum, Curaçao liqueur, Orgeat syrup, and lime juice. Beverly had to come get us as the restaurant manager wouldn't give Jim his car keys.

Kaiser had Don Snellman escrow one million cash as good faith, and they agreed that the closing would be when *The Wall Street Journal* ran the Edgar Kaiser Sr. obituary. We could visit the boat by appointment at the family compound on Orcas Island, Washington, in the San Juan Islands. So, we chartered a Seattle seaplane with Jim Chrysler and headed for Orcas Island.

Kaiser forgot to tell Snellman that Tongsun Park of South Korea was at the compound. Tongsun Park was the poster boy for graft and corruption in South Korea. He was under investigation for bribing members of the United States Congress. He did bring the shadow of organized crime to the U.S. House of Representatives. Otto Passman of Louisiana's 5th Congressional District was tied to Tongsun Park and charged with conspiracy, bribery, and income tax evasion. He was acquitted.

Guns and bodyguards faced us as we arrived. Tongsun Park's security detail would not let us off the plane after we taxied to the dock at the compound. Don Snellman had just deposited one million dollars in Rainer Bank as good faith, and now some Great Gatsby asshole from South Korea was not letting us on the dock!

We left and flew back to Seattle.

When Edgar Kaiser Sr. died, *The Wall Street Journal* ran the obituary. Kaiser Jr. agreed to deliver the boat to the dock at the Bay Club in Vancouver, British Columbia. Snellman had not forgotten the snub at the dock on Orcas Island, so at the Bay Club, Kaiser decided not to attend. He was busy with his NFL team in Denver. He sent two young lawyers instead.

Now I'm standing with Snellman as he sees the chink in the armor. We walk aboard and do a cursory walk-through. Snellman says, "This is not the same boat that was represented. I will not transfer the money."

Then he reaches into his pocket and hands a punch list to the lawyers. It was for $100,000 of defined missing equipment. They had no idea how to react. The list was likely an invention by Snellman. The lawyers call Kaiser. Kaiser, who is with visiting press corps before a Denver Broncos football game, gives Snellman the money.

13

In terms of private jets, there's a big difference between the Bombardier Challenger 600 and a Learjet 24. There was to be a meeting at Flightcraft at Boeing Field in Seattle between Ron Rivett and Bill Belzberg. Flightcraft is where I had a tie down for my plane, so I knew the operational side of business meetings next to airplanes.

Both men were captains of industry. Belzberg self-made savings and loans throughout Canada. Rivett also self-made when he and a buddy decided to take a couple of claw hammers and stack up a motel in Aberdeen, South Dakota. They called it *Super 8*.

Belzberg, listed in *Fortune* magazine among the richest men in the world, was in the Bombardier Challenger 600.

Rivett's Super 8 organization had just made the *Inc.* 500 list, and he was in the Learjet 24.

Both were driving their egos to this meeting. What my experience lacked was how to not plan a meeting between two business giants when one is driving a patrol boat that he will need to park next to an aircraft carrier. That seemed to tilt the tone of the meeting.

Within days after the Flightcraft meeting, Rivett was sitting in his own Bombardier Challenger 650. My lesson was to understand Einstein's theory of relativity. Energy equals Mass times the speed of light squared ($E=MC^2$). Rivett's quick jump to the Challenger should have been my indicator that he understood the theory. As the Rivett organization grew, I was growing also, but through a different lens. So once again, I missed how to equate Energy to Mass. Rivett was opening a new Super 8 Motel every seventy-two hours. I was still seeing him as a contender, but not on the main stage. He was *new money*—much different than *old money,* where I spent most of my time.

One day I came across a distress yacht situation, I thought fit the Rivett profile. The deal made my eyes water. The sale would go down to $280,000 under the market. I got on the phone and called him in South Dakota. I gave him an exhaustive pitch on this incredible opportunity. My big favor to him from a world-class Yacht Broker.

He let me finish before he said, "John, I lose more money than that off the backs of my trucks on their way to the jobs every morning."

The Ron Rivett answer was my next learning after Gene Hackman. There was personage and style, but there was also relentless power. Yacht buyers came in many stripes. Unlike Rivett and Belzberg, some of these players were either not-so-solid citizens or psychotic.

The *entourage* was the opening mark of endless self-absorbed doublespeak walking through the door.

We had a first-time *Gold Record* rock star come in with a set of directors and camera crew so they could record his yacht purchase. The crew would position him on his "best" side to ask questions. His questions were about the camera on my desk—not boats. The yacht purchase footage was functionally useless. Instead, he left, went to a camera store, and ordered every item Canon Camera Systems sold—Everything!

We had a suit come in looking for a tugboat because he planned to have a horse off JZ Knight's ranch placed in a stall on the aft deck to copulate with a blonde woman, thereby producing the rebirth of Ramtha. To his family's New York Stock Exchange (NYSE) listed credit, they sent lawyers in after him. I never did call JZ Knight to ask WTF!

Another guy was starting a church. He needed a boat as his cathedral. He was the spiritual leader of *The Alive Church of Harmonious Living*. His followers ate potatoes—only potatoes. I asked if he had ever studied Irish history. He said, "No." I sold him a surplus Freezer Ship. The hull was all cold storage. It seemed a good fit. He agreed.

A woman came in one day and made a (bad check) deposit on a Hatteras Sport Fisherman. She asked for a demonstration ride. She had a small boy with her. I knew the check was bad, and something about her got us out on Lake Union and into Lake Washington. We talked on the fly bridge as her boy used the instrument array to spin himself into another dimension. She was losing custody of her son and was on the run. She wanted him to have a good last memory of his mom. The police and Social Service agency people met us at the dock. Even now, I can't stabilize my emotions through those last moments.

A guy with a brown leather hat and gold neck chains said he was moving to Seattle from New Mexico. He wanted to live on a boat. We called around and, from our bank, found him a 58-foot Hatteras Yacht Fisherman that was being held in foreclosure. The leather hat wanted to know which bank. From our office, he called our bank's Trust Department and told the manager he was moving into Washington State and would like to move some trust funds to Seattle. The Trust Department was delighted.

Then he called the Marine Finance Department of the same bank and told them he planned to buy a boat and would like financing. They invited him downtown. He said, "I'm a little short on time, but if you call your Trust Department, they know who I am." The bank was Rainier Bank. The Marine loan officer was Greg Hull. He was a good guy, and we moved money through his bank. So, Greg called the trust officer and was told, "Oh yes, he is coming to Seattle and moving a great deal of money into Rainier Bank."

We got the boat ready for sale.

The guy with the leather hat and gold neck chains told us he would be back in three days to survey and close. We proceeded accordingly. During that three-day period, he found a local print shop and convinced the owner he would buy his shop. He stayed after shop hours to get acquainted with the layout. What he really did was fabricated counterfeit certificates of deposit. They were not perfect, so he photocopied them.

We go to close the sale at the bank.

The leather hat guy slides a large envelope across the table to the bank officers. They open the flap to find photocopies of CDs. The leather hat goes into a rage accusing his New Mexico bank of incompetence. "I said send the certificates—NOT COPIES," he exclaims.

The marine loan officers say, "No problem. We will handle the Certificate transfer," and with the vision of a major trust account in their heads, close the sale.

In a day or so, Greg Hull calls me. He is talking, but there is no voice. That left hours earlier. We scramble to reverse-engineer the last few days. We call the U.S. Coast Guard, and they mount a helicopter search out the Straits of Juan de Fuca toward the Pacific. They find him, and so do the police back at the dock.

A guy driving a coin gold Mercedes 600 pulls up in front. The same model the Vatican staff uses for the Pope. When he walks in, he is tall and well-spoken. His story is that he is the general contractor for the new United Airlines building in Seattle. He wants to live on a boat but maybe try one overnight—kind of a sleepover—to see if he likes it. I call Bob Reed of Reed Sand and Gravel. He has a boat in our marina that is always for sale and never for sale. I figure these two guys can at least shop talk, and maybe a boat deal results. The shop talk happens, and the Mercedes 600 guy comes out of that conversation with Bob Reed agreeing on his own company letterhead to be the sand and gravel subcontractor for the new United Airlines building in Seattle.

In the business community of Seattle, being tight with Bob Reed was a very big deal! The 600 Mercedes guy has just reached a kind of parody with Reed. Now it's Christmas Eve, and the Mercedes guy is at the flagship Downtown Nordstrom buying Christmas gifts. He has selected $25,000 worth of jewelry for his lady friend. At the counter, he starts to pay with a vest-pocket personal check. The store employee says she is unable to take a personal check. The Mercedes guy asks for someone from the C-Suite to intervene. Then he produces the letter from Bob Reed that establishes himself as the contractor for the new United Airlines building, and in the letter, Bob Reed is the subcontractor. Nordstrom takes the check and the jewelry walks out the door.

The following Monday, I am on the phone with Bob Reed and Bruce Nordstrom. Once again, we reverse-engineer the weekend and manage to tag the girlfriend. She tells us the jewelry is *hers—too bad*. We up the tone of the conversation making her an accessory. She produces the jewelry and the location of her boyfriend. The Seattle Police Department (SPD) gets in the act and starts to chase the Mercedes 600 boyfriend. He pulls up in front of the office again and runs inside. He tosses me the keys to the car and runs out the door. Two detectives are running on his tail. They zip-tie him on the ground about a block away. From the police station, he makes his one call—to me. He gives me his car for the trouble.

The whole story was fake—top to bottom. I didn't want the car, so I gave it to my lawyer. He stored it in a rented garage, and I never saw the car again.

Years later, as new money and old money mixed, I spent fifteen weeks managing the sale of Ron Rivett's 200-foot research vessel after he completed seventeen movies for Discovery Television, and Bill Belzberg would reach in his suit vest pocket and write me a check for $36 million for a position in a residential business compound in Moses Lake, Washington.

14

Large transactions, from my perspective, were like living on a one-lane street in the core of a large city. The transactions mirrored the traffic pattern on the street. Sometimes one car drives straight through uninhibited. Sometimes two cars enter simultaneously from opposite ends, and one gives way to the other as a courtesy, drivers waving to each other as they pass. Sometimes cars enter simultaneously and drive grill to grill in their demonstrated attempt to dominate the lane.

The most extreme case of lane domination was when one owner barricaded himself in his yacht, threatening to commit suicide if the transaction went through. Or, in anger, took the vessel into deep water and tried to sink it. In this case, we had an owner who, under the grip of a low offer, took a large trawler into Puget Sound and opened all the through-hull fittings to watch his vessel sink away from him. I think he figured his insurance payment would be better than the offer. He forgot to check the level of his fuel tanks—they were empty—therefore served as flotation, and the boat did not sink.

Sometimes a yacht is a great equalizer. Self-admiration can be the driver of a large transaction. Humbleness, humility, and modesty are not to be found. It's a case of manufactured privilege when single rich men firewall themselves against women by having a woman sign a prenuptial agreement before a date. Of course, she would be picked up in a long black car; however, any self-worth she might possess unfortunately left the room.

We had a circumstance where one of these men placed himself aboard his new boat and decided to cruise around Lake Union as opposed to going to the locks and out into Puget Sound. The boat was large and had a deep draft. Onboard, he had his entourage of followers. Within the first fifteen minutes of his maiden voyage, he put the vessel aground in Lake Union.

In terms of embarrassment, that would be like the owner standing naked in a Fifth Avenue window of Nordstrom. Not just the day-to-day workers around Lake Union but the entire city of downtown Seattle watched as Mattson Tug & Barge, along with various divers and maritime experts, tried to pull this guy's new yacht out of the mud and silt. The project went on for days. It was just perfect.

In the quest for big yachts, executive jets, and fast cars, there are extreme examples, and as a broker, one must always carry that reality. One day I was approached by a fellow who wanted to build a steel yacht. He had plans, and the plans represented the boat to be fifty feet in length overall. I had no experience with construction in steel, so I looked around for an option. I found Tacoma Boatbuilding. The yard was a military repair and refit facility that handled new construction for the Navy. So, I went to the yard with my plans. I was a walk-in with no appointment, but I was lucky enough to get in front of Tacoma Boatbuilding's chief engineer. As we faced each other in his office, he appeared to be just like the shipyard. After so many years of shipbuilding, he somehow looked like some combination of aluminum steel and hot rivets. He smoked constantly. His fingers were yellow. He had simply become his product.

He was cordial as he invited me to unroll my plans. He was at his desk, and I was standing in front. I laid out the boat's plan profile. He looked for a moment, then sat down and said, "We can't build that."

I asked why.

He said, "The boat is too small."

On his office walls were pictures of ships—just ships. Ships for the Navy of the United States, and Korea, and Taiwan. I pointed to a picture of a Navy frigate right behind him.

"That ship on the wall behind you—if you built that and painted it white, could we call it a yacht?"

"Yes," he said, "you could call it a yacht."

I stood, clearing my head for a moment, and I asked him again, "So, if we commission you to build essentially a warship of steel and the paint scheme is white, then that becomes a yacht."

"I don't care what you call it—anything you like as long as your checks clear."

With that piece of check-processing humor, I drove back to my office. I was on my own now. McGinnis Yacht Sales was behind me. Leaving McGinnis was easy. As his top producer every year since I joined his company, I wanted to talk about working my way into some McGinnis Yacht Sales equity. He turned me down. I left, opened my own office, and took his Office Manager with me. Beverly would now keep me on my own set of rails. "LaCasse Marine Group" was underway.

Karen is in a big house in Mill Creek. She is wrangling the boys. John Patrick is captain of the tennis team. Jeff is being campaigned by Cornish College of the Arts to become a student—pulling out all the stops. Bob is refining his mind to become a journalist, and Erik is selling golf balls to Mill Creek Country Club members—balls that he picked out of the rough along the fairways. A very successful side-hustle that got us in trouble with the club management. Erik was an early used golf ball adopter who was taking a bite out of the Club's market share.

We have two Mercedes-Benz (one gold and one black) and a black Fiat Spider. We are members of the Country Club, Tennis Club, and the Swim Club. We are the first in our community to build a deck supporting a hot tub. Our Christmas trees are too big to put in stands, so we hang them from the overhead beams in front of panorama windows.

With all this middle-class day-to-day action, I decide to get into the new yacht construction business. I couldn't get the white battleship/yacht idea out of my head. I wasn't Teddy Roosevelt, but hey.... I had experience managing new construction up to fifty feet. But this was going to be a major jump in size and complexity.

There was no deciding. I didn't make decisions that way; I just reacted. I began to run the idea past people I knew in the industry who would fill the gaps in a complete project. I knew I had the platform at Tacoma Boatbuilding, but I needed an interior. I went to Delta Marine. Jack and

Ivar Jones agreed to contract my interiors with the Yard's permission. Tacoma Boat agreed. For interior design, I turned to Teague Associates Inc. in Redmond, Washington. They did Boeing interiors. I needed to associate all of this with an international brokerage house, so I made a deal with David Fraser of Fraser Yachts. Now I had my team. We named it "Trilogy Yachts."

But how to begin? I needed a rendering of our boat. Teague came up with a 152-foot boat drawing that looked like a badass private fighting machine. They scribed in Darth Vader at the helm. Perfect topper.

I contacted the Fort Lauderdale Boat Show management and reserved a twenty-five-foot corner booth. Convinced Teague to design the layout and provide the staging. Delta Marine sent scale models of their construction. Greyhound bus transport moved all our stuff and equipment to the show. A few days before I left, I checked in with Tacoma Boatbuilding to see what promotional material they might have. The engineer said, "I have some VCRs." I drove to Tacoma and collected them.

We are at the booth the day before the show opens. I am there with a designer from Teague and a broker from Fraser Yachts. We are assembling glass and chrome stations, rolling out carpets, and sweating in the Florida heat.

I decided to preview the Tacoma Boatbuilding promotional material. I load a player, and the tape opens with a Navy frigate doing crash stops in widely rough sea conditions. Then the scene changes to another ship doing flank speed while shooting deck guns in rapid-fire. There is brass rolling around on the deck and the *Whump-bang / Whump-bang* of the deck guns roaring like a World War II "Uncle Sam Needs You" commercial. The only thing missing was real smoke coming out of the VCR.

With that ration of smoke, I instinctively knew Trilogy would be successful. The sales pitch focused on the strength of a Navy ship couched in a private yacht. Safety at sea. Protect your family. Let your family feel safe in the open ocean. If it's good enough for the U.S. Navy, it's good enough for your family.

We began running the deck gun tape with sound at the opening bell. People began to gather around our booth. The Teague influence was pivotal because, suddenly, we were providing a yacht warship with a Boeing-quality interior. We were name-dropping everywhere. We had contracts for two 150-foot yachts built to U.S. Navy specifications for private parties by the end of the day.

Local television crews came to our booth, turned on the hot lights, and ran the interviews. We had done more business in one day than most yards do in a decade. The first contract guy was San Puglia. He brought in super yacht designer Gerhard Gilgenast. The boat became the "Sea Falcon II."

We come home and go to the yard. We get our hard hats, our own offices, and our engineering staff. We take breaks when the whistle blows. We have project managers, compliance officers, and Navy liaison officers. I'm thinking, *why do we have Navy liaison officers?* That was because we were sharing space with USNS *Hayes* (T-AGOR-16)—a super-secret acoustic ship designed to recover submarines. They were our under-construction partners. For them, it was refit; for us, it was all new. However, in conversation with these guys, we learned how to keep our rhetoric on the table about keeping one's family safe.

For example, we could electrify the rails so when a pirate comes over the side, he fries in the wire, and the owner could simply broom sweep him off the deck as required. The list was long. We could route raw gas and diesel to the fire hose so when a pirate boat comes alongside, the ship's crew sprays them with a mix of gas and diesel, then hits them with a flare. We designed bulkheads with breakaway silhouettes of AR-15-223/556 COLT M-4s. The yacht crew could resemble a rifle company in a matter of minutes. We were becoming the darlings of offshore cruising. Tacoma Boatbuilding was also feeling the excitement, as well as some investors in Washington, D.C. These were M&A people in D.C. who could smell a roll-up of two yacht builders that could stand in the light of our enormous success. The other two organizations down range were Striker and Burger—two legacy yacht builders looking for some lift. We, in the eyes of the investors, were the solution.

The back channel story was Tacoma Boatbuilding was selling to this D.C. group, so the roll-up was Tacoma Boatbuilding, Striker Yachts, Burger Yachts, and we were a high-end customer, not a principal. We didn't pay much attention to the business of Tacoma Boat and the new investor group, except we began seeing Striker sport fishermen taking shape in another building at the shipyard.

We are cutting and riveting—there were over three hundred employees working on the Tacoma Boatbuilding yacht projects. *The Seattle Times* asked me for an interview. I agreed, and the *Sunday Times* did a double-truck above-the-fold story. The article featured me pictured in a workman's helmet next to welding sparks against the headline "Yachts of Money—Luxury ships for super-rich a growth industry in Tacoma."

The next day I get a call from Charles (Chuck) Pigott, the CEO of PACCAR. He wants to have a look at our Gilgenast design under construction. *Oh, my God*, I'm thinking, *these guys are Kenworth trucks, railroad boxcars, and Sherman tanks. Are we hot or what!*

It's raining when Charles Pigott arrives. He's driving a new Jaguar sedan. There are potholes full of water. I'm outside waiting to direct him in. He stops his new car at a barricade in front of some standing water. I advise him to go back around. He thinks not—he is short on time. He drives forward, and his new car disappears up to above the floorboards. Now I have the CEO and Chairman of one of the largest companies in the world up to his ass in a mud puddle.

We bring a truck and pull him and his car onto the dry. Now he is out of time, starts his car, and heads back to Seattle. I needed a way to get back to him that was more interesting than a phone call. I went to West Marine and bought a new life preserver PFD, still in plastic. Gift-wrapped it, attached my card, and headed for PACCAR's home office. I walked into this reception area and handed my box to the "gatekeeper" at the desk. "Give this to Mr. Pigott. It's for his car."

As the weeks passed, we became working friends with the Navy staff. Lots of fun and very knowledgeable about security upon oceans. We took the stories to our customers. Among the ensuing ideas was that we established a private system of war games. Electronic targets to be built into our yachts along with electronic guns (not lasers), and our owners would meet from time to time to establish the winners. Open ocean private battles. The whole Navy guns-to-plowshares thing started trending among the super-rich.

While this was going on, the new owners of Tacoma Boat were tossing multiple balls in the air, trying to jumpstart their adventure into yacht construction. The lag time was more than they planned. The welder's union didn't care. These were Union shop welders, and they get paid, or they walk. Revenue was good, but it was all Navy. The new yachts were lagging. We were fine because we were outside the Striker, Burger, Tacoma Boatbuilding deal but sharing yard workers.

The Navy, however, was not so fine. Their contracts officer began to suspect he wasn't getting his money's worth. He called for a serious meeting and put the yard on notice that an investigation was underway, and the Navy would pull the Hayes out of the yard if his suspicions were correct—that federal money was being siphoned off the Hayes to support Burger and Striker.

The day the story about me and Trilogy ran in *The Seattle Times*, I took the newspaper to the Seattle Athletic Club and sat in the restaurant all morning with the paper spread in front of me, hoping someone would tag me in the story and make a fuss. Didn't happen. What did happen was the Navy contracts officer decided the yard was cooking the books and sent a team of sailors over that weekend to grab their ship and return it to the Navy Yard in Bremerton.

The yard was closed. Everyone was laid off or fired. We were looking through the fence at our work in progress. Sam Puglia, the customer for Hull Number One, had the chops to take control of Building Number 16, where we were; go back into the skilled labor markets and find enough people to save his investment and deliver his own yacht.

Gerhard flew in from Europe to review options. When I met him at SeaTac International Airport, he was limping. We did a photo shoot in the main terminal and moved into town. He was in pain. We took care of business, and he returned to Europe. He was dead two weeks later from bone cancer. He didn't know—thought it was arthritis. Kept ignoring it.

All the spoils got spread around the industry. No one recovered.

I sat staring at the wall for days.

15

Being a yacht broker is not all crisis management. At least not a serious case of crisis management.

Not long ago, I got the word that George Shultz died. He was the Secretary of State under President Reagan from 1982, a position he held for six years. He was one of only two guys who served in four cabinet positions in his lifetime. Under President Nixon, he served as Secretary of Labor, then as the first Director of the Office of Management and Budget, and as the Secretary of the Treasury, which is when I knew him. On July 15, 1978, he and I were sitting on a boat, a big boat; it was an 80-foot Stevens, on Lake Union in downtown Seattle. He was in town to open the King Tutankhamen exhibit in Seattle, and we were providing the boat for him because we knew him. And, of course, because he was Secretary of the Treasury, we spent the afternoon having him sign dollar bills. But anyway, that's not the point. The point is that we drank all afternoon on the boat, and his wife at the time was deaf, so there was signing going on. And she knew that he had to open the King Tut exhibition that night, and he was getting hammered. And, of course, so was I, and so were some of our friends.

So, late in the afternoon, after they got done signing each other and stuff I couldn't understand, but it couldn't have been good, she comes out, and she addresses him in whatever way that they do, and Shultz is there with us, and what had occurred to her—I think her name was Mary. Anyway, he'd forgotten his tuxedo pants. He had a tuxedo with a top and no pants. And now we're like an hour away from having to go downtown.

We had a full security detail that was assigned to our station there at the boat, and one of the guys was a Washington State highway patrolman. And he had a pair of very dark blue stripe-down pants. They were kind of dress officer's pants that looked sort of close to tuxedo pants. So, we make this decision, this command decision that we're going to trade this officer, this highway patrol officer, his pants for a pair of George Shultz's pants, that will be khakis.

We make the play. We ask the highway patrolman if he would be willing to trade his pants for George Shultz's pants. Now, this is the Secretary of the Treasury asking this, and so, of course, the officer said, "Well, of course, yes, sir. I mean, I'm assigned to this. Do you want my jacket too?" So, anyway, that worked. We all go down below, and we get this tuxedo out, and we start swapping pairs of pants around till we get something that fits and it works right. And then to downtown, we go to open the Tutankhamen exhibition with our signed $1 bills. George Shultz, a hell of a guy. He was one hundred years old, and he passed away at Stanford, California. He was one of those icons that stood strong and tall. I'm going to miss him.

16

Privilege has its own cache, be it in money or station. The first morning I am in Seattle, I have coffee with Bill Boeing. The first month I'm in Seattle, I'm doing a deal with Edgar Kaiser. Eventually, I'm sitting on a boat getting drunk with George Schultz. One day I pick up a call, and it's from Mexico—the President of Mexico.

I'm at the Olympic Hotel, and this guy walks up to my table. He wants to talk about boats. He is Frank Orrico. He owns sixteen shopping centers. Not least the Ala Moana Center in Honolulu. Orrico recognized me because I had just run a Two for One Yacht Sale in *SEA Magazine*. Indeed, two yachts for the price of one! People up and down the West Coast saw the humor, but this guy brought it to my table. We built two new yachts. One for Frank Orrico and one for his buddy Harry See. Our builder was Tom Nelson, who managed a place known as the Boat Yard. He was experienced and perfect for these guys because he understood privilege as *good for them—but not one of them*. We all had to be that way.

Orrico brought Harry See (See's Candies) as part of my two-for-one sale. See's Candies is now part of Warren Buffett's portfolio. And that might be because I got a call from Charlie Munger from their jet. I had a question about a NASCAR deal (new track). I thought they might like that also had some interest from Bill Belzberg. But I was cranky because Harry See's two Rhodesian ridgebacks (dogs) had just eaten my new Cole Hawn shoes. Harry and I were playing cribbage at his lake house. I thanked Munger for the call and passed along Harry See's regards. Eventually, Buffett and Munger owned Harry's company.

The story around See's Candies is that there was never a "Mary See." She was an invention of the See brothers because nobody would believe they were making the candy—they weren't that creative—or so the solid citizens thought, anyway. How it all began was the See brothers made a bad sugar buy. They were in the commodity business. They couldn't unload the sugar. So, the brothers decided to make candy. They just couldn't sell the idea that they were the wizards behind the product. When they noticed a woman's torso graphic on an apple box, that became Mary See, the originator of See's Candies.

One night, Harry See was playing poker with Max Wyman. Among other things, Harry owned the Silverado Winery in Napa, California, and as a hobby yachtsman, had built the largest fiberglass boat in the United States up to that time. It was named after the vineyards, the *Silverado*. The table stakes were high, and Harry was short at the table. Everyone knew Harry was good for the money, but no, instead Harry put up his boat and lost the hand. Max Wyman now owned the *Silverado*.

My first $25,000 glass of wine was in Harry See's wine cellar. We were shooing the geese off his deck. He lived on Lake Washington in Seattle. "Would you like some wine?" he asked. I'm thinking that would be fine so we go downstairs. Harry reaches into a kind of hole and comes out with a bottle of wine resembling the Vatican's version of a piece of the true cross. Lots of dust. He lights a candle. Holds the bottle to the candle. There is a chandelier of glass grapes hanging over the table. The room is dim to accommodate the candle. Harry opens the bottle and pours the wine through some cheesecloth into a decanter. He stares at the decanter for a long time. I am quiet, just standing. I know this is going to be an important glass of wine. And then, with the candor of losing his yacht in a poker game, he pours me a glass and speculates.

"About $25,000 per glass, I would say."

▲ ▲ ▲

One day, the phone rings. On the line is John P. Doolittle, USAF Colonel retired. His brother James, Vice Commander of the Air Force Flight Test Center at Edwards Air Force Base, California. Their father, General James Harold Doolittle, was no longer available. John wanted me to sell his boat—a 42-foot Grand Banks. I did.

17

I'm in Osaka, Japan. Why am I here? Because Mitsubishi heavy industries decided to build a yacht. Why not get in the yacht business? My guess: Mitsubishi heavy industries are in the transportation business. Multiple divisions are moving stuff everywhere. It's part of a shipping industry using five million barrels of oil per day to move material across ocean routes. In a year, that's eight hundred million tons of carbon dioxide into the atmosphere. So, someone in their C-Suite decides, let's change the public focus to something less invasive—yachts. The project will be only a part of one maritime division but will have the face of environmental concern, however oblique.

Because this company had generations of experience, the assumption was that its engineering department would come up with the finest yacht in the world. So, they did. And that ended up being a case of: *Be careful what you wish for. You might get it.*

When I arrived in Osaka, I grabbed a cab to the Osaka Air Terminal Hotel. Essentially a building built of stainless steel and tile with traditional trappings. Businessmen love the Osaka Terminal because it's in the middle of everything, although the bathtubs are a bit short for American men.

Every morning, breakfast is served on the 20th floor. I suspect that's to get the international business crowd above the morning fog. During the 1980s, work in Japan was all day, and play was all night. I don't know when these guys slept. The gaming sounds of the pachinko parlors permeated the night air, and the business community maintained a black suit posture twenty-four hours a day. I had to commute a couple hundred miles out of Tokyo and would look down the tarmac to see rows of Boeing 747s with endless lines of black-suit, black-briefcase men staging for a commute. It may have been business-as-usual, but visually, it was a dystopian version of army ants on a mission.

Mitsubishi had spent millions of dollars on a 112-foot motor yacht to the finest specifications known. And, of course, if it's good enough for commercial ships, it's good enough for yachts. So, they built the yacht with a double hull and a round bottom—just like a tanker. Odd-looking to an average yachtsman, but it got better.

Mitsubishi builds to ClassNK, a maritime classification dedicated to ensuring the safety of life and property at sea. Strong stuff, good welding, advanced fire systems, bulkhead transits that do not leak and, of course, what every yachtsman wants: a complete fire system with canvas hose and brass nozzles where necessary, including over the bed in the master stateroom.

Nothing more comforting than a fire ax in the bathroom. I'm sure, as an owner, you could become comfortable with that kind of safety gear, but on the open market, this Mitsubishi yacht, known as the "Devil Queller," was bringing no offers. So, I show up with interest from the United States.

The Japanese businessman named Mike Nakamura is my contact. He arranged the first meeting. We get a cab that has the traffic side doors welded shut so passengers don't step into the flow. I think of it as an interesting control mechanism. Nakamura takes me to a waterfront outside a location where there are wooden seats against a barrel. Three black suits show up. The five of us sit down. The lead in the black suit says to the American at the table, in reasonably good English, this *is a* "cash on the barrelhead deal."

I'm thinking to myself, *in the Old West, that used to work in the taverns, but how do you get your ship on his barrel?*

Mike Nakamura vectors the conversation to how we would like to visit the boat before we discuss the price.

I have two buyers. The first is Keith McCaw, the youngest of the McCaw brothers of Cellular One, later sold to AT&T, and Jimmy Krause, a Harley-Davidson dealer—an aggressive young man always swinging for the fences. I had met him on a Taco Tuesday, the day when motorcycle people get together for socializing at a local bar. He invited me to go riding. I had a Harley-Davidson Dyna Wide Glide, a street version of a Chopper, in yellow and black with flame on the tank. I agree, and we set a time for a ride to Port Townsend up at the curve of the Straits of Juan de Fuca as it becomes Puget Sound. On the ride, I was stuck between balance, wisdom, and power, but all I could see was the White Horse of Death. The guy was insanely reckless on his bike.

Keith McCaw, my other buyer, was interested but tentative. The motorcycle guy wanted me to be aggressive. Like, *do not offer more than we can sell it for scrap* kind of aggressive. But I am in a foreign country with no social support if I start playing hardball. The following day, Mike and I go to the boat. The three men at the table the day before turned out to be bankers. The bankers who wrote the construction loan for the boat. The original buyer was a straw man who took the deal on the speculation it was a slam-dunk for a profit because the builder was an international maritime behemoth.

And, as they were finding out, everything was wrong with that picture.

Although I had good photography, the actuality of the boat was like a diorama of museum-quality safety gear. The boat felt like a trade show sample where every option was stuffed into a booth-size model. Like a member of the Cascade Walking Club gets his membership card and then goes to the REI flagship store to buy one of everything to hang in his bathroom. The most extreme example of "more is better" I had ever seen.

So, I tell the bankers that for this boat to be marketable as a yacht, all the good stuff must come out, be capped off, or hidden in some fashion. We break for the day, and I go back to the Osaka Terminal to pencil in some numbers. At this point, we are in Japan on Day 3, and as I walk into the lobby, I'm approached by some official-looking fellow who is holding a hotel bill—pointing and saying, "statement, statement!" He hands me a bill for $5,000 U.S. dollars. I say something very American-like, "You must be fucking kidding!"

He bows, and I continue to my room.

The next morning, I meet Mike Nakamura on the 20th floor. We watch the sun do its second rise over the pollution. The first rise, nobody sees. He tells me that the $5,000 was most likely an estimate going forward. Mike speculates that "statement" and "Yes" are the only English the lobby man knows. So "you must be fucking kidding" would be confusing. Mike and I make a desk stop on our way out, and I, through Mike, establish how I will cover the associated costs.

We are back at the barrel head with the banker suits. They expect cash put on the barrel. And I do not recognize the quality. I find this amazing. I tell them I will do an international bank transfer. No cash on the barrel head. So now, regardless of cultural differences or distortion, I'm tired of their barrel-head gaslighting. I offer $1,000,000 U.S. As-Is on the dock in Osaka. I will handle the delivery to the USA.

Later that day, I'm told all three bankers hung themselves in a local hotel room. That hotel rafter version of seppuku gave me my first case of cosmic consciousness. I fly back to Seattle with no answer.

Five weeks later, I'm back at the Osaka Terminal. Someone upstream accepted the offer, and Mike is helping me find a ship to deck load the "Devil Queller" to Seattle. In the lobby, the same guy approaches with his manager's estimate for my stay. He smiles, "I fuck you for your room," he says.

"Not bad," I say. "Maybe a little more practice," and move to the desk where I handle the cost going forward. The boat arrived in Seattle, and there was some confusion at the port that was about to cost us $16,000 per day. I said, "I don't care where you put the boat. Get it the hell off your deck!"

The refit began, and eventually, the boat launched for a second time. However . . .

Associated with the *Devil Queller*

The three bankers hung themselves in the hotel.
The buyer manages to get killed on his jet ski behind the boat.
Keith McCaw drowns in his hot tub.
So, is fate the hunter? Or was there just something in the name?

18

During the days of building the Alaska pipeline, contractors came to Seattle with bags of money. Alaskan contractors are not like contractors in the Lower 48. These guys come in like the sourdoughs that they are. Their expectations are high. They love to drink, and they're good at it. They were each some versions of Jack London's White Fang. Each man played out his wild ancestry by tossing back shots of Jack Daniel's Sour Mash. This was in the back of the ride from the airport. Always a bar in the trunk. Always fresh ice. Never a question. They would look out the car windows like children with noses pressed to the glass in an aquarium. Then they would pull away and kill every bug in their throats with 80 Proof Tennessee Whiskey. Then back to the windows.

This was a group of men whose demonstrated bravado was so strong that they walked in a thunder corona, the far northern latitude tough guys who could burn through life just like they burnt through jobs with a bulldozer and contractor shovel.

Contracts were handshakes. Equipment lists were on matchbook covers. Sometimes these men would drink themselves to sleep on the boats they liked. In the morning, I would open the main saloon door and sing my dad's limerick: *"Drop your cocks and grab your socks. It's rise-and-shine on the Luckenbach Line!"* And then some sleepy-eyed guy would crawl out on the deck and say, "Well, I slept with her last night. I guess I better marry her," and we would pencil a deal over coffee in his new-found galley.

Prime contractors were a yacht broker's dream. They made and lost money in equal shares. So, we would sell them a boat on the upswing and sell the boat on the downswing. The broker's standard distribution curve for planned obsolescence and they would duplicate the process repeatedly.

Then there was the keeper of the money. Elmer Rasmuson, President and Chairman of the National Bank of Alaska, and his friend Joe Columbus of Sand and Gravel, in Anchorage. If the pipeline contractors were on the spectrum, these two *were* the spectrum. They were a show of private power. Celebrity came often, but a deep dive into the style of economic power was rare.

Imagine sitting with Don Vito Corleone, the Godfather. How the head swings, how the hand moves. Soft-spoken. No bravado. No fingers steepling. Just power. "What do you think of the new Long-Range Cruiser?" Rasmuson would ask. Columbus would lean in like Tom Hagen to be sure Don Corleone understands the answer. After my response, Rasmuson says, "I think I will have one of those."

I walk to the phone and call North Carolina. "One 58 LRC for Mr. Rasmuson, National Bank of Alaska."

And the answer on the line was, *"Done."*

There is a twist, however, in male bravado. Sometimes it's a matter of style instead of power. A great deal of our activity was moving boats through the Hiram M. Chittenden Locks, or Ballard Locks. They are a complex of locks at the west end of Salmon Bay, in Seattle's Lake Washington Ship Canal, between the neighborhoods of Ballard to the north and Magnolia to the south. They were established to normalize the water level in Lake Washington and Lake Union. Boat owners must transit these locks from time to time as they begin or end a cruise in the Salish Sea. The locks are manned and managed by the U.S. Army Corps of Engineers.

For most new boaters, the locks are a scary place. Enormous concrete walls form a channel with closing steel doors at each end. Army Corps people walk the walls with fifty-foot lines to help boat captains and crew fetch a bollard for a tie along the wall. If they miss, the boat can drift off the wall and get sideways in the lock. That equals a hell of a lot of damage and embarrassment for the boat owner.

Considering the locks are a major public attraction in Seattle, hundreds of people can be watching as the hapless captain stands hollering at his crew as they miss the bollard, and the boat does a bouncing pirouette along the wall.

But here's the problem. The alpha male captain doesn't want anyone to know he is afraid of the locks. So, the process continues. Every weekend of every year to infinity. Men in their boats are being scrambled in the concrete and steel locks. Their wives are standing in stunned amazement as their perpetually dilettante husbands squander household capital by the Sisyphean task of going through the Ballard Locks.

In my case, with a new owner, the process of *New Captain through the locks* was simple. I would get on a bullhorn and announce to the Army Corps of Engineers and the five hundred people standing alongside, "Attention, Lock Master, we have a new captain on board, and we require assistance on the wall."

I would do that before the newbie captain had a chance to push on regardless and trash his boat. Now we would be on the wall, the bollards and cleats positioned properly. The Army Engineer staff would be out in front to welcome the captain to the locks, offer advice, and admire his boat. The spectators would clap and cheer throughout the process. All was well, and his angels were happy.

Except, of course, when the captain turned to me and said, "Don't you EVER do that to me again!"

Yeah, right. . . . under my breath, of course.

After a broker has gone through the locks a couple hundred times, the process becomes automatic. Sometimes more automatic than others. It rains in Seattle from time to time. And sometimes, a night transit is in order. But who wants to go out on the deck and manage the lock lines in the dark and in the rain? So, I came up with a lovely answer.

Before leaving my dock, I would loose-lay the lock line over the rails both fore and aft. That way, the line was ready to pay out as required. Then I would pour two highball glasses of Seagram's VO and place each on the rail—fore and aft. As I entered the locks, the sweep of the Army floodlight would find my setup. The lock attendants would come out and, with a boat hook, work my lines off the rails. They would enjoy the Seagram's in the dark of night, replace the glasses, and we would exchange snappy hand salutes as they worked me off the well and on my way.

I never left the bridge deck.

19

The television programs *Yellowstone*, *1883*, and *Lonesome Dove* all memorialize Montana with excellent camerawork, editing, and A-list actors. It's simple to understand why. With that kind of power behind the landscape, a Montana ten-acre patch of pine trees and dry grass can sell for four million dollars in today's money.

This romance is not lost on those who lived there. I am among them. In between business contracts and strategizing beside Max Baucus for his first congressional seat, I decided to take my family into the Bitterroot down above the Yellowstone River and try ranching—maybe it was farming, maybe it was just rural living. We did have seven horse corrals and room for five hundred chickens on one hundred and ten acres.

The area I'm referring to is known as Stevensville, a small town between Missoula and Hamilton on the way to Yellowstone Park. Stevensville is nestled next to the Bitterroot Range, with St. Mary's Mountain and its peak looking straight into the valley, which is laced up by the Bitterroot River. The Paramount television series *Yellowstone* does a great deal of work in that area.

So, even though I was more interested in boats than I was horses, I thought it was a good idea to give Montana tradition a try on my second time around in the state. The first time I left, it was 54° below zero, and I simply walked into the JCPenney Company looking for a job. On this day, the weather didn't have the same influence.

As I was a native-born guy from Montana, one would expect I understood the ways of cowboy hats, leather vests, cinches on saddles, and half-ton trucks. None of that was true. I was a dilettante cowboy and accomplished pool hall flutter. I was, however, accomplished with a Winchester Model 70-270 and a razor-sharp 20-degree taper four-inch blade. Sometimes they go together, but, in this case, they didn't. Regardless, I packed up my family and headed for the country.

We drove down our gravel half-mile entry road in a teal blue Ford station wagon packed top to bottom with personal belongings, three preschool boys, and a dog. Even the color of the car was mismatched by the environment. The house was a one-story, turn-of-the-century, salt box-looking white wood rambler. There were outbuildings, including a barn for the horses and chicken coops flanking the house opposite the stables. The property looked straight at St. Mary's peak to the east, and a federal game preserve to the west.

When we parked in front of the house for the first time, I let our golden retriever Chien out the back of the station wagon, and he did some running and sniffing around the house and yard, around several trees, and then across the fence line to the neighbor's field. Chien was running a clean arc around a fifty-foot diameter circle when a shot rang out, and dust rose adjacent to our family pet. The dog stopped with the second whip-snapped shot, yelped and dropped to the ground. Chien was crying, my boys were crying, my wife was screaming, and I was over the fence running for the dog.

Robert (Bob) Crossley was a friend of mine and a veterinarian, and that's where we ended up—at his clinic, still packed from the trip, and now wondering what we were up against. On the way to the clinic, we used compression with T-shirts and paper towels. There was blood all over the inside of the car. The bullet entered Chien's upper chest and nicked the top of his lung and out. So, Bob moved quickly into thoracic surgery. I held two self-retaining retractors in Chien's ribs, having no idea what I was doing, and I was looking at beads of sweat growing on Bob's summer tan forehead. His hands were steel-steady. He did not stop for a cigarette. I might have been dizzying around in my brain—but I wasn't. All I wanted was for Chien to make it out alive. I suspect in today's money, we spent $70,000 on that stainless steel table. But it was Bob Crossley's table, and he said later when we were washing up, "You owe me a beer!" Chien lived and lived some more.

I never approached the guy who shot my dog. I figured there was no way that could end well.

After we moved in, I would sit on the back steps and look across the federal preserve. Lots of geese. Then I would look back at our coops. No chickens. The kids would play on tree swings with black tires and hemp ropes. Carol would read. Our family and friends were in a kind of curiosity queue. Like we were on a ranch with a no-ranch lifestyle. We could have been back in town. The commute would have been better, for sure.

My dad called Pin Larsen at the Stockman's Bar. Told him we needed some chickens, and like all my dad's calls on our behalf, the chickens found their way to the Stockman's Bar. Three chickens in a tied tan canvas bag. I picked them up at the bar. Who do you know who walks in and then out of a bar with a bag of live, squawking chickens?—*right*.

When I got home, I entered the coop and opened the bag. Out they came, all a-flutter with noise. Only fifty years later would John Lewis teach me about chickens! But, on this day, I told the chickens not to worry. This was their house, a very big house indeed. The next morning, I went to the coop to see if they were settled. They were dead. They were helter-skelter along the fence with no heads. Something came in the night, and as they stuck their heads out of the wire, whatever it was snapped off their heads. So, okay, I needed to do some research into chickens and how to handle their environment.

Carol decided we needed a cat for the mice. She was abnormally afraid of mice. Her fear is why this will be a short story. The cat was a black American Burmese. Heavy for their size and hyper-tuned to movement. We named him Sam.

I opened an account at the First State Bank in Stevensville. Don Scothorn was the owner/manager. He said we should come to town for the 4th of July Parade. We could stand by the bank. We did stand by the bank, and the floats and tractors and fire engines started up in the center of town. The first pass was so we could all see one side of the floats. Then they all turned around and came down the street in the opposite direction so we could see the other side of the floats. It was a very small town. A bank, a drugstore, and a bar.

We had another neighbor, a young guy and a hunter. We enjoyed our conversations, but one day, he poached a moose. He was afraid the

Department of Fish and Wildlife (DFW) would spot him, so he quartered the animal and dumped it in our water well. That was nice!?! Then he apologized for that, noticed we had a skunk under the house, and shot it. It let go of its scent then and there—permeated our house for days.

I heard Carol screaming—way out-of-control screaming. She was up on the dining room table. Sam had a mouse—not dead, just for fun. Carol was holding a large kitchen knife. She swung the knife around. I don't think she realized she was windmill-ing the blade in all the diameter degrees available. I was scared she would drive the blade into her body as she stood screaming wildly out of control. I talked her down as Sam and the mouse got the hell out of there. She had no recall of swinging the knife or how she got on the table. We had a problem because, in fields of grass, mice are everywhere.

I finally bought a horse. The kids should have a horse—at least one horse, I surmised. The horse came with a blanket, a saddle, and a hackamore (a bridle without a bit, operating by exerting pressure on the horse's nose.). So, no bit. The horse guy came with a trailer. He backed out the horse. Stood there, waiting for one of us to take control of the horse. We didn't move. Nobody moved. The horse guy looked at me. He extended his arm, holding the reins of the hackamore. I took it out of his hand and stood looking at the horse.

"Thanks, Dad. Gee, thanks, Dad," coming into my senses from all sides.

The horse guy left. I spoke to the horse. "Hi, a horse," I said. *"You are a horse."*

I figured I would sit on the horse. No saddle, no blanket, just me. Show the boys the legendary connection between horse and man. So, I got a stool. Put the stool next to the horse. I wrapped my arms around the horse's neck and got one leg on the horse's back. Then with one body thrust up, I went. On the horse. "Look at you!" Carol said.

The horse began to trot—then run. I kept my arms around the horse's neck. I leaned forward as the horse broke into a galloping run across one hundred acres of grass. I'm thinking, *Holy shit, this is not good!*

Then, like the best cutting horses you have ever seen in the biggest rodeos in Texas, the horse stopped—stopped dead. I kept going. I was fully airborne and rotating like a kite with a broken stick. I hit the ground and a rock at the same moment. I could feel my pelvic bone crack—sort of snap. My glasses flew off my face in front of me. Chien had been following us across the field. The dog licked my face as I lay in suspended tension on the ground. Chien, the dog, mouthed my glasses and picked them up. Then Chien the dog and the horse with no name ran together toward the federal game preserve.

Carol came out in the car. I could barely walk and was in extreme pain. I said, "Let's just get me to the house so we can get a handle on what's wrong."

"Oh, no," Carol said. "I'm not going back in that house. There's a mouse in there." Sam had brought in another mouse.

20

I always thought his outfit was an overreach, but that was when I didn't understand the mechanics of celebrity. To sit across the table from Jacques Cousteau and to my immediate right, Jean Michel Cousteau, was exactly what one would imagine. For, you see, it doesn't matter what imagining comes to mind; it's accurate—all of it.

We were at the Rainier Club in Seattle. Cousteau had a couple of reasons to be in town. *The Calypso* (his boat) came from Seattle, and around Seattle (the Salish Sea), we have the biggest octopuses in the world.

The Calypso was built and launched in Lake Union /Lake Washington Ship Channel in 1942 as Minesweeper BYMS-26 from the Ballard Marine Railway at the foot of 24th Street. *Calypso* served in the Royal British Navy during the Second World War and then became surplus and into Cousteau's hands with the financial help of Loel Guinness, the owner of Guinness Brewery. So, ordering drinks at our table was easy. *"I'll have a Guinness Draft, please."*

I don't know if the Rainier Club usually carried Guinness Beer, but they carried it on that day.

There was a decided contrast between father and son. Jean Michel, the first son, sat understated in monotonous variations of black and gray. He became the authentic environmental activist his father compromised to meet the strain of maintaining international celebrity. Jean Michel would not be produced or directed. His father became both. The overriding question became: do production, fame, and environmental activism need one another to stand the gaff of opposition?

Maybe both. Over lunch, Cousteau mentioned that the Naval Undersea Warfare Center Division Keyport contacted him regarding a woman who was using a chain mail swimsuit to repel, i.e., discourage, sharks from taking off her arm while diving on the Great Barrier Reef. She was Valerie Taylor, without a doubt among the most accomplished divers in the world. Her shark-repellant suit caught the Navy's attention.

The image: Special Operations Command (SOCOM) Frog Men, now Navy Seals, with a five-foot, drop-dead attractive blonde, who swims in this testosterone engorgement fashioning these BUDS Class (name your number) boys into swimming the last mile without being eaten by sharks—it's almost funny.

To Cousteau, she was the real deal. What he didn't know was I was about to be her dive partner/escort in a run through Agate Pass in Puget Sound, aka the Salish Sea. I let that slip at the table and watched the red skullcap do a sort of Moulin Rouge dance across Cousteau's forehead. It is reasonable to assume every scuba diver in the world had a secret mental love affair with Valerie Taylor, even Jacques Cousteau. The acknowledging signal was when Jean Michel adjusted his head a little left when he realized I had some involvement with Valerie Taylor.

So, while the Navy was deciding about Valerie, I was on my way to Agate Pass, a high-current tidal strait connecting Port Madison and mainland Kitsap County in Washington State. As it turned out, she wanted to have a swift cold-water experience. And we had the perfect spot. I was selected from a group of Puget Sound divers to escort her through the pass. It's a one-mile strait, about twenty feet deep, with a six-knot velocity (7 mph). On land, not a big deal. Under cold water with limited visibility, it's a hell of a big deal.

Valerie was in 1/8-inch neoprene—what she brought. We told her she needed ¼ inch neoprene, or her ass would simply freeze and fall off at the end channel marker. That was risky, but she laughed and laughed. We were off to a good start. Then I noticed she didn't have weights. I told her she needed weights.er answerHer Her answer: "I'm naturally buoyant. Don't need weight."

I said, "But the ¼ neoprene will change that."

She said, "I'm not changing."

I leaned back and cocked my neck forward, "OKAY, no problem, we are going to dive."

Various dive organizations were poised with inflatable boats along the route with a pickup Zodiac at the final channel marker.

We tested the water, checked regulators, cleared masks, and started a slow descent toward the middle of the channel. I'm behind her by ten plus or minus feet. There are other divers on my flanks with me on the point. Valerie is the beauty of expression as she extends her arms toward the taxonomy of darkness in fast water and sea phylum.

Then, in what seemed microseconds, she is upside down and sideways. The metal bands around her mask flash in the limited light. It was Dr. Jones in Warner Brothers' *Gravity* spinning detached into the black of space.

I cranked a right leg—then a left. I swam every day and rode STP in one day, so I had quads to handle the burn rate. Valerie was facing me and drifting back into the current. At the half-mile point, there were cement caissons supporting the Agate Pass Bridge. She knew that going in. As I close in, her eyes are wide—but in control. After all, the only difference to her usual self was she was drifting backward and upside down in fast dark current—freezing her ass off while approaching, in the blind, a bridge caisson at flank speed, aka she was out of control.

The comforting reality check would be Valerie Taylor played herself in *Blue Water, White Death* and *Jaws*. All the boys ran the gaffs, but it was Valerie who swam with the sharks—the real sharks, not the plastic replicas.

In the green/black of swift current, this red form in front of me extends and compresses like an octopus. Then jacks herself into position. And we swim on like it's just another day in paradise. At the channel marker, she was snagged by the pickup boat. I inflated a buoyancy compensator and cleared my mask. I watched her swing over the side, then turn toward me. She smiled. I smiled. They spirited her away to be the celebrity she was. I swam to shore and waited for another pickup.

The Navy sniffed around the chain mail suit, and some of us got SEAL fanboy hats. Cousteau found his way to the biggest octopuses in the world. And I got to swim with Valerie Taylor.

21

Working as a broker on the Seattle waterfront was a little like having a cryptocurrency portfolio. As a yacht broker, your primary customer base had money that was supported by the Federal Reserve. Your own currency was supported by the story you could produce.

When people came to buy a yacht, especially if it was a family, the entire process was about the dream. Husbands brought wives, but NewCo captains of industry brought girlfriends. Both combinations looked to the broker for guidance as well as discretion. In the case of wives, there was universally a conservative approach that the family did not need to drop between one and ten million dollars on a recreational toy that required management and insurance and only represented one percent of the family's time.

When it was high-powered businesspeople bringing girlfriends, the money would drop into the master stateroom, and the discretion had to follow it down. As a broker, I was a "Breaking Bad" fixer. No recognizable power, yet more power than any owner wanted to admit. A walk-around man who knew where all the bodies were buried. It's hard to write about that in a matter-of-fact way. The frailty of the human condition drives the curiosity over everyone, depending on the circumstances of the moment.

Money and privilege tended to remove social constructs that would stand in the way of stolen moments potentially out of harm's way. If it was socially sketchy, it was also funny. Girlfriends who used hair curlers owners did not plan on. Young, naïve women who refused to go home.

Women were willing to leverage threats to see how long they could hold their ground against the matriarch in the other house.

Men who would come face-to-face with the complications clouding the playing field after drinks and a few moments in the bunk. Erratic talk and unpredictable decisions that by themselves could represent fifty percent or more of the owner's estate. All of that for an evening of fun behind the drawn shades on six-million-dollar yachts.

When not prospecting for listings, I was arranging airport rides for women with light luggage, spying on yacht owners' children at college fraternity parties, warehousing weapons that could not cross into Canada, and arranging for fuel tanks to be converted into whisky storage.

I found it fascinating that these guys were willing to pivot toward risk for retrospectively small amounts of excitement.

So, what else would they do?

I was sitting at Franco's Bar after work when one of my owners wanders in. We join up a couple of stools and talk. I tell him I am fed up with the mechanics of the yacht business: chasing people, pouring drinks out of my trunk, stashing hair curlers, walking dogs, and keeping college students (children) from fucking their girlfriends in the old man's boat.

He laughs.

Then he says, "Okay then, become a niche player. Do what nobody else does in your industry. Like me. People think I'm in the aviation business, but all I do is make aircraft door locks."

He goes on, "What do you think makes these guys rich? Is it putting money in the bank?—hell no! They are diversified all over the board. Take any one of your key customers/owners. They own equity in all sorts of high-risk, high-growth new companies, or they hold hard assets to support their old portfolio. Old men with more stuff than they need, and they can't afford to off the stuff for the capital gains. You become the 'all I do is aircraft door locks' yacht broker, and that will make you rich."

Over the next few weeks, I become Socratic among my customer/owners. One question after another. About their business, their interests, their portfolio against risk. And would they trade any of that stuff for a boat? The answers were varied, but "yes" enough times that I could see the potential. I started reading Joseph Stiglitz's ideas on world order, globalization, and asset offsets. I went back to read *The True Believer* by Eric Hoffer. I surmised that my customers were practical men of action in the context of asset offsets. They fed off each other, and that reinforcement made them a collection of true believers.

My research found that my confabulation was known as *countertrade*. So, in an instant, I was credible. The World Bank cataloged the process; almost all big manufacturing companies traded commodities for supplies. Asset trades involved companies and governments—countertrade was everywhere.

While the rest of the industry maintained a traditional cash transaction policy, I began to catalog owners' portfolios as possible asset transfers in exchange for large yachts. My portfolio of other people's money and assets began to grow exponentially. Whenever a customer opened the door for a large yacht transaction, I would never discuss price. I would simply discuss asset trades, e.g., *what have you got we can trade?*

In my countertrade portfolio was the ocean liner *USS United States*. I also had concept cars. Street-legal cars were produced by design companies as pitch platforms for future automobile market rollouts. I had ore deposits of molybdenum and thousands of acres of standing timber. I was quickly becoming the manager of my own country.

In the easy-to-understand category, I had catalogs of executive jets and platted residential subdivisions. I made it clear to members of the transaction that I would accept equity instead of cash, should that be the case.

So as a yacht broker, I began playing in the franchise motel business as an equity partner in Alaska Salmon Charters, in a new formula for roadway pavement, and in a kinetic energy company. I ended up negotiating a position in bank ATM cash machines for a research ship.

Eventually, Boat International USA found me out and coined "The Kingdom of Countertrade." They broke it open—cracked the code, so to say. They ran a picture of me in front of my Porsche next to a Lear 24 Executive Jet. They stacked that with 105 West Highland Drive. A new six-story top-tier residential building I was sliding into my countertrade mix. The article talked of spread and circumstance. Sixty commercial acres contiguous to the city of New Orleans, a ninety-four-unit residential subdivision, and a high-grade iron-ore aggregate in Michigan.

Boat International USA wrote: "With more than two hundred million trading since the first of the year, the breakdown looks like this: $140 million in property, $90 million in yachts, and $10 million in durable goods."

A *SEA Magazine* page read: "In this industry, the phrase 'doing the deal' and the name John LaCasse have become synonymous." It went on to read: "John LaCasse does not have contacts. John LaCasse is contacted."

I became the Yacht Broker version of *I only make aircraft door locks*.

I told my customers to clean up their master staterooms. Tell their concubines to buy different hair curlers. No more airport midnight dashes.

Then I told Bruce McCaw, for whom I was holding a $900,000 deposit check, to "Stop calling me at home after nine o'clock!"

At that moment, I knew I was finished with the yacht business. So did he.

22

Any average person observing my $900,000 conversation ith Bruce McCaw would have thought I had been relieved of my faculties, and they probably would be correct. However, my life has been the function of reaction, and that was my reaction.

I had one more sale in the process, which took fifteen weeks to survey and close while having me live on the boat at the Orange Coast shipyard in San Diego. I had a consistent Great Blue Heron friend who hunted for fish every morning off the side dock. After weeks of being together every morning, I nicknamed it "shy poke." This bird would fish with delicate precision. I could be watching the bird's head rested in shy repose in the morning sun. Then, in an instant, no head. A quick poke, then back into my visual frame, shaking the momentum out of a fish and swallowing it whole. Watching the space-time geometry precision of this creature was a recurring moment of awe.

Life aboard big yachts and small ships takes a person away from the normalcy of stick-built houses with drywall interiors. The constant drone of machinery becomes irreducible beyond a certain dB. My eyes still glaze over with the comforting sound of a generator's wet exhaust. The constant noise, companion with the throb and water line splash, has put sailors comfortably to sleep for over one hundred years.

The boat was 183 feet in length overall, and it carried small boats plus a helicopter, its most recent history being the platform for seventeen adventure movies on Discovery Television (*The Adventures of Quest*). We had the comings and goings of Andrew Wight. He was flying helicopters for

James Cameron as *Titanic* (the movie) was in production. His observations of Kate Winslet and Leonardo DiCaprio being "once you see it, you can't unsee it" came to make movie history. We had a short crew, so Andrew and I took advantage of the space, swapping flying stories and making our breakfasts without the unhinged cook deciding what was available.

It was a high-impact afternoon in February 2012 when I learned Andrew was killed, along with his cameraman Michael deGruy, in his helicopter near Jaspers Bush, Australia. Still with Cameron—this time on the documentary "Deep Sea Challenge." Lawsuits ensued, but I didn't follow the story, as my friend was simply dead.

I had an occasion where I was encouraged to sue for the wrongful death of my son. I didn't. There is nothing in existence that can weathercock perspective like the death of a child. In my case, two children, and knowing what a firestorm of gut-wrenching pain this was going to be.

I was on my couch, a nine-foot Lucca light-brown saddle leather Henredon. It was a $15,000 idea I had had years before. Silly idea maybe, considering the depreciated value of furniture; but for thinking, napping, occasional sex, telephone calls, and light reading, it was worth every nickel. John (my son) and I were having a phone conversation about exercise. He was a competitive sailboat racer (Santana 30) and felt that keeping in shape was an ingredient for success. There is a great deal of exertion involved with sail trim while holding off the mark and doubling down on speed for long periods. He was good at this, and it was clear he was one to be watched among West Coast competitors coming through the yacht club circuits.

Even though he was working hard to capture as much forearm and shoulder power he could develop, he was having difficulty with his right side. A friend noticed as they were both working the cockpit during a race that John was having trouble working the primary winch on the starboard side. This was his power side and was a logical position for being quick and effective. And, yet, for all the practice, he could feel there was something up with his right arm.

Most people do not have a good reference point for limited weakness in their limbs. We come and go from ailments that are passed off as stress, fibromyalgia, or just plain nothing except waiting for it to be better the following day. I also don't believe people tend to accelerate routine body pain to crisis proportions as a matter of routine. However, in John's case, there was another trigger that happened while he was sitting on the cockpit coaming after a race. He reached down to unscrew the crown on his Rolex so that he could adjust the date, and he was not able to manage his fingers to get that done. That was the trigger.

I didn't know any of this as it was happening. There was no reason for him to alert me. Enough time passed so John could consult with a physician team at Evergreen Hospital in Bellevue, Washington. From what I understand, there was a great deal of testing, some remarkable and some unremarkable, as these things go. Finally, John and his wife Wen went in for a conference with the Evergreen medical team. The diagnosis was tentative because the physicians at Evergreen Hospital were not experts in this medical circumstance. They suspected that John might have Amyotrophic Lateral Sclerosis (ALS), commonly referred to as Lou Gehrig's disease. The recommendation was for John to transfer his case to Virginia Mason Hospital in Seattle, where there was a team of physicians studied in progressive neurodegenerative disease, specifically ALS.

About a week after John got the diagnosis from Evergreen Hospital, and he made his way to Virginia Mason for a second consult, he gave me a call. He told me he had Lou Gehrig's disease and was wondering if I knew anyone who had it that might add some light on what to expect. His voice tone was low but controlled, and he seemed directed toward getting additional information from any available third parties.

What do you do when, after a one-sentence exchange, you know a person is going to die? When that person is your son. When you've been through this before with his younger brother. When you already know what a firestorm of gut-wrenching pain this is going to be. When children die first, it's never right, and I'm unaware of a circumstance where you can understand why.

Jim Geraghty of *National Review* put our situation in perspective. "A dire death diagnosis, with pain and suffering to follow, is something that makes the road ahead look unbearable, so hopeless, that a quick self-imposed ending appears perversely easier."

As John and I spoke on the phone, there came over me nausea. I began swallowing for air and tightening my stomach muscles. In my mind seeing him as my little boy. Oh, my God, my dearest little boy, my wonderful little boy. I remembered how he would wave goodbye to me as he piloted his Santana away from the dock at Shilshole Bay and north toward Port Townsend. I would envision him walking toward my boat, then walking away. I once told him that sailing alone was like being a lone rider on a horse. The horse and the boat have a magic relationship with nature.

I was quickly losing my ability to sound normal, and I didn't see well through the welling tears in my eyes, so I told him I would get back to him shortly with any new information I could round up. I told him I loved him and lowered the phone. I sat up erect in my seat, cupped my hands into a fist, held it against my lips, and began to pull my arms close to my body. I was forcing my arms in as tight as I could manage. I began to breathe in and out of my fist. I looked out the window to the sky. I stayed motionless. Stoic. Breathing.

I had been here before. In this state of grace, a place where our body's circuits begin to shut with staggering speed. The body's race to survive. The murky world of quick-time slow motion. The place where options end, and there is no choice but to maintain course and speed.

In February 1989 (21 years earlier), I was asleep on my 54-foot Maple Leaf motor sailor at the Port of Seattle. Early in the morning, the phone rang, announcing what all parents consistently describe as "their worst nightmare." My son Jeff was at Harborview Medical Center. He had been in a car accident.

My dark-of-the-morning trip to the hospital was filled with a general curiosity about his length of stay, the costs, whether it was his fault, and if others were involved. I could begin to see the lights of the hospital floors ladder their way higher as I drove up Boren Avenue. I parked the truck and found my way to the Emergency Room entrance. I walked quickly to the ER while announcing my name.

The eyes of the nursing staff began to dart all around. One of them said, "If you stay right here for a moment, I will be right back." She hurried into the hall and, in a few moments, came back with three green-gowned doctors. Their masks were each hanging off one ear; one of them was still gloved. The other was holding a piece of equipment. We all sat down. They jockeyed through the conversation. However, the message was they wanted me to know the situation was severe, that I must be prepared for a shock when we entered the critical care unit where Jeff was being "positioned," and that they were prepared to support me at any moment.

As I am rifling this memory through my mind, I am taken by the contrast between the doctors in the ER for Jeff and the matter-of-fact conversation I am having with John. I guess in Jeff's case, serious as it was, death wasn't on the table. In John's conversation, the fait accompli was death right out of the box. The lead-in is desperation. So, I am masking how I feel, like an airline pilot on a direct approach to the side of a mountain. *"Seattle Center, this is 311Quebec Heavy. It doesn't appear we are going to clear the north ridge."*

The doctors and I walked toward the Emergency Room, where Jeff was in isolation. As we entered, I could see him at the end of the room. He was tilted up, then his head would disappear, and all I could see were his feet. There was nursing staff moving seamlessly through the hiss and gasp of pump pressure that ran the equipment. I saw several beeping monitors with wires, some with tubes. One was alarming as it looked like a tracheotomy, and it was. He was secured to a metal table that was moving in a slow circular motion in a 4-axis routine—head up, then down, while simultaneously rocking from side to side. There was a stainless-steel halo ring around his head with long steel screws positioned into his skull. He was asleep.

There was no blood, no bandages. He was draped with a sheet, but a good deal of his body was exposed. His solid muscle tone stood in stark contrast to his restrained body. It seemed an odd dichotomy on a 20-year-old body. One of the doctors said that they were unable to get an X-ray yet, but they suspected he had a C-6 fracture at the base of his neck. One of the doctors turned to me. He said the special table was to "maintain hemodynamic stability and stabilize blood pressure values, as well as steady his spine." I imagine my eyes were trying to engage my brain as I watched him speak. Only later did a nurse tell me what he said.

As I stood next to Jeff, I had long since lost my ability to breathe involuntarily and was now moving air in through my nose and pressuring it out through my pursed lips, desperately trying not to descend into hypoxia and drop to the floor. I was clammy and cold. I was shaking and utterly terrified.

In both these cases, my sons died—Jeff in thirty-three days, John in about two years.

My last conversation with Jeff was at a moment when he opened his eyes as I was standing over him. He winked—his eyes hard-focused on mine, then he fell back to wherever he was. I left his side and walked to a window in the corridor. I could see far to the west—all the Olympic Mountains in high resolution.

A nurse approached me. "You must come now," she said. Jeff was on his way. The equipment was flat-lining, then silent. I ran my hand through his hair, leaned through my tears, and kissed his forehead. I took some tape scissors and cut away a lock of hair, stuffed it in my pocket, watched his body get covered and wheeled away, went to my boat, sat on the deck and drank beer until I fell over.

My last conversation with John was by text message. I was at Staples, making a Bluetooth exchange for my computer. John was unable to talk but could text me using an electronic relay attached to his forehead.

Me: You, Ok?
John: Yes
Me: ;-)
Me: Reinstalling Dragon and Service pack 1.
John: Which one?
Me: Calisto for Savi Go
John: Wish I could be there.
Me: Not the same without you.
John: Too bad, my Savi Go worked great.

The exchange stopped. Shortly, John began to choke and died of hypoxia.

Later that week, I opened my phone and typed, "I will love you forever."

23

In 2007, Washington Governor Christine Gregoire allocated $1.4 million in her supplemental budget for the construction of an eight-foot-high suicide-prevention fence on Seattle's Aurora Bridge to help reduce the number of suicides off the rail. Construction of the fence began in the spring of 2010 and was completed in February 2011 at a total cost of $4.8 million.

But in mid-September 1983, it was a different story. The bridge had a standard rail and walkways on both sides, with 230 suicides off the rail since construction. What triggered this reflection was that, more recently, I moored my Beneteau sailboat at the canal entrance to Lake Union. That put me close to a position for a vertical drop off the bridge. It was from this position that I begin my reflection on the woman on the bridge. The woman I grabbed before she could let go—she was like cold steel—rebar, I thought at the time. She was short. Had short gray hair. A lightweight cotton kind of jacket. She fought with me to let her go. She was in a kind of quiet hysteria. That's how I felt anyway.

I first noticed her as I was driving. It was visually obvious she was over the rail and, with the simple release of her hand, would fall to her death in the ship channel. But the drama of the moment is in a different context. *Holy shit . . . !* and I drive my truck into a smoking, screeching stop. I jump out, leaving the door open. As I head toward the woman, I see a Metro bus coming at me. I signal by laying my right hand to my head with my little finger at my mouth and my thumb by my ear. My other hand points to the woman. The bus driver knows immediately what's up. As he passes, I can see him pick up a microphone/receiver combination, so I figure that's a call to the Seattle police.

I come upon the woman quietly but quickly, trying to keep a bridge light stanchion blocking her view of me. By that time, two of my associates, who were driving behind me on the bridge, also stop, and they are coming in behind me. Without any hesitation, I am over the rail, with my arms around the woman, hanging on as tight as I can. First to grab onto me is Dan Colby, a 6'5" giant of a man—with the full intent to save both me and the woman. His intention cracked two of my ribs.

Behind Dan Colby is Ann McAllister, so now we have a committee saving this woman. Ann tries to speak with her—no luck. Just *"You don't understand"* is the woman's response. Quicker than I imagined, the police and fire are on the scene. Both men and women. A woman officer has her hand on my back.

"We've got this," she said. Then a couple of firemen. I hung on to the woman until I was satisfied that they did, in fact, *have this*. The responders' efficiency had the incident under control in quick time. An officer took our names, and we went on to work. Ann asked if she could visit the woman and was turned down. Later that day, *The Seattle Times* sent over a news photographer and writer. Dan and Ann, and I were photographed under the bridge, and the story ran. The news story gave us credit for making a tough call in a crisis. Later, the Seattle SWAT Chief Hostage Negotiator was interviewed, noting that *Mr. LaCasse saved the woman incorrectly.*

The impact of that day remained with me—it's still with me. It got tattooed on my brain once again while standing on my dock watching a young woman jump. She hit the water with a smacking sound like a rifle shot. She was about thirty feet off my stern. The police were already in position, but she was dead on impact. Her jeans were rolled up halfway to her knees. Her hair was in a ponytail. Her hair was summer ash brown—light. As the police boat approached, her skin was turning black—some blues, mostly toward black. Arms and legs apart. Her jacket adrift. The Harbor Police slid her body into their boat and slowly made their way back to the police dock on Lake Union. There was a crowd gathered on the dock. No one spoke. Not a word. I guess everyone just went home to give someone a hug—and say I love you.

24

Fifty years after the close of the Second World War, surveyed out-of-service military boats became yachts for project-minded boaters. Actor John Wayne and explorer Jacques Cousteau are notable examples. The same with WWII fighter pilots. They flew Grumman TBM Avenger Torpedo Bombers for the U.S. Forest Service. The torpedo bay was converted to carry Borate slurry—a red chemical the USFS used to put out fires. Pilots who were pretend bombing just like the old days. Now it was forest fires instead of enemy bridges and bunkers.

Yachtsmen were little different. These were men who remembered manning *stations* instead of modern bridge controls. It was a visceral command of raw tonnage that kept recurring in their memories. So, they bought Survey Ships and Minesweepers. Freezer Ships and Army T-Boats.

Unlimited manpower is a hallmark of manning the original equipment. So now we have a surplus warship. Bow, stern, and breast lines to the dock. The big brass key for the wing doors. Ladder ways everywhere. Hatches to the engine room, wherein resides an engine as big as the biggest GM dually truck. Tubes and handles and shafts with oil seeping through the cork gaskets. Water and oil under the engine only to guess how deep. And these guys were thrilled with the whole package—oil and water, gears and handles, little round brass port lights, and gray peeling paint. And all of this for the command of a man and his wife. Not thirty-five active duty sailors. No, for him and his wife.

"Look here, honey!" he exclaims. "LOOK AT THESE" "Look at these. . . ." "Wow," his voice drifting on . . .

His wife steps to the bridge deck, approaches the wheel. Her arms don't span the wheel. Her eyes don't quite look over the spokes.

Her name was Sally. The first time I met Sally, she was with her husband, Tom Aparo, in my office. Tom had retired from his contracting business. His dream to live on a boat was now available. Plenty of time. Travel the Inside Passage to Alaska. Catch fish. Catch crabs. Tom was discharged from the U.S. Navy in 1947. He met Sally during the war. She was a Wave Nurse trainee. Tom was a Gunner's Mate. Guns and bullets are for Gunners' mates. So, Sally was Florence Nightingale, and Tom was any Captain out of Patrick O'Brian's *Master and Commander.*

Tom decided to sell their house. "We will go to sea," he told Sally.

Sally asked if he was sure of his decision? "Are you positive this is the right decision, Tom?"

Does Sally ask? Yes, repeatedly. The house gets sold. Tom has $110,000 to spend and buys a surplus Navy Minesweeper.

All old surveyed-out equipment applies. Oil, water, peeling paint, broken lines, twisted wire, foggy glass, and rising deck planks. Dream home by any measure. The engine is a Fairbanks Morse direct reversible. That means that for the boat to go in reverse, the engine must be stopped completely, the camshaft switched to the other side of the block, and the engine restarted in reverse—backward. That takes twelve to thirty seconds. It also takes compressor pressure because these processes are done with compressed air through brass nozzles directed toward a flywheel. It is a Capt. Billy's whiz-bang operation and found nowhere in Sally's emotional wheelhouse. But Tom Aparo decided Sally would love it.

The ship was surveyed by Marine Surveyors Inc. of Seattle, WA. Herbert (Herb) Johnson got the job. I knew Herb well. We enjoyed professional protocol.

We didn't talk over a job but sometimes rolled our eyes. This time Herb took me aside. We stood next to the Gudgeons aft. "You can't be serious," Herb says.

"I don't know, Herb. It's their deal. It's not my call. The guy is crazy, but it's not my call."

"John, you must talk some sense into these people!"

"How about you, Herb? You're hired to render an opinion?"

"On the boat, John. On the boat."

We had eight deckhands on the sea trial. We cleared the cut and ran the mile marker on the Evergreen Point Bridge—got seven knots at 600 RPM. Not much smoke. No vibration. There was a little water through the planks in the forward locker. Just dry from age. No problem. I put two men in the engine room with hand-held radios to the bridge. We ran the compressors up for max air pressure to the flywheel. We were north on Lake Washington by the old Sandpoint Naval Air Station. From the bridge deck, I pulled back on the control, and the engine room answered. We went to a full stop—zero RPM. The engine crew transferred the cam and hit the flywheel with high-pressure air for a start in reverse. The period was about fourteen seconds. Not bad.

Maybe this will be good for the voyages undertaken and the cargo to be transported, I'm thinking. *This may fit in the common definition of seaworthiness if enough manpower is applied.*

Tom and Sally must have friends and relatives who would love the experience.

Sally was on the forward deck. Looking at her, I couldn't decide if she was happy or trying to be happy, but she was smiling. Tom was pacing from deck to bridge, to engine room, to deck. He remained on the weather deck. He never went above. My crew was ready for beer, and Tom was ready to take command.

"The ship is yours, Tom," I announce and step away as the crew restarts the engine forward. Everyone found their way to the weather deck. We opened the galley and beer all around. Slowly Tom took the ship's wheel and installed a long sweeping turn. The move was graceful and smooth. We were all relaxed and headed back toward the Montlake Cut and into Lake Union. The boat speed was about three to four knots. Low engine RPM. I could see the Husky Crew Shell House coming up on the right. University of Washington (Husky) Stadium in the background. A perfect day.

As I leaned on the taffrail, I could feel the boat's stern change. We were starting a turn. I shouted out, "TOM, what's going on?"

I dropped my beer and began running along the starboard deck. "TOM, what are you doing!?"

"I think we should go by the house in Madrona," he said.

"STOP your turn, TOM. STOP your turn! Bring it back around."

I hollered at Culley, a friend, seasoned hand, and Alaska fisherman. "We are going to hit the bridge, Culley. Get your ass into the engine room."

Culley dove through the hatch and looked for some flywheel air. The pressure was low. He could stop the engine, but he couldn't transfer the cam. I was back on the bridge, giving Tom a shoulder block away from the wheel. I saw Sally frozen on the forward deck. Two deckhands appeared like eagles on a salmon and grabbed Sally in mid-flight. They put her on the deck and rolled her against a hawsehole cleat. The west end of the Evergreen Point Bridge was too low for the ship to pass. So, now thirteen hundred tons was on a slow glide into the west end overpass. Sally screamed for God. Tom put his fist through the bridge deck door glass—I think he was aiming for the wood. He started to bleed.

The crack and snapping sound of timbers and members began. The top of the house was coming off in splinters. The mast snapped back and stuck itself through the stack. All the bridge deck glass had started breaking and falling. We ground to a stop. No fire. No smoke. Just stopped.

Culley had the compressor running, and the air was up. He slammed the cams, started the engine, and all thirteen hundred tons began to back away from the bridge. Nobody stopped on the bridge. They just kept going between Bellevue and Seattle—just another day commute.

The ship had power, and the rudder answered the wheel. In stunned amazement, we started down the cut toward Lake Union dry dock. Sally was crying and wrapping paper towels around Tom's hand.

Culley saddled up next to me and said, "I might have broken my arm on the engine room hatch."

Everyone else was quiet. I got on the radio and called Hobby Stebbins at the dry dock. He arranged for an SFD Medic One to stand by. Hobby was waiting on the dock. We hit the face a little hard, and Hobby fell over. He got up and took the bow line.

Tom put his good arm around Sally. I don't think she ever stopped crying.

25

Every Christmas season, Argosy Cruises and Seattle Parks and Recreation (REC) combine with Yacht Clubs and Cruising Clubs to form and conduct the Puget Sound Christmas Cruise. Music and cheer for all to enjoy around the Salish Sea (Puget Sound)—about 4.5 million people. This is a Seattle tradition that runs from mid-November to just before Christmas. Seattle Parks and REC arrange for beach fires at selected locations. There is live music and fireworks for the final gathering on Lake Union. KIRO (CBS) televises the final night.

I'm starting this story with these mechanics because the effort by all parties is extraordinary, and, of course, being in the big boat business, we got to play. Various owners among our customers were in some way attached to the sponsors and would offer their boats as platforms for guests to enjoy the music and cruise. Our participation boats were usually plus or minus 80 feet, so their presence was noticeable among the smaller yachts in the boating peloton. I get it about bikes, but I love the word, so for me, a string of anything is a peloton. Besides, I was a Seattle to Portland (STP) Cascade Rider in one day.

So, going forward, a parade of boats in my vernacular is a peloton.

But that's not why we're here. This is a story about how privilege gets trumped by metaphysics. The staging areas for the boats are scattered around the Sound with rendezvous points for the official night cruise to beaches where Parks and REC had fires burning, waiting for us, and the music of the Argosy lead boat—a small ship.

So, we would stage at the Marina Mart, Westlake Avenue on Lake Union. Then travel through the Hiram M. Chittenden Locks (Ballard Locks) to the north or south sound locations or Gasworks Park on the final night. The arriving passengers were typically lovers in pairs, children in clutches, parents with dark rings under their eyes, and old people, worried and cautious.

The big notice for us as the crew was that none of these people had much experience with boats. It also became apparent that we were looked upon as special people with privilege. Not like Washington State Ferry deck hands. That was public transportation. Those guys get paid to be nice and professional. State employees they were. No, we were private parties who liked to donate our boats to this cruise. We were indeed special in the eyes of our passengers.

But that perception had a causal effect as well. Among passengers, we were barely approachable. People of privilege throw little nuggets of goodwill to the pedestrians. We were expected to wave to the crowd with the slightest hand movement, lightly eating a butter cookie as we moved our hand. Maybe they thought this was like High Tea at the Empress Hotel in Victoria, British Columbia. I don't know, but it was as it was.

It became more uneasy when they had to use the head (go to the bathroom). Using a marine head is not like the porcelain American Standard at home. On 30-meter boats, the toilet is a macerator pump immediately behind the flush. So, instead of the pleasant sound of swishy water removing fecal matter quick and away, there is a loud grinding noise. Sounds like a starter motor in a 350 Chevy V-8 that won't engage the flywheel. Just grinds away. It can scare new people. And, because of the mechanics involved, toilet paper is considered a hazard and should be placed in a separate container, not in the toilet bowl.

So, now we have fifty guests on board, most of whom haven't a clue about what to expect, and after we do the head explanation decide to poop in their pants. That will be easier. The rest of the night, the bartender and servers are making book on which guest has the most pressure and won't use the head.

In this vortex of social construct, we sing and laugh and drink and marvel at the lovely beach fires. We are, in fact, people of privilege. We are accommodating these pedestrians with our wealth and charity. It will be over soon, and we can go back to the swill of our three-olive gin.

Except, one night, I'm leaning into the helm chair, and a woman approaches me—asking permission to enter the bridge through the starboard wing door. I step down and invite her in.

"What can I do for you?" I begin.

"Well, sir, pardon me, sir, is this okay?"

"Of course..."

"My sister and I brought our mom and dad on this Christmas cruise."

I agree that "that is very nice."

"*We wanted to do this for them—we've never been able to do anything for them—and this is their anniversary. They have been married fifty years today. They were married in 1930. Those were hard times,*" she says. "*We do not have much money, and my sister and I saved for this cruise. My mom and dad have never had a vacation that we can figure—always worked, always helping us. We were wondering if, maybe, you would speak to them?*"

I can't explain the peculiar unreality of the next few moments.

I immediately dressed my hat to my forehead. Shook off my pants. Adjusted my coat and fixed all the gold buttons. I stood straight. Looked down at my shoes. They were polished. I looked straight into her eyes and said, *"It will be my pleasure."*

Her parents were on a teak bench against a deck locker on the aft port side. The other sister was standing next to her mom. As we cleared the companionway, the mother saw us immediately. She reached for her husband's hand. He looked down—then up—and our eyes locked. I slowed my walk. His daughter moved out ahead of me. As I approached him, he stood. His eyes blinked and blinked again. His eyes had gray rings around the pupils. He was fully weathered. He had a navy suit coat that was too small. His black shoes laced and curled.

I extended my hand, and he, his hand. As our hands engaged, I could feel decades of hard work across his skin. He thanked me for coming back. He introduced his wife and daughters. We all shook hands. His wife said, "We are so enjoying such a fine trip. Our girls are so wonderful."

I told the family that it was our pleasure to have them on board. That they were the very people who should be here. That I wanted them to enjoy another fifty years together. Everyone smiled. As I stepped back, I asked him if he would like to come to the bridge. He said, *"Oh, no, thank you, Captain, I've already been there."* More peculiar unreality.

I nodded to the woman who came to the bridge. I swept my eyes across the family. I turned toward the companionway. It was but a few feet to the door. I placed my left hand on the door stile, turning to say goodbye. The bench was by itself, and the space was empty.

26

Walking away from the yacht business was crazy from an economic perspective. Telling an A-List customer to effectively take his million-dollar deposit and *stick it where the sun don't shine* may not have been my finest hour. But there is some social construct behind that kind of decision. When ordinary people budget and save for boat show tickets while billionaires have you meet them on the perimeter so you can pass free show passes through the fence, there is something fundamentally wrong with the whole shittereee.

I remember toward the end, I changed my magazine ad content to reflect my attitude. I advertised a two-for-one sale where I ran a double-truck in *SEA Magazine* with two Mega Yachts for the price of one. Another time I was to set a catered meeting between mega titans on a Delta 70 Long Range Cruiser. I set the table with bottles marked "DOG WATER" and had Hostess Twinkies for the entrée. I told them that *at the highest levels of negotiation, the food served should require no introduction.* The owner dismissed me and asked me to leave the boat. Of course, I did. We never spoke again.

Midpoint of the spectrum, there becomes a tear between the established wealthy and the antebellum gentry, who are deciding whether to advance or hold. I was standing at my office window with Bill Culliton. We had motored the *Wind Star* through the locks and into Lake Union. She was there a side tie at Latitude 47. A big ketch she was—almost one hundred feet. Fancy everywhere. We noticed the waterline stripe wasn't showing on the hull. That made no sense.

We walked to the Latitude 47 dock and made our way on deck. The boat was showing a slight list. We went below. There was water to the floorboards. We called the fire department. Since the boat was new, just out of the yard, there was an investigation. Eventually, a shipyard worker was tagged as going aboard with a brace and bit. He quietly drilled a hole in the hull well below the water line. His reason was a thrown insult by the owner.

The shipyard worker felt powerless to meet the yacht owner on common ground, so he became an urban terrorist and tried to sink the guy's new boat. It happens a great deal as free enterprise devolves into a class system.

27

After fifteen weeks in the Orange Coast shipyard for the American Bureau of Ships (ABS) marine survey and trials, I was back in Seattle from San Diego. I was on the bed, staging my brain for coffee while relaxing my eyes toward Lake Union. Our house was the entire top floor of a new condominium on 6th Avenue. I was looking through seventy-five feet of glass windows and doors facing a deck festooned with trees and Adirondack chairs and crows on the rail. Inside, the surface tops were white marble, and there was a white marble bathroom for looking in the mirror and a bathroom for shaving. A bathroom for singing and a bathroom for sitting. If our house transformed into a table in 8-Ball, on the *break*, all the balls would find a bathroom. Every morning was sunrise, and every evening was a glittering panorama of Seattle to the North Cascade Mountains toward Montana. The level below was our garage, where we kept a white GMC K-series pickup and a Coin Gold 928 Porsche. Two Eddyline kayaks and two Greg LeMond championship bicycles. *The Wall Street Journal* was on my step every morning. On this day, I was managing my left foot into some cargo pants, and my phone chirped next to me. The text message was, *"Turn on your TV."*

The entire political and economic structure of the world changed on that day. It was like a geopolitical asteroid struck the earth. The shock waves were non-discriminate. Everyone could feel the burn on their face. In an odd way, it was America's finest hour. We *took one for the team,* so to say. The moment of greatest impact on me was when I learned that United Flight 93 passenger Todd Beamer's last message was "Let's Roll!"

as he and others forced the aircraft into a crashing death roll in Somerset County, Pennsylvania. Unbounded heroism is impossible to match.

The sky over Seattle got very quiet. Only an occasional F-16 flyby from McChord Air Force Base in Pierce County. Domestic flights in traffic zones were directed to land where they were. That put a great deal of USA equipment on the tarmac in British Columbia. Civility and cooperation were surfacing everywhere.

As the world stood still and priorities were being realigned in orders of magnitude, I realized that this force majeure was not being lost on me. I was right in the flow of change. My brain was involuntarily realigning like racks of clicking key sets. I couldn't think backward two weeks and come forward with how my career choices met who I was. Or, who I thought I was. I was running on emotional empty. I didn't care about anything and didn't know why.

The person watching all this was Christine. My live-in girlfriend/motorcycle (two up) buddy/kayaking partner/ Alaska fishing lodge owner. We'd both had friends who were predicting we would eat each other alive—didn't happen. Christine spent a good deal of her life in floatplanes on scud-runs around southeast Alaska. She shouldered a Winchester 300 Magnum and could place a shot at one thousand yards. Her most circulated picture was of her standing buck-ass naked in a Geronimo pose riding an ice flow in Glacier Bay, Alaska.

So, with that kind of deck, she said to me one day, "Why don't you go back to school."

I was just hollow enough and fed up enough to fall straight into that vortex with no Q&A required. However, it was among these moments that I was forced into reflection on a previous University of Montana transcript. The one that would reflect my major was drinking beer and shooting pool. That I was on academic probation until the U of M imprimatur was out of the question.

So, regardless of my drifty-colored background, I walked completely away from yachts and started looking for a university.

28

So, I'm a seasoned international yacht broker with gray hair deciding to become a college student. My yacht transaction range was between $350,000 and $12,000,000. In Countertrade, I was rolling $150,000,000 in executive jets, property, and trade credits. I was trading subdivisions in New Orleans for giant yachts in San Diego. I was working with aggressive private companies and Fortune 500 C-Suite Executives. Sometimes heads of state.

Now, I'm talking to college recruiters. I have an embarrassing transcript from the University of Montana. On every call, I hear, "We will not accept your transfer credits," and I need 120 credits to graduate Bachelor of Something.

I am about to take a pass on the whole idea when I find that the U.K. will allow students to open a master's program without a first degree. No BS or BA required. Within minutes I'm out of the pits and onto the track.

I find Heriot-Watt University in Edinburgh, Scotland, offering an online MBA under the no BA/BS required U.K. protocol. *Perfect*, I say in the mirror. *How cool is that? I leverage my experience into a famous university in Scotland—walk out with an MBA—I'm happy again. I will vindicate years of college sloth in one fell swoop.*

I begin dropping *University in Edinburgh* in my conversations. I don't mention the school's name so my listeners can let their minds run with the romance of the Scottish Highlands. I am now a foreign student, except it's backward. The school is foreign, and I'm domestic.

The admissions people in Edinburgh tell me they are aligned with the University of Washington, where I will be taking my end-of-term tests in a proctored environment. I didn't know what that meant, exactly, but I got that handled with the UW.

The study material arrives from the school, and I begin. No class. No nothing. Just read for the test. A classroom of one. The tone of the text develops a variety of strategies around a human frame with emerging evidence . . . and so on. I presume the "human frame" is a person—maybe a customer. I find out that I *must invest in people, or they will feel neglected.* I laugh out loud.

I think. *You must be kidding;* I speculate over the approved text. *Is the guy a high-grade bullshitter? Can he afford to be in this deal? Does his wife have all the money? Wait! No, that's his girlfriend!*

The textbook tells me that my *environment is my source of raw materials.*

I think *absolutely. This guy is going to dance his way into the emotions of his girlfriend, knock-her-up at the Airport Hyatt Regency, and a month later call me for instructions on how to off her into an abortion. Let's see; I wonder if she will feel neglected?*

Beyond the human frame, we move to the political frame. Coalitions of various individuals. This is where the people *"come alive,"* it says. *Where they gather up scarce resources.* I *speculate that would be when a Ponzi scheme perp makes a fake deposit on a motor yacht so he can hold an aft deck meeting for his investor marks later that afternoon. They come with three-quarters of a million dollars, and the Ponzi provides the address of a shared office in the Columbia Tower.* Of course, silly me, those shared office spaces are scarce.

So, this continues as I read and speculate in the arena of graduate school in Scotland. I can't get away from my mental sarcasm as I read chapter after chapter on the *artistry of leadership.*

I'm thinking, *how in the hell do these people survive?*

They are providing mind maps of techies and middle managers and top managers and front-line workers. I've never heard of any of them. All my guys were top of the pyramid unless they were operationally active criminals. Even then, they were usually on top of their game. Customers like Johnny Carbone fully understood business. Racketeering was his business model, and arson was a form of supply chain management.

So, I read on. Eventually, I'm scheduled to be tested at the UW for the Heriot-Watt University Master of Business Administration online series as Test number one. So, I arrive at the appointed room, pick up my test package, and the proctor TIs start the clock. I open the book and find I am to write *a structural scenario including managerial grids on contingent theories for first-level supervisions.* I lean back in my chair. Then I lean forward in my chair. I look at the clock. I look at my hands. I look at the door into the hall. I synchronize my Rolex Submariner with the clock on the wall. I spin the bezel to adjust for synchronous lead or lag. I calculate how long it will take me to get to Franco's back bar. I have time. I place my hands on the Blue Book Page One and write, "Show up for work and get the fucking money!"

The Business Dean called me from Scotland. Yes, he did. . . .

29

The business school dean at Heriot-Watt University was from California. When he called, he was reserved, and then he started to chuckle, then laugh. He choked on his words: "Mr. LaCasse, you know you can't reenroll?!"

I agreed. Trying to talk my way back in was a bad idea. But then he said, "Your astounding disrespect for higher education will forever reside in my top drawer. A reminder of how universities are perceived through the elementary common man lens."

I thought to myself; *I can buy this guy with my petty cash.* I had a fresh $300,000 in my wallet from the research ship deal in San Diego. I'm living in a penthouse that spans the entire top of a building on 6th Avenue in Seattle. For the last four years, Christine and I have been living on our new 47.3 Beneteau from San Rochelle, France. *And this academic pencil-necked troll tells me I'm an elementary common man?*

Then what struck me was I was justifying my actions with the trappings and lifestyle I was trying to leave. I am rolling this around in my head, thinking, *How big a stack of hypocrisy is that! I am working toward another social construct in a love-hate relationship. Just a different arena. So, where is the problem here?*

Christine was comfortable with my decisions because we were relatively new together, and, after all, I was successful. Christine wanted a new car, so I bought her a 928 Porsche.

Pat Rhodes, my friend and CPA, called from Italy and told me he got his nose full of red wine and raised his hand at an auction. He told me the auction item was to stay at the Fiat family villa with the architecture faculty of the University of Washington Rome school. Someplace called *Civita di Bagnoregio*.

I tell Christine to *pack a go-bag. We are catching a flight to Rome.*

I am walking around like Cock Robin and drinking my way out of reality. I'm knocking back a fifth of Seagram's VO a day. Lacing that with a pack of whatever smokes from Liggett and Myers. Wake up every morning at two A.M. dehydrated, so cure that with some *hair of the dog*.

The affair begins to dial into my High-Performance pilot's metaphoric brain. I am pushing the aircraft's envelope, coming every time closer to a flat spin—the death spiral all pilots fear the most. I am right there. All my instrument needles are dancing. My existence is shuddering. And, any moment, I will drop a wing and watch the ground approach as I count the seconds to my death. I am totally fucked-up!

30

So, I quit everything. I quit laughing. I quit smiling. I quit talking. I quit society. I became a stone-faced recovering addict as thirty-five years of Seagram's VO sweat its way out of my body. I ran around Green Lake every night. I jumped in an Olympic-sized pool at five A.M. every morning and clicked off laps.

I was living on the phone with more sober time on my clock. Sometimes two phones at the same time. My office manager, Ann McAllister, decided to create a desk plate that read, "John doesn't do drugs; he does phones!" Brokers began to refer to me as "The Shark."

As my sober synapses began to come back, my life transitioned into quick time. I was walking away from the yacht business, but I was not. I did not know how to get out. I managed to tell billionaire customers to *stick their deposits where the sun don't shine* and then pivoted into a blank wall. I was becoming a powerful sober train wreck. My test book answer for Heriot-Watt University was substantiation.

This attitude was becoming public and began to play into cross-border negotiations in the global mega yacht business. I was considered a prime player, as were David Fraser and Dave Christensen. Fraser was brokering in the USA and Europe, and Christensen came to yacht building after being a prime contractor for Hilton Hotels. I'd met Ronnie Hilton on the research ship in San Diego, and Barron Hilton kept a boat in Poulsbo, just across the Sound from Seattle.

Christensen was looking for traction in the mega yacht arena, and hooking up with Fraser was a likely way for him to get in without a long apprenticeship. He could build hotels, but could he build yachts? No doubt in his mind, but this was about the "market." So, Dave Christensen came to my office. He was a classic big-time contractor guy. Square body, big attitude. When he cleared the door, he said, "I want to speak with LaCasse, LaCasse, and LaCasse!"

When I rented the bottom floor of the building, the owner gave me the entire building façade. That included the side of the building as well. My name was stuck to every possible maritime option. I was "LaCasse Maritime." I was "LaCasse Yacht Sales," and I was "LaCasse Engineering." All with subtitle options in raised silver leaf across the front of the building.

When I walked out of the conference room, Christensen asked, "Are you LaCasse, LaCasse, and LaCasse?"

I agreed that I was, and with humor and candor, the games began. What I didn't know was that David Fraser was jockeying to represent Christensen while at the same time selling his company to his bud Carlo in Monaco. So, the Fraser brokerage company would end up in the city-state of Monaco in Europe. There was drumming among the major houses trying to see if a pony might come out of the straw pile. I was ushered into the game because my countertrade profile dwarfed all the big players, and they couldn't figure out how I was putting up one hundred and fifty million year after year. It's amazing to me how binary people can be. These guys were stuck on "here's the boat; where is the money?"

Conversely, my office was, "I understand you own sixteen shopping centers and fifty-five movie houses and that you sell more popcorn than anyone in the Lower 48.

"Ever thought of owning a mega yacht? Your jet? Hell yes, I'll take your jet—Lear 34, you said?

"Let's meet in San Juan. . . . I have an idea out of the water at the San Juan shipyard, and the Dupont Plaza Hotel Casino has the deepest Baccarat tables in the world!"

The boys at Fraser and Dave Christensen learned through Boat International in London that I was spinning these deals, and they wanted in. This intrigue was driving Christensen to find a lever against Fraser while romancing him at the same time. I was too busy to realize I was being used as a pawn by both of them.

So, in the fine tradition of chess—control by dominating the center of the board—Dave Christensen offers me the exclusive right to sell Christensen Yachts in America. That made me an acquisition target for Fraser, who was trying to bolster his stable in advance of the boys in Monaco. Fraser tells Carlo that he (Fraser) is considering acquiring my organization, and Carlo should give me a call to better understand my scope in large yacht transactions. Carlo does not call. Instead, he has one of his brokers call. *I still don't know that I am in the acquisition X-ring.*

I get on the line with this guy, and he begins a scenario around a large transaction covering cross-border buyers and sellers. He says *Fraser recommended me as the best of the best in sophisticated deals.* I'm okay with that. I'm talking to a broker in Europe who is name-dropping all over Europe, Africa, and the United States. How could this be bad? Except it was. This guy is way over his depth. Worse, he is getting lost in his own story. He is wasting my time. Being the professional that I was, I tell him, "You are full of shit! Good-bye!"

Carlo calls David Fraser and makes it clear that my book of business is interesting, but LaCasse himself must go. So, with Dave Christensen in the wings, David Fraser approached me to somehow jack me out of the deal and take over my company.

The situation was getting dicey. Very awkward.

As I began learning over my life to come, this moment-to-moment smack down with Fraser and Christensen had me against the wall, and yet, indelibly appearing in the Eleventh hour, some transcendental hand snatched me from the fire, and I lived to play another day.

During the meeting, the office phone rings, and Ann McAllister edges in with animation. "You better take this," she says. The men at the table nod in agreement, and I pick up the receiver.

"*Hello, is this John LaCasse of LaCasse Maritime?*"

"Yes, it is."

"*I have Rainier Louis Henry Maxence Bertrand Grimaldi on the line— Rainier III, Prince of Monaco, holding. Would you be available for a call?*"

"Ah . . . Yes!"

"Hello, Mr. LaCasse. This is Prince Rainier." And the conversation continued. He wanted me to come to Monaco and advise him on a large Motor Sailor project. His yacht. Would I be available?

The room and everyone in it turned to salt. Prince Rainier just picked me out of the crowd.

I guess Carlo forgot to tell the Prince that I was an asshole.

I could not stop laughing. I just couldn't stop laughing.

Four people from LaCasse Maritime left for Monaco.

31

Once again, I was staged and upright with control I didn't want. Prince Rainier III of Monaco had blown the apostate angels' game plan out of the box. I was again flying high in the canopy inside an industry I was trying to leave.

Now that one observation moved me from *jumping the shark* to an entirely new life. I was about to reinvent myself as the amalgamation of my experience. One day, as I was spooling up for another contest between men and money, Christine looked at me and said, "You are incredibly unhappy! You have become a dying caged bird. You must . . . you must . . . change, or you will hit the ridge and explode."

I instantly knew what she meant. With both of us having experience in planes, she knew she could get my attention with a plane crash metaphor. Christine spent several years traveling in float planes in Southeast Alaska, from one village to another, as she managed state and federal programs for Alaska native children. Then she spent another thirteen years as owner-manager of George Inlet Lodge at Mile 12 South Tongass, Ketchikan. Before that, she taught K-12 in Juneau.

Christine patterned herself after Sylvia Ashton Warner, who, from New Zealand, became the famous benchmark for understanding education in old cultures and new nations. Christine's students learned through metaphor. Mathematics from the scuba dive table. Biology under the dock at low tide. She grew up as a Valley Girl in Los Angeles. She played well in every spectrum frequency.

Instinctively, I knew her admonishment was correct. I grabbed two sets of leathers and a couple of helmets and said, "Let's ride." We took the Harley (Harley-Davidson Wide Glide) and headed north. We put the kickstand down at Harvey Field, a small airport in Snohomish County, Washington. We parked in the grass and lay down like two people on a beach ball spinning through space. Our first run at being in perspective with the universe.

I began casting around for two things: A university that would take me and a job/lifestyle aligned with my perception of who I was. Neither of us considered changes brought on by the loss of income. This was simply about living in the light instead of the dark.

32

We got back to our nest on 6th Avenue—the penthouse that occupied the entire top floor. The one that had the best seat in the city for the 4th of July fireworks on Lake Union. The one that had our garage under our unit housing a 928 V-8 Porsche. A total custom skiff designed around a Gig off the *Dorothy Luckenbach* in 1925 with gold leaf on the bow. Road bikes by Greg LeMond, American cycling legend who has been diagnosed with leukemia as I write this. Expedition kayaks that we used to circumnavigate around the United States' San Juan Islands and to the headwaters of Toba Inlet in British Columbia, Canada, where we hung them vertically on a rock cliff face to abate grizzly bears having their way with all our equipment. . . . Now reflecting on the retractable gear high-performance Piper Turbo Arrow I had tied down at Flightcraft Boeing Field.

We couldn't afford this stuff anymore. We had symbolically strapped on a hair shirt and walked into the desert. A great deal more fun on a Harley-Davidson, but that didn't change the situation. Walking out of the dark and into the light exposed my moment-to-moment lifestyle. Money was a renewal resource. Easy to make, so why squirrel any away for a rainy day? All of us front-line brokers were that way. We spent money like drunken sailors—and in some cases, we were.

Within days, maybe hours, the expenses were overriding income. We began missing house payments. I decided to start offing my toys.

I flew the airplane for the last time with my son John Patrick in the second seat. We rotated off Boeing Field, One Three Right (13R).

That's a runway, and straight out to Mount Rainier. It was beautiful—the snow—the ice. At fifteen thousand feet, we could see the ridge lines in high relief. We strapped on oxygen and kept circling. I knew I was seeing Mount Rainier for the last time. I didn't want that to fade. John was pressed to the window, looking forward and backward across the wing. I banked right and put the tip of the wing on Camp Muir, so John could see it all—everything.

I was quietly crying as John was fixed on the mountain. What a pair we were. The dad flying a fancy airplane; the son in the wonder of it all. It struck me that I could have all the boys on this flight, but I didn't plan in that way. Each boy was the sentinel next to his own tree. So, on this day, it was John and me. Back at Boeing, I put the plane away and gave John a ride home. It was a good day in a forlorn kind of way.

The following morning, I took off on 13R, banked, and headed north. I had an appointment for the plane at Paine Field where it would be detailed and with a broker to offer it for sale. I left the pattern at Boeing and began a slow ascent against the eastern slopes of the Cascade Range on my way to one last landing. I could see from Snohomish County, Washington, to British Columbia, Canada. The sensory reward for all pilots. I remembered that Mount Baker has the most measurable snowfall in the lower United States. An astounding 1140 inches in 1999. I was one of those *who knew* those kinds of factoids about the Pacific Northwest. From Artist Point to Mount Shuksan and up into the blue glaciers. I was sad once again.

As I changed the pattern to cross Martha Lake and Interstate 5, I felt an abrupt drop in engine RPMs. I looked quickly at the panel and then up to the windshield. I was losing visibility. The windshield was covered in oil, splaying itself across the view forward. My pressure kept dropping, and the engine RPM continued to fall. Within moments, I couldn't see anything forward.

I called Seattle Center about the situation. Center linked me to the tower frequency at Paine Field. They had me identified from the Transponder—altitude, direction, and speed. In a series of quick decisions, Seattle began directing me for a straight-in into Paine Field. Once they got me on a glide slope, it would be up to me to look out the side and gauge my descent to touch down with a rollout that kept me on the numbers.

This was my second emergency approach. Years earlier, I had called for a *straight-in* into Missoula County Airport in western Montana. That was a Salt Lake Center call with all the same FAA professionalism. That time, it was from a blown turbocharger but still related to oil and pressure. In Missoula, the Tower decided to "Roll the Equipment." That means that fire engines and crash trucks are your new best friends as you collectively roll down the runway upon landing. A great deal of happiness at the end of the rollout. You can bet your ass on that.

So, Paine Field, Seattle Center, and I (P1131Quebec) are crackling back and forth, and I am trying to see out the side window on approach. I know *I am flying into the teeth of the tiger,* but my mind is on yesterday. On Mount Rainier. What would this be like on the downslope of a 14,000-foot mountain? John Patrick and I would be dead today. None of this would be happening because it all happened yesterday. We would be dead—dead! I couldn't get off that thought.

I could almost smell the screech of black rubber smoke as the plane found the runway. I began s-curving between the lines to a taxi lane. The plane was happy. I was happy. Relieved, more like it.

I kept doing pirouettes to see and kept rolling. The Tower closed the flight plan, and I stepped off the wing at the Aviation Flight School at Paine Field.

"My oily plane is ready for a bath," I tell the line boy.

"Yes, sir," he says.

I look for a cigarette. I forgot. I don't smoke.

33

Christensen and Fraser continued to circle. They wanted each other but were not going to let either pretension show. Christensen wanted an early entry into big-time yacht construction, and Fraser needed control of market share to get maximum money for his company. I was *Lucky Pierre in The Middle*.

My interest in heavy yachts was getting thinner by the day. Eventually, Fraser and I had another sit-down around cooperation between us. Most likely, there would not be another mid-meeting call like Prince Rainier. Unless, maybe, the Pope wanted a new car. I had a Gold 600 Mercedes-Benz off a yacht deal in my garage. The 600 is one of those in-your-face kinds of cars. They only work for dilettantes in the finals for German Chancellor—maybe Roman Emperor. Driving around in a 600 Mercedes without a full-stack security detail is just plain laughable. Although Dick Kelleher (my lawyer) and I drove it around one Halloween until we were too drunk to drive. So, we parked it at Green Lake and fell asleep. The cops were courteous. Must have been the car.

Fraser wanted Christensen more than he wanted me, but I had the Christensen contract. We were a pair. I was like a Scorpion to Fraser. The strike was unpredictable, and the venom was deadly. Not the kind of reputation built on a solid foundation. I didn't care. Fraser was dull. He had a great smile and enjoyed the socialization of big yachts. That notwithstanding, his intellectual curiosity had flatlined.

So, David Fraser and I decided on a working compromise. I would keep the facility, and he would put his marquee on my business. For all who looked on, I became Fraser Yachts in Seattle. That gave Fraser the Christensen contract by default. Both Christensen and Fraser were happy. I got rid of overhead. Now they had each other in a kind of shotgun marriage, and I was the Deadwood preacher.

David made frequent trips to Seattle and Vancouver/Portland, where Christensen had his plant. There became an ongoing battle between Christensen and Fraser about construction quality. Fraser thought Christensen was building the equivalent of backwater floating hotels, not high-seas yachts. Christensen accused Fraser of elitism, underwritten by shallow research. They were both right. Fraser knew how a yacht was supposed to look and feel. Christensen knew that hydrostatically it makes little difference where he placed the propeller shafts if they were under the boat. Between the three of us, I was the only member of the Society of Naval Architects and Marine Engineers (SNAME), and I was dancing with two teenagers trying to swing the biggest dick. Clearly, I was becoming fed up with both.

Back on Westlake Avenue, everyone could sense I was going to walk. I was aggravated and aggressive. I rode up to my office on the Harley, wheeled it into the office, and parked in front of my desk. I was pushing the envelope in every direction, *but for what* continuing to erode my mind. Everyone walked around me as if I was a short-fused explosive, and I was.

I sat at my desk; my eyes focused on a nail in the wall. It was all the way to the head. Silver on gray. Almost sunk into the drywall. Then I panned through my stuff. Pictures, awards, furniture, guns, braided line, and my motorcycle in the center. The engine was still hot. At the ready. My motorcycle was my ticket out of here. The same ride we took to Harvey Field, and that was the *ride* I was taking out of here.

I picked up the phone and called Newport Beach—David Fraser. When he got on, I puked the whole company right on my bib. "David, if you want to keep your name on my building, you can have it there for the lease. I'm going back to school; I'm done."

He said, "you're *what*!?"

"*I'm done.* You tried to kill me for Carlo trying to get your deal, and I carried the day. I got Prince Rainier, and you got a hockey puck between the teeth. Now, I'm leading an impossible life between you and Christensen, even when I win. So, my friend, this is my incandescent flash. I am no longer related to this business. I'm done.

"Do you want the space or not?"

David said, "Absolutely! I'll have some papers drafted, and we can meet up there."

"David, I am about to get on my motorcycle and ride out of here. If you want this office, you call Montgomery Elevator and get yourself on the lease."

He said, "I think we should have an agreement."

"Fuck you and the horse you rode in on, David! You are on, or you are off. My next call is to Northrop and Johnson and/or Ardell" (competing houses on the West Coast).

We agreed to meet.

The next morning, David Fraser called me from the 6th Avenue Motel in Seattle. We met in their coffee shop. He had an agreement in hand. I took it from him and set it aside. I never saw it again. Dave Christensen called while we were at the motel. "Fraser called last night. You know about that?"

"Yep."

It's remarkable how hunger limits choice. I was hungry for change. In my mind, all I had was a slice of *cut-and-run*. It's impossible to overstate the value of that kind of healing foundation. Fresh. All the lines are empty; the pencil is sharp. Life becomes a bardic minimum. Freedom is everywhere.

I was off to college—among other things.

Shakespeare and Company was a gathering place for the great ex-pat writers—Joyce, Hemingway, Stein, Fitzgerald, Eliot, Pound—as well as for leading French writers. It's where John most likely met the manifestation of Simone de Beauvoir who decided he should read Alexandre Dumas and *The Count of Monte Cristo*.

Place Saint-Michel (Paris) where Thomas Aquinas and John LaCasse walked to have coffee after Aquinas first manifested himself out of the light spectrum and river mist on the Seine River of France. Situated in the Latin Quarter (Left Bank), the Place Saint Michel represents centuries of Christian dogma as the yin yang of good and evil. A symbolic Christian artifact for Thomas Aquinas to begin his assessment of John LaCasse.

John LaCasse at his desk with John Patrick and Robert Charles. As John began to get traction in the early years of sales, his boys, soon to be four, were in his sphere. Like his father before him, his boys were laced into his day-to-day. Regardless of schedules, he and his boys were like monkeys in a barrel. They slept on the floor together. Sailed together, went alpine climbing, and sat making plans on upside-down Zodiac rafts—stacked with loaded scuba tanks and regulators.

Armosa LaCasse and John LaCasse. Grandmother and Grandson reviewing LA PRESS newspaper from Quebec, Canada. French was the language of the main house, and the French newspaper was a daily delivery. Armosa was a day-to-day caregiver for John. She held her counsel close as the matriarch of the family. The trinity of parents and grandparents left John with ramrod confidence.

Zodiac. The primary tool of John's water life. He is known for heavy yachts, but he sleeps under the stars upon the Salish Sea. After crossing the Strait of Juan de Fuca people want to know what yacht he's from. He simply smiles, and they say, "You must be kidding!"

For the first 20 years in western Montana.

John B. LaCasse and John L. LaCasse (Father and Son). Born in 1904, John B. LaCasse was a bootstrap Renaissance man, with a family from Canada and France. He left home early and rounded the world three times as a U.S. Merchant Marine Lifeboat Man. John, the son, followed, becoming a Merchant Marine Master (CAPT). That aside, they spent 20 years together in the mountains of Western Montana. That was who they were one to the other. Living with nature, under the canopy of the overland.

Marie LaCasse (Mother). Marie J. Sparrow's (Sparrowvich) family came to Montana from Dalmatia Croatia and Austria. Marie grew up influenced by restauranteurs in Europe and America. She practiced a Hinterland work ethic while watching her parents learn the ways of American culture. She brought her son the arts, music, theater, and culinary art. Whenever John was away from the outdoor life, he was in the theater with his mom. She took him to Michigan where her privileged estate was expanded. John became a commuter during and after the 2nd World War. Montana to Michigan and back in multiple rotations. The families LaCasse and Sparrowvich mixed and matched two completely different cultures, John becoming the after-effect of both.

At the Pont Neuf Bridge, walking between Île de la Cité and the Sorbonne, University of Paris, and three hours before Aquinas decided LaCasse has the qualities necessary to help subvert the Seraphim, John LaCasse finds himself dead by the hand of Doctor Angelicus Aquinas on the streets of Paris.

Wikipedia contributors, "No good deed goes unpunished," *Wikipedia, The Free Encyclopedia*, https://en.wikipedia.org/w/index.php?title=No_good_deed_goes_unpunished&oldid=1130513092 (accessed January 9, 2023).

Michigan quickly became John's center of upper-middle-class culture. Fancy cars and big cigars. John had his own houseman with a brace of German Shepherds. Michigan's juxtaposed life from Montana evolved into a hallmark of John's understanding of wealth.

John's little boy commuting between Montana and Michigan was punctuated by style. Here he is the Troop Train Traveler as a returning officer from the theaters in Germany and France during the 2nd World War.

In his father's early tradition, John became a U.S. Merchant Marine Master.

EQUITY FUNDING REAL ESTATE STOCK EQUITY SECURITIES WALL STREET JOURNAL 144 SECURI

In this industry, the phrase *"doing the deal"* and the name John LaCasse have become synonymous. If your next transaction calls for something more sophisticated than "show me the money," for example 144 Restricted Securities, then it is time to talk.

If your broker needs to walk like a realtor, talk like a lawyer and think like a stockbroker, you are reading the right ad. After more than 24 years in the trenches, doing successful deals, John LaCasse does not have contacts. John LaCasse is contacted.

A broker with Fraser Yachts, John LaCasse is also President of Striker Pacific Corporation, Director of WMA Group Holdings, L.L.C. and Senior Partner of Capital Exchange, L.L.C. LaCasse did his undergraduate studies at the University of Montana and completed his L.L.B. degree in Law at Blackstone College of Law in Chicago in 1973.

LaCasse is a United States Merchant Marine Master and has been a member of the Society of Naval Architects and Marine Engineers,1978; the Institute of Marine Engineers, 1979; and the Northeast Coast Institute of Engineers and Ship Builders, 1979. For additional information, please see the *International Who's Who in Professional Management*, 1996.

93' PUNAT LRC 1968 • $1,800,000 cash or consider 144 Securities with free trading shares • $10.00 or mark to market with personal guarantee.

98' QUEENSHIP LRMY 1993 • $5,750,000 or cash to mortgage and consider Fannie Mae or Jennie Mae derivatives at market with short-term maturity and additional strips for risk.

103' RMS CUSTOM MY 1990 • $3,950,000 or cash to mortgage and consider any net quick asset funding instrument in domestic markets.

107' BARATTUCCI YF 1992 • $4,375,000 cash or consider derivatives or 144 Securities who's free trading shares are active or commercial real estate improved or un-improved.

Fraser YACHTS WORLDWIDE

Contact Worldwide Central Agent John LaCasse
1500 Westlake Ave. No., Suite 118, Seattle, WA 98109 U.S.A. • Tel: 206-282-4943 Fax: 206-285-4956 • E-mail yacht@msn.com

Sausalito　　　Seattle　　　Newport Beach　　　San Diego

John turned Fraser Yachts into an international player in Countertrade.

Around the World

Patrick Goes it Alone

■ Ruth Merritt, president of Merritt Knowles Design Group has announced her retirement, leaving vice president Patrick Knowles to go it alone under the new company name of Patrick Knowles Design. Clients will be pleased to know they can find Patrick at the same location and can be reassured that all current projects of the Merritt Knowles Design Group will be completed.
Contact: Patrick Knowles Design
1650 SE 17th Street Causeway, Suite 210
Fort Lauderdale, FL 33316
Tel: (954) 832-0108 Fax: (954) 832-9951

Burger with CNI

■ Burger Boat Company is now represented by Camper & Nicholsons International. Three new yachts to be unveiled shortly are described by Burger president David Ross (above right) as "specifically for the international market." George Nicholson (above left) of CNI rates aluminum semi-displacement Burgers "the finest quality vessels in their class."
Contact: Burger Boat Company
1811 Spring St, Manitowoc, WI 54220
Tel: (920) 686-5104 Fax: (920) 686-5101
Camper & Nicholsons International
25 Bruton St, London W1X 7DB, UK
Tel: +44 171 491 2950 Fax: +44 171 499 0111

Michael Ahrens

■ Following eight years as marketing and sales director for Abeking and Rasmussen and five years in the same role for Moonen Shipyards, Michael Ahrens has moved on to become chairman of Heliyachts International SA and Heli dd. The latter, a shipyard in Croatia, was founded in 1995 and has completed repair contracts, and the construction of a 32m sailing yacht *Dat Helja* delivered in 1996. Heliyachts International in Lugano, as general contractor, will offer marketing and sales for the shipyard as well as financing, registration, consulting, brokerage and management of yachts.
Contact: Heliyachts International
SA, Via Tesserete 67, CH-6942 Lugano/Savosa
Tel/Fax: +49 421 15727 or
Heli dd, St Polikarpa-Str 8
52100 Pula/Istria, Croatia
Tel: +385 52 216633 Fax: +385 52 216634

The Kingdom of Countertrade

Countertrade is a commercial arrangement in which the buyer pays for his purchases, wholly or partly, with something other than money. Very often countertrade deals include some cash, but a significant portion of the transaction is settled with commodities or services. Countertrade has been employed heavily and successfully in trade arrangements with communist nations and Third World countries, where shortage of foreign exchange might otherwise preclude trade.
Over 100 countries worldwide now impose offset obligations in both defense and civil sectors. Because of this, offsets are becoming important to exporters, and thus are becoming more varied and creative as they become more widely used.
Because yachts fall into a category of commodities in use throughout developed countries, and because yachts are usually owned by individuals or corporations with an income stream able to support commercial activities well beyond the yacht itself, countertrade and offset contracts of both yachts and executive jets have arrived.
Striker Pacific Corporation of Seattle, Washington, headed by John Lacasse (above), has become a major player in countertrade. With more than two hundred million dollars trading since the beginning of the year, the breakdown looks like this: One hundred forty million in property, ninety million in yachts and ten million in durable goods. The typical spread in a yacht transaction would be a 94-unit residential subdivision; a jet turbine aircraft and half a million in cash. In one case the entire transaction developed around a joint venture for 60 commercial acres contiguous to the city of New Orleans. In another deal, five two-million-dollar contracts were developed for high-grade iron ore aggregate in Michigan.
The secret to countertrade lies in the ability

The garden unit of this new building at 105 West Highland Dr, Seattle, worth two million is available for countertrade

of the transaction to develop full equity for the trade goods. For example, if a yacht comes to market for seven million dollars and is receiving offers of four million, the owner becomes distressed at the prospect of a capital loss. The countertrader will develop a relationship with a companion company that has the resources usable by the yacht owner and re-negotiate the offer. Earlier this year a company in a similar circumstance, had a large yacht for sale on the West Coast with offers coming in at about seventy percent of the value. The yacht owner, while not willing to accept offers in this range, was simultaneously developing a new regional distribution center in Sacramento, California. The countertrader became a combination of cash for the yacht and enough trade credits to supply construction material for the distribution center. In the end both parties had what they could use on the table. Although the use of yachts in trade credit transactions has been considered by the yacht industry as a complicated counter culture phenomenon, the face of the industry is changing. With almost all multinational corporations using countertrade both domestically and offshore, this sales tool will be found in greater numbers in the future.
Contact: Striker Pacific Corporation
2170, 6 Ave N, Suite 301, Seattle, WA 98109
Tel: (206) 301-0864 Fax: (206) 301-0170

John was rolling over $200,000,000.00 in Countertrade for Mega Yachts.

When John turned the U.S. Navy Ship Builder into a Yacht Builder.

Jim Chrysler and Steven Hawking get in the white plane. John gets in the blue plane, and off they go . . . John spends the night jawboning with Hawking over Existential Physics.

Christine took John aside and said "If you don't stop, you are going to die." And John spent the next 17 years rearranging his life in college to become Dr. John LaCasse Ph.D.

John was unique in the yachting industry because as a U.S. Merchant Marine Master, he could both sail them and sell them while understanding the psychology of wealth.

Through multiple trips to Paris, Dr. LaCasse got close to the culture, spreading his time to the street, gentry, and research—intellectually understanding by then that the physics of time could be spread like butter.

In the Helicon Days of Countertrade Yacht Transactions.

On deck when all the boys were still alive. Front row: Jeff and Heidi. Back row (standing): Erik, Rene, John, and Bob.

Brian sorting Spanish treasure.

Merrilee of the Trinity.

Kelly of the Trinity.

Jacqueline of the Trinity.

Ratifying the Education Exchange agreement with the Confederated Tribes of the Colville Reservation for the Moses Lake Project involving Benedictine University, George Washington University, and The Administrative Government of The Peoples Republic of China.

PART TWO

BREAKING AWAY

34

Going back to school when you are middle-aged is not Fraternity parties and Cheerleader Pompoms. I was, by some measure, an old man. Older than many faculty I would encounter. Coming out of the *"You get to eat what you kill"* business sales tranche, I had an attitude. Salespeople like me did not receive a base salary. We got paid at closing. That posture kept us sharp—like a wolf pack in winter. Hunting and hungry. Stacked on that was how I leveraged yacht sales into a global countertrade phenomenon. I had a business history and *chops*.

The problem with that mix, and the people in it, is staying in context. It becomes a narrow formula for success. There is little or no need to become expansive. Good salespeople become siloed in their success. That was never me. I would finish a transaction and try to escape. But to where? I never could see *where*. And that didn't change even when I was in the middle of change, like starting school. When I went back to school, I watched students ruminate over homework, jobs, parents, social structure, and sex partners.

Not me. I ended up forming three academic groups to build a new university campus as a cooperative between The George Washington University, Benedictine University, and The Confederated Tribes of the Colville Reservation. And that mix would become a post-secondary student exchange with Guangdong University in China. Yeah, how's that for a confabulated fraternity party with new sex partners? No problem! But that *was* my problem. I could never see the ground in front of me. I was always looking at the horizon.

Every time I encountered a situation, I would transform it into a force multiplier opportunity. And that got me in front of amazing people. So, I'm not sorry because the rest of my life became running headlong into opportunity with no Harvard Business School (HBS) advance team flying cover. About walking into a casino. Sitting down in front of a guy wearing full Native American regalia. The Chairman/Chief of twelve Indian Tribes. Being scared shitless. Placing my forearm across my chest—then holding up my hand and saying, *"How."*

To have him lean in and say, "I've studied Law. I have an MBA. I'm writing my dissertation for a Ph.D. in Biomass Sustainable Practices, and I speak English."

35

By the time I sat down with Mike Marchand to have him tell me he went to school and spoke English, I was already in graduate school. I'm not going to up my burn rate here by analyzing my opening to the Indian chief. I do have some ideas, like too much time with Hopalong Cassidy. Even Hoppy had more style. To this day, I don't know how—or why—I arrived at hand gestures and smoke signals during our first meeting.

Mike was indeed in charge of a bunch of Native Americans who were market economy capitalists ranging from gaming to timber and mining. I was studying for my MBA at Benedictine University in Lyle, Illinois. That's *Chicago Land* in midwestern parlance. Benedictine was my third graduate school because I was summarily dismissed out of the first two. As you reflect on the stories in this book, it becomes easier to understand how I could be tossed out of anywhere. I was not risk-averse, so following my version of Sun Tzu and *The Art of War,* anything short of death was a win.

In each university dismissal, I came up against policy in an eleemosynary culture. I remember after being dismissed from the University of Maryland, the recruiter at The George Washington University asked, "Mr. LaCasse, do you understand who has the power here?"

None of the graduate school recruiters could understand how I could be dismissed with such a high GPA. Like, wait. What?!

In actuality, I was a misunderstood anomaly. At the University of Maryland, one faculty member tried to recruit me to help him carve out a division of U Maryland (University College) and take it private. I told him he was way over his depth, and furthermore, he had no business trying to recruit a graduate student to attack the school like a barbarian at the gate. Even If I liked the idea, the guy was dumb as a stump. The kind of guy you won't let drive or babysit your kid. So, he gave me an "F," and that triggered the Registrar and Provost to review my transcript. Earlier in my University of Maryland career, I had had the same kind of run-in with another faculty member. I challenged her on just about everything in the course. She gave me an "F," so I had all "As" and two "Fs." That was enough "Fs" to get me dropped from the program.

So, back on the street with ninety graduate school credits, looking once again for a school. That's when I checked with The George Washington University at Foggy Bottom. I could slide into GW and come away with a Master's in Education Administration. I passed the graduate admission test once again, and my first class was my Education Administration Internship. I matriculated in an odd year, but that didn't seem to matter. No classroom experience, but turn him loose on a middle school and see what happens.

The school was expecting a twenty-year-old graduate student in education administration. What they got was a crusty reprobate full of compliance scars. When I arrived, the Principal was stumped for an assignment.

I said, "How about I monitor a few general classrooms for a little get-a-feel-for-the-environment?" She agreed.

It became quickly clear to me that the entire school was leveraged toward special education. The Special Ed classrooms were packed with teachers, and a large percentage of the overall budget landed in Special Ed. It looked to me like all the students were on the short bus to school. So, I brought it up in a meeting. I hit pay dirt right out of the box. The teachers in this school were, in some cases, third generation. They had their "way," and I was an interloper.

One woman walked up to me and, with her index finger, poked me in the chest, reminding me who was in charge. They were originally comfortable with me because I looked like a colleague. Now, however, they were uneasy about my nose under their tent. After some digging around, I brought my case to all the general classroom teachers and parents.

"You guys are being isolated out of most of your operating budget in favor of Special Education. I suggest we start integrating Special Education students into the general classroom. Spread the teachers around and let the students comingle so General Classroom and Special Education reach some kind of staffing and economic parity."

And I advised that the Special Education and General Education students would be fine, just like a Dog Show. In their cages, all the dogs want to bark and fight. In the ring, they are fine—no problem. Might have been a mistake using that comparison, but I made my case, and the bifurcation of money and talent was about to fall into entropy. I had everyone's attention, and there were action plans aplenty. Except for the Special Education teachers who were forming up in a wedge. I didn't receive death threats, and nobody sent me a bloody horse head for my bed, but I received a scarlet letter for my forehead.

Within days, I got a call from the Dean of Education at The George Washington University. She thought it would be best if I dropped the program. So, she gave me an "A," and I did not re-enroll.

Back on the street looking.

By now, I was looking for traction outside education. My prospects as a graduate student were not looking good. Then I had some sort of angel-driven spiritual epiphany. Catholic schools, maybe. I got thrown out of a Catholic high school. That must count for something. My uncle was dicey enough that he ended up in Boys Town with Father Flanagan.

I once went out for a pass—on the field—at Notre Dame. Bought the ball in the student union and talked my way into the stadium and onto the field. Once again, it was: *what do we do with this guy*? And I said, "How about I go out for a pass?" . . . and I did, and a helmet with pads did, in fact, throw me a nice little screen pass. So, does that mean I played football at Notre Dame? Maybe.

So, I started looking for a Catholic college. A place for disenfranchised interlopers. On the catalog page for the President of Benedictine University in Chicago was the picture of a guy standing in a fireman's full fire suit. Like double canvas and helmet. Gloves and pike. YEAH, that's my guy! Bill Carroll, President of Benedictine University in Illinois.

We talked. I applied. I'm accepted, and I am on my way to my MBA in International Business.

None of these education adventures were taking that much time, so I was nosing around in business. That's how I tagged up with Mike Marchand and the Confederated Tribes of the Colville Reservation.

36

One of the advantages of being thrown out of school as a truant, as opposed to the skid-road of academic probation, is your reputation lingers in the faculty lounge. Even though you're dismissed, your odor remains. I had about a year to go at Benedictine when I found my way to the tribe. The prompt was Benedictine University had an active student exchange with China. And the China project was a favorite of Bill Carroll (Ben-U President).

Being a businessman more than a student, I started looking at Bill Carroll's student exchange thing as scalable. I also had my own China connection. One of my associates nominated me to be the American Business guest speaker at a trade conference in Detroit. The event was centered round the big three auto makers along with their inside technical people from Ricardo Engineering. I came to Detroit alone. The Chinese came with a planeload of executives.

Before the opening, I met the Governor of Guangdong Province for tea. A long table with white cloth. He was on one side with twelve associates. I was on the other side alone. We smiled. I told him that the table must have parity. He should send six of his people to my side of the table. That way, we have balance. I was winging it with my version of *feng shui*. Maybe it would stick if I could say it right. He smiled and sent six people to my side of the table. We had a great time laughing and talking. Then we all went to lunch and sat together.

After my speech, at the end of the conference, a woman (Calisa Chen) approached me. "Mr. LaCasse, we have gold gifts for you from

China." She handed me two (real) gold dioramas (keys to two cities) and a gold and red certificate with a red CCP chop star.

"Governor Hon appointed you The United States Representative to the Bureau of Foreign Trade and Economic Cooperation, Zhaoquing/Gaoyao, PRC."

"Yeah, right. . . ."

So, I had a China connection, and I grew up trained like a white man Indian. That is as close as we get outside the wire, but my dad had me tracking and trapping for the first twenty years.

Coming from Montana and remembering my dad's interaction with the Blackfeet and Crow, his curiosity around gambling at the Saint Ignatius stick games, and his overall understanding of Indian culture, I was channeling my dad as an opportunity to add Indians into the Benedictine University China program. Undergraduate two-year USA and two-year China. But I needed an ad hoc location—a branch school—some kind of bridge to handle a trifecta of students from the Midwest, the Reservation, and China. And a way to navigate through truckloads of gatekeepers.

Looking like an Indian helped. One morning on Creek Street in Ketchikan, Alaska, I was walking out of Parnassus Books. A couple of Native men spotted me as a fresh face and asked what tribe I belonged to. That remains today as a top-tier moment.

I also had some carry-over yacht connections that I maintained after the fact. Among them the Belzberg family in California. They were fast deciders with quick cash assets. That relationship remained after Bill Belzberg and I struck out with Jennifer Granholm and the UAW to rehab the Cadillac Stamping Plant in Grand Rapids, Michigan. Bill and Fred Joseph came to the table with three billion dollars. Sitting down with a couple of guys who can reach in their breast pocket and cut you a reader for three billion dollars becomes tattooed on your brain.

But it was his brother Sam who made the point. He bought a mega yacht on the east coast and had us bring it around—six thousand miles on open ocean. Upon arrival, Sam brought his wife down the dock to welcome her aboard. She stopped at the boarding platform—stepped back, looked up, said, "I don't like it!"

Sam looked at me and said, "Sell it," and they both walked off the dock.

Or maybe it was Sam's brother, Bill. We met for dinner at a Beverly Hills Italian restaurant. When we cleared the door on the way in, everyone stood up. Yeah, probably it was Bill.

I was also reflecting on how I left The George Washington University. As a troublemaker with an eye for change. That lingering feeling happened when the Education Dean cut me loose. I got the feeling that wasn't her decision. She was under pressure from some higher order in the academy. I intuitively knew that down the road, I could dial her number, and she would take the call.

So, I was walking around with this mental bag of contrived cohorts.

As the pieces of this puzzle came together, it was a game of leverage. It's like a free trade environment where all the parties have a strategic value but no single player the entire value.

Mike Marchand knew I was coming, but he wasn't sure why I was coming. The why of that equation was my private speculation that he would like to get access to a major interstate highway. His Colville reservation was in the center of the State of Washington. Four thousand square miles of raw timber laced up by the Columbia River. A big slice of God's Country through any lens, but a casino on Interstate 90 could bring in some cash quicker than the trees. I wanted to spin his casino interest into a branch campus university from Benedictine University in Chicago.

At the table, I was talking, and Mike Marchand was listening. We were in the center of the spectacular Clearwater Casino Resort, the only waterfront casino around The Salish Sea (Puget Sound). There were Native Americans all around us. This was a business meeting of twelve tribes, but it wasn't on Colville land.

The dress code was color, leather and feathers. Marchand was the Number One Indian, and he was sitting there focused on the white guy who stumbled over his words after he said "How" instead of "Hello."

I told Marchand I knew an old customer who knew a lawyer who knew a family in Japan. They quietly owned the raw land from the shores of Moses Lake to Interstate 90 east and west in Grant County. I said I thought it could be taken for around forty million dollars. Mike Marchand, Chairman and Chief of Twelve Tribes, leaned back in and said, "And?"

He didn't say, "Thank you for coming, I have another meeting." No, he said, "And?" He just flat-out called for the question. In an instant, I realized I was sitting in front of the platform money that would support the whole shitteree.

37

As I defused my brain driving away from the casino meeting with Chairman (Mike) Marchand, my mind was spinning around my thoughts of a joint venture between universities and Colville. It was not lost on my research that the U.S. Army et al decided to re-educate Native American students beginning in 1884 with the Carlisle Indian Industrial School in Pennsylvania. Precisely where, "America the Beautiful" began its unfortunate tarnish with "Indians must be taught the knowledge, values, mores, and habits of Christian civilization."

Studies done in the 1970s showed that up to twenty-five to thirty-five percent of all Indian children had been removed from their families and placed into non-Indian care. The plan was to "Kill the Indian to save the man."

There was an effort to turn Indian women into The Handmaid's Tale. Government-sponsored posters advertised Indian women's marriage availability. Marrying Indian women to white men impacted how the population of Native Americans decreased. Canadian enrollment laws for Indians used to only allow Indian enrollment to follow parental lines. If an Indian woman married a white man, she lost her "Indianness." This reduced the numbers of Native American people because children of women married to white men were no longer considered Indians. All being a kind of selective obsolesces in reducing the Indian population. Then, of course, there was the U.S. Army's effort to rid the Great Plains of all buffalo—the primary Indian food supply.

And now, the white man John was going to ask an Indian for help. I was thinking the international university exchange between my school (Benedictine University), the Colville, and China would be a benchmark deal in my business history vernacular. Besides, being a graduate student without a project was boring.

The problem was my typical full stack of complicated issues to make a project work. My yacht broker contemporaries in business would simply ask for the money. On the other hand, I would ask for a subdivision, a jet, and some cash. But I was thinking my style could serve me well in this trinity of culture and education. First, it was legitimate. We would not be gerrymandering Indians away from their culture. We would be adding international culture to the overall mix. That was a good thing. The China segment worked for me, considering I was in the mix with the Peoples Republic (PRC) Bureau of Foreign Trade. As a usual graduate student, I was not. *So, I had to be careful not to make somebody angry and get thrown out of school—again!*

By now, I had completed my MBA at Benedictine University in Chicago and passed my Comprehensive Exam (that's the halfway point) for my Ph.D. As it turned out, Mike Marchand and I were completing our dissertations for doctorates—Mike from the University of Washington, soon to be rated the Number One research university in America, and I at Northcentral University, a Carnegie Think Tank, where a committee of faculty doctors did what they could to make your Ph.D. some academic version of "Hell Week" at a Basic Underwater Demolition/Seal (BUD/S) class in the U.S. Navy.

In the end, both of our dissertations were published as books and are available at fine bookstores everywhere, as well as the Library of Congress and ProQuest Academic Libraries. So, Mike and I had that developing in common as we moved through our relationship.

I was maintaining contact with Bill Carroll, President of Benedictine. He and I believed we could put together a satellite campus near the Colville Reservation (Moses Lake) and begin an undergraduate exchange program with China. He was already doing just that, so I was going to school on his experience.

Carroll began to realize that going to school for me was more of a game than a quest for the irreducible mind. He knew I'd been bounced out of George Washington University for blowing the whistle on the gerrymandering in my internship middle school and that I was a *Walk on* at Harvard University Graduate School—just because I could. But it was Bill Carroll himself who overnighted my MBA diploma to me in Seattle because he knew, by then, that if he didn't get the *sheepskin* in my hands fast, I would forget about it, and my résumé would never enjoy its glitter.

I told Bill Carroll that I felt we could get some support from GW faculty even though I was asked to leave. I felt the education school dean believed I was stuffed in a box of academic featherbedding, but the local political optics would never support my position.

When I called for the question—at GW—about teaming up with us for a satellite university and exchange with China, the response was immediate and positive. We had ignition. Every key faculty member of The George Washington University Education Administration program was on the call. Tough guy that I was, I started tearing up. They had pegged me for the real deal all along, and their payback handshake was on the wire for the idiosyncrasies of an eleemosynary enterprise.

None of this was going to happen, though, if we couldn't put together a physical plant and State approvals for an out-of-state satellite university. During one of these conversations, Chairman Mike Marchand reminded me about land owned by indigenous peoples. Immediately, I began drinking from the fire hose of The Bureau of Indian Affairs, The Bureau of Land Management, the United States Forest Service, Weyerhaeuser Corporation, Plum Creek Timber, and the Confederated Tribes of the Colville Reservation.

There are old saws in business about create an odor. Like animals use odor to attract mates, business organizations create odor to attract interest. I was unwittingly in the business of odor. While I was dancing with three universities on different continents and Native Americans who operate in two hundred years of tangled American law, there was a more pedestrian crowd sniffing the air for maybe a windfall around the magnanimous. They were interlopers who were grasping the idea that something big was in the wind. An odor of big development.

The land in question that Mike Marchand and I discussed at our first meeting made the distance from State Highway 17, Moses Lake, north toward Interstate Highway 90, toward Blue Heron Park. Even as a stack of dry sagebrush and coyotes, it was worth around forty million dollars.

Like everything in my life, anything short of death was a win, and money is a renewable resource, so I started casting around for some heavy cash. I called Bill Belzberg in Beverly Hills. He and Fred Joseph, the former Drexel CEO, were avoiding the Drexel Burnham Lambert bankruptcy. Michael Milken, the current Drexel Chief Executive, would end up in Junk Bond jail, but my guys were clean.

I told Bill about the project—at least as I had envisioned it. He told me he was interested, and I flew to California. Bill's office was on Wilshire Boulevard, upstairs sandwiched between Yves Saint Laurent and The House of Gucci. Going to see Bill was like going to Costco to buy a rotisserie chicken, and you walk out a thousand dollars lighter. As I write, I'm looking at a red leather Saint Laurent shoulder bag on the back of a closet door. Some guys have 401-Ks for retirement. I have this Wilshire Boulevard bag.

Bill called himself Westminster Capital. He was a founder and board member of The Simon Wiesenthal Center, a global Jewish human rights organization that confronts anti-Semitism, hate, and terrorism; promotes human rights and dignity; stands with Israel; defends the safety of Jews worldwide; and teaches lessons of the Holocaust for future generations.

He was a co-founder of Yeshiva University High School of Los Angeles (YULA) . . . served in important leadership roles with the Los Angeles United Jewish Federation. He also served on the Board of Governors of Cedars-Sinai Medical Center and as a board member of Claremont College.

I report this today because he is deceased. When I received my doctorate, Bill contributed to the Simon Wiesenthal Center in my name. When he was dying, I gave him a priest-blessed Rosary I picked up at the Vatican. I said, "If the Jewish thing doesn't work out for ya . . . here is a fallback position."

That's how it was between Bill Belzberg and me. But on this day, it was about money and land.

Everyone was seeing big development while I was seeing satellite universities. Bill asked what the land was worth. I speculated at forty million. He asked if I was in the deal. I said, "Only as an idea." He asked, "Who else?" I said "Benedictine University in Chicago, The George Washington University at Foggy Bottom, and The Confederated Tribes of the Colville Reservation—I hope."

"What else?" he asked.

"I don't know" came straight off my brain.

He said, "That's a hell-of-a-lot-of-land for a satellite two-story undergraduate university campus!"

I reported my thoughts on culture and recreation and international exchange.

Bill said, "You know some solid citizen yacht people, don't you?"

"Yes."

"Call them," he said.

Then came that once-in-a-lifetime moment when a tall, well-coiffured businessman reaches in his suit coat breast pocket and pulls out a dog-eared, tuck this plastic flap under the carbon, get 'em for free at your local branch, personal checkbook, and cut me a 2.5" x 6" *reader* for thirty-four million dollars.

"Try this," he said. "See if it buys the land."

▲ ▲ ▲

Back in Seattle, I was on the phone with Mike Marchand. I told him Belzberg was taking a run at the land and liked the university idea with some additions. Marchand was typically Indian—million-year timeline—ho-hum? I reminded him we spoke of this earlier. He remembered. I told Mike I was going to contact the lawyer representing the landowner with the offer. I also arranged to meet Mike on the reservation so "we" could make the case to the Tribal Council. He agreed.

Now I was punching way over my pay grade, but I kept going.

The lawyer for the landowner invited me to his office in an industrial park south of Seattle. It was not a law office. It was the developer's office of the landowner. Drawings and maps, and models of a resort city on the land I planned to use. I asked him *why the land was for sale with all this stuff in the works.* He told me the family was focused on Japan. At least for now. *But something just came up that might change that.*

He told me the National Association for Stock Car Auto Racing (NASCAR) had a couple of representatives in town looking at the land for a Pacific Northwest racetrack. I didn't know how to react. I just stood there.

The lawyer reminded me that I had an offer on the land. I recovered from NASCAR shock and played it at thirty-four million. He turned it down. Then he talked to me about how he could disassemble and reassemble a Chevy 350 V8 engine in an extraordinarily short time. So, I started to catch on about why NASCAR might be in town.

I drove back to the city, trying to get my head around what was in play here. So far, my original satellite school idea was sucking wind. The universities were willing to discuss. The tribes had nothing on the table to consider. I didn't have any leverage to push my Belzberg offer. The landowner's representative was a stock car mechanic masquerading as a lawyer. And I was some out-of-pocket graduate student who was flying by the seat of his pants. "What the hell am I doing?"

Belzberg would not come up on his offer; however, The Colville agreed to have me sit before the Tribal Council and present my case. So, now I knew Mike Marchand was getting in the mix. He would not set me up with the Council if he weren't interested. *So, maybe I have a crack opening for my plan.*

▲ ▲ ▲

The Colville reservation is east and north of Seattle over Blewettt Pass. A long drive into three million years of Ice Age history and ecosystems. Tan sandstone terraces where ancient people scouted for game. The snake of the Columbia River lacing it all together. Plateau after plateau of small game eyes watching and deciding who should enter this domain. Hot or cold. Not moderate. Natural resources aplenty, with old-growth standing timber on top and Molybdenum underneath. The largest Moly deposit in the world, they say. Steel-producing stuff for centuries, and nobody touches it.

Mike was inside the Tribal Center when I arrived. The Council was in session. He walked out, and we spoke in a traditional Western way. We didn't look at each other; rather, we leaned on a fence, looking at the ground in front of us. We both had Western boots. We used our boots to figure in the dirt. Our legs moved our boots—the toes drawing lines in the heavy dust. Front and back if we agreed, and side to side if we were cautious or disagreed. We watched each other's boots to get a line on the conversation. Looking up was always away—looking away, then back down to the boots. Eventually, the boots stopped moving. Both parties had established their thoughts, and what appeared to be a normal meeting began. The reality is the entire conversation had been outlined in the sand beforehand. That's just how it is on the ancient sandstone plateaus. I had come a long way from hand sign language answered with ". . . and I speak English."

▲ ▲ ▲

My first on-reservation day-to-day contact was a Native guy who had been a vocal stand-in for the rock group Red Bone. He had been living in Hawaii and was a recent transplant on the reservation. So, his talk was laced with a combination of White men / Indian men. He was sort of a jive-talking caricature of a television Indian. I liked him. The kind of guy you know right away has your back in a knife fight. I miss him a great deal.

Early on, I received a call from Chairman Marchand informing me my inside contact was dead. Then another call that I was invited to his funeral. I had to come quickly as tradition keeps the body in its natural state to be returned to earth. I drove all night. Got lost in the dark of the reservation. Found my way again in daylight and parked on yet another high plateau overlook of the Columbia River. The cemetery was a kind of horizon overlook. Classic forever kind of place. A heavy smell of sage. I was the first to arrive. I sat in my pickup and felt the sun now rising about twenty degrees off the horizon. The sky was clearly showing a sharp contrast with the land. The power of the river was moving quietly alone on the valley floor. The cemetery was old. Dozens of decades in gray stone. Family names of hereditary chiefs.

As people arrived, mostly wearing red, green, and black blankets, they looked at me. Not everyone knew why I was there. Out of place, for sure. Then I was acknowledged by the family, and some smiles appeared. The burial was Mother Earth authentic. The body lay in a raw white pine casket box—open. Wrapped in a red Colville Indian Honor Blanket open to the chest. We passed by, some placing mementos in the casket. Then the cover went on. The casket was lowered into the ground by men using ropes. We were asked as a group to take our hands and push the dirt back atop the casket to close the site. I was in a navy-blue sports coat and tan slacks. I ruined them both. In the end, I was asked to speak. I spoke of this Indian man's legacy in this white man's mind.

In my life, I have come to watch the release of death. The transition of pain and mourning, and the wonder of it all. How we all shoulder the risk of death.

◂ ◂ ◂

Marchand and I decided we needed to walk the land before meeting with the Council and decide for ourselves what we might have. In this case, it was drive the land because of its size. I got permission from the owners' lawyer, and a caravan of interested parties ensued, including the lawyer.

We had three trucks formed up as a White GMC Short Bed, A Red Jeep Wagoneer, and a light tan International 4 x 4 antique. Obviously, a project. The land was in degrees of swales in every direction. Like rolling ocean waves tall enough to miss the trough but not high enough to obscure vision. Mike and I in my white GMC. Several Colville Tribe elders in the Jeep, and the lawyer plus a couple of suits in the International.

Everyone seemed to have an agenda for what was the forty-million-dollar question. The lawyer et al. led and opened what seemed endless fence lines. The land was parceled up in cattle leases, but it was more like multiple feeder lots because there wasn't much to graze. We drove toward the lake from Interstate 90. For those among us who had been to Mongolia or Russia, the roads were passable. For the rest, there were no roads. I imagined we were part of the empire caravan in *The Wind and the Lion*. Or maybe *The Man Who Would Be King*.

For some reason, I was not thinking Indian. Just desert, Arabian horses, and camels against a backdrop of Sean Connery, a Berber Chieftain protecting Candice Bergen. Her predicament triggering Theodore Roosevelt to come up with The Great White Fleet. Maybe we could sing shanties of history as we walk. Although I didn't recall ever hearing Sean Connery sing. Mike looked over to me every few minutes, making sure I had both hands on the wheel. The dust was stacking and falling down the windshield into the vents. It was just lovely by any measure. Finally, we stopped and began walking.

As we walked, the suits kept pointing like they were already aware of what was for them in our outing. And they were shortly correct, obviously having been here before. That was a large section of low valley already formed like a racetrack. Truly a surprise considering the easy visual association. These were NASCAR people scouting.

Mike was nonplussed about NASCAR. He figured there was enough land for everyone. I was so focused on the university that I was missing the reality of universities, casinos, hotels, retail malls, and racetracks. The players seemed to think we were standing in Las Vegas as a practical matter.

As we walked, we could smell the lake—the fresh cool water. When we saw it for the first time, it was blue. Like a permanent slash across the endless landscape. The Wind and the Lion fit perfectly. Big and striking and alone in its splendor and power. As a species, we could kill this lake. As its position in space and time, we weren't even there.

The Indians who were traveling in the jeep were grouped in some kind of conference. I looked at Mike. He was somehow different. I knew he was prepared to best the Belzberg offer to thirty-eight million dollars if the land worked for the overall plan. But he was, at this moment, in another place. Mike, as well as the elders, were focused on a shallow ridge line to the north. Just a sliver of a thing on that swale top. As I focused my eyes, I was transported to Wales. To the 30th century before Christ. To a Carn Gosdog outcrop. I kept looking at Mike. He moved his left hand to his chin. Then quietly said, "We better have a look."

The elders' heads made a weathercock to Marchand. All the Indians were hit with the same strike. We might be on sacred land. At the time, I was writing my dissertation on transcendental teaching styles. I was researching the impact of the fourth dimension. My focus was on the

International Baccalaureate in Cardiff, Wales, U.K. The place where the Romans, Druids, Saxons, and Vikings, and maybe King Arthur and his buddy Merlin, made rocks very special. And that is what we all of a sudden had on the top of the ridge. A pile of rocks.

▲ ▲ ▲

As we made our way to the rocks on the ridge line, Bill Carroll of Benedictine University was in China visiting Calisa Chen, the Vice Mayor of Zhaoqing City. She was my contact for the Bureau of Foreign Trade and the connection to where we might go with Bill's existing China Exchange program in Chicago.

At the same time, the Colville Tribe had privately aggregated interest among the Council members and indicated a willingness to send a delegation to China for discussions. The Colville, in turn, sent a message to the Vice Mayor of Zhaoqing City that a China delegation would be welcome at the reservation. They included a suggestion that an interesting cultural time would be during the Omak Stampede/Rodeo. As we were walking, I got an international call from China. It was Calisa Chen telling me the China delegation was wondering if they could ride in the Omak Stampede Parade while visiting the Confederated Tribes of the Colville Reservation. She was researching Omak on the strength of the tribe's message and liked the idea of cowboys and Indians, and so on.

So, now I was walking toward a pile of rocks as an event planner. Mike was smiling. He knew what the call was about. He was just smiling. Then he turned to face me and said, "How about we invite them to the Omak Stampede Death Race?"

"Yeah, right!" I said. "That's one way we can get the Fed involved. I can see you before the Senate Committee." *"Chairman Marchand, members of the committee were wondering how you decided that putting members of the Chinese delegation on horseback and racing them down a 62-percent grade 210-foot slope to dive horse and rider into the Okanogan River was in our international interest?"*

▲ ▲ ▲

As we got closer to the rocks, they began to shine in high blue relief, but they were dark gray. The rocks were taking a shape—not a pile anymore. We were facing a closed circle about four feet high and fifty feet in diameter. Mike had his left hand back on his chin. Everyone was quiet.

▲ ▲ ▲

The rocks were of varying sizes, about a foot in diameter—not small. They were purposely placed, calling for the question: Could this place have a unique story? The Indians instinctively knew the answer. However, the suits were on their phones looking for intelligence regarding indigenous sacred sites. What everyone could see were the rock features that could have ties to transcendental metaphysics. Unique stories, rituals, and practices. That was my personal speculation, but I could feel in the wind what was up. . . . The project was in trouble right out of the box. I was a Ph.D. candidate doing research in this very mix. We were standing in sacral traditions with already legislated government restrictions. I knew it. I could feel it. And so could everyone else, save the lawyer and two suits from NASCAR.

▲ ▲ ▲

I know we were moving into archaeologist territory. Radiocarbon dating Carbon 14 compared to Carbon 12. No amount of clout changes that. Organic material can be carbon traced. Mike announced that he would have the tribal archaeologist make the trip to the spirit circle. And there it was for the first time. Mike said, *"spirit circle."*

"For Christ's sake," said the lawyer. "This is probably a cattle or sheep pen."

Mike saddled up to me and said, "I can still buy the land and exempt the circle.

"That's my call," he said.

I could see he was fingering an envelope. *Got to be his offer*, I thought, *and I know it's going to be thirty-eight million.* The NASCAR suits walked toward Mike. They were smiling. Like Mike Marchand was their new best friend. It was becoming clear they were free riders on whoever bought the land. NASCAR would be in the deal for their experience and talent. Not their money.

▲ ▲ ▲

So, now I had the president of Benedictine University in Zhaoqing, China. The Colville Council was ready to go to China. China was ready to be in the Omak Stampede parade. The Chairman of the tribe was ready to buy the land, regardless of the rock circle. And they were looking to me for some direction. So, true to my history, I triggered the trips. China comes here. Tribe goes there. Universities bless the deal. We get financing, and *boom*—a new university with benefits like gambling and racing. And before Mike could say, "you're crazy," I reminded everyone that from where we stood, we could damn-near throw a rock and hit the old Larson Air Force Base—now, Grant County International Airport.

Larson Air Force Base had as its host unit the 4170th Wing of the Strategic Air Command. Four runways—one long enough to be an alternate landing site for the Space Shuttle. Three runways long enough to handle any big thing that flies. All concrete enough to handle a direct hit from an atomic bomb. B-52s used to park inside concrete bunkers loaded with nuclear weapons, ready to be in the air within twelve minutes after the alarm. Flight crews were on constant alert and would come out of the ground like someone kicked an anthill at the squawk of the bell.

I collectively asked, "Do ya think that airport might be handy for a full-on city that includes a new top-tier university, automobile racing, resort hotels with spas, and platted commercial and residential subdivisions in all directions?

"Well? Do ya think?"

I suddenly jumped from university graduate student to merger and acquisition broker. I was doubling down on my old style—sell the package, not the product.

Back in Seattle, we were arranging the international protocols for the trips. Calisa Chen was back on the phone. "Mr. John, you come China, we send long black car!" Gifts were being arranged. The Tribe Council members traveling would stay in Zhaoqing City, an area of southern China strategically positioned between Hong Kong and Macau. Three hundred thousand people in light manufacturing feeder organizations for U.S. Foreign Trade. A well-developed example of modern China. I was still inside my appointment as Economic Advisor to Gaoyao for the Bureau of Foreign Trade and Economic Cooperation. So, the long black car was within the scope of the position. There were questions like whether I wanted United States flags on the fenders. I, of course, said "yes."

So, I was mentally swimming in the ozone international business, a trinity of universities, the matter-of-fact process of radiocarbon dating, and free riders trying to grab a wave and ride the deal as far as possible. Through all this exhilaration, a group of antiquarians and archaeologists were on the site lifting samples of Lichen off the rocks. They were also looking for past movement along the stack. With an implied understanding that the deal was in play, three members of the Tribal Council left for China. Mike Marchand and I remained in the USA. We were trying to figure how to handle a coming Chinese delegation in the Omak Stampede Parade. Do they walk? Do they ride? And will there be people with experience around livestock? We had yet to tell the Omak City Council what we had in mind.

Bill Carroll returned from China with positive news from Shenyang Jianshu University for an undergraduate Junior and Senior exchange with the Benedictine University and the satellite campus in Moses Lake. The George Washington University faculty were ready to lend their gravitas to the project.

▲ ▲ ▲

Mike Marchand called me from Nespelem. The Lichen on the rocks is Paleoindian. Once again, in a moment, I was transported to the blue rocks 175 miles from Salisbury Plain. To where the Romans, Druids, Vikings, Saxons, and maybe King Arthur and his buddy Merlin decided the rocks were magic. Our stone circle had not been touched for five thousand years.

I could tell Mike was undecided about what to do. How to proceed. I gave him my best business advice. "There are no contracts in place. It's all speculation." We decided to meet in Moses Lake. Walk the site again. *Smell it. Touch it. Talk to it,* he said. I alerted the lawyer for the owners, and we spooled up another visit.

I got the word out to all the travelers. *We have a situation. Stand by.* The travelers in China were having so much fun I don't think they remembered why they were there. The China delegation had yet to leave the Peoples Republic. All the rest were marching in place.

The ride into the property was as before. Some from the tribe are different. The rest, the same. Same dust, same road ruts, same sagebrush, same landscape strike of blue water, and one mighty fine 5,000-year-old rock circle.

Mike and I stepped out of my truck. The International came to a stop. So stopped the jeep. Everyone stepped out. Nobody wanted to touch the rocks; an amazing change, I thought. The lawyer was leaning on his truck. The NASCAR guys were now in Charlotte, North Carolina.

In the middle of the spirit circle stood a Coyote. A Disney Studio, Industrial Light and Magic, perfect Coyote. The Coyote is the spirit animal for the Confederated Tribes of the Colville Reservation. The Coyote lowered its hind legs and sat down. Didn't run. Just sat there. Mike and the Coyote became fixed on each other. Then Mike said, "I don't think there should be a developed project around here."

The lawyer for the owners opened the driver's side door of the International and vomited on the ground—some on the fender. Everyone was quiet.

38

Mike Marchand and I didn't tag up again until we both finished our dissertations. In each case, we were measuring the dangers associated with the authoritarian personality. Mike was making a researched defense for the Native method in the use of biomass, and I with findings based on the transactional nature of secondary education. In both cases, our findings became books.

We were both making cases on path analysis, but I was about to step away and into the arena of education and metaphysics. It was not lost on me that the Coyote in the spirit circle carried the day and saved the land. Or that in his mind's eye of *The North Water*, the codices based 163 years earlier, author Ian McGuire describes Patrick Summer saving himself from certain frozen death by gutting a polar bear and crawling inside. Then meeting the cosmic doppelganger of the same bear in Berlin five years later.

Or, my dad, fearing the prospect of frozen death, gutted an elk and crawled inside for safety from the Montana temperatures running minus 54 degrees Fahrenheit. Then talking with the elk every Saturday morning for the next fifty-nine years.

Or that for twenty years, I had a recurring dream that my son Jeff was in grave danger as he uncontrollably fell through high voltage wires—dodging as he fell. Then he broke his neck, and thirty-three days later, he was dead. The dream stopped.

Or that Libby Kelleher was drowning in the Snake River—under a raft—and was willing to let life go, to die. She believes she was given the option. Then she met her yet-to-be-born daughter, who told her to be a mother, to stay alive. To let her be born. So, Libby fought the water again and made it to shore. Molly was born, and the story continues.

Or, when Don Martin's brother, Patrick, died, Don had a dream the same night. In the dream, Patrick and Don were on the bridge of a large ship. Patrick was telling his brother he would be happy here. The bridge deck was green, festooned in brass. Years later, Don became a cadet at the California Maritime Academy. He went on to become the head of all U.S. Jones Act Operations for ConocoPhillips. The day Don Martin stepped onto the bridge of the training ship *Golden Bear*, the bridge deck was green, festooned in brass.

What I was realizing was that nature allows information to be time-reversible and deterministic. That Rupert Sheldrake was correct when he declared that there are no constants in nature. That nature is habitual.

I had spent twenty-six years dealing with captains of industry. Then seventeen years studying how transactional education drove future decisions. Then I heard Terence McKenna, who billed himself as a shamanologist, respond to the popular science around the Big Bang. The beginning of the universe from a primal particle/element. An explosion that, from its primal core, became responsible for the evolution of everything. McKenna said, "If you believe that, you will believe anything."

I found myself in a kind of developmental vortex. I was swinging in the business community, calling in cards based on my previous experience, but success was fleeting.

But now I was a doctor. A man who had the answers to everything.

39

After seventeen years of qualitative research outside the purview of algebraic equations and rational coefficients, I could feel the mind-like aspect of my surroundings. I do, and must, give credit to hard science for bending their fact sets in coefficients—the fudge factor. Or maybe there is more to this than mathematical polemicists would have us believe.

The Spirit Circle Coyote was not a student of neuroscientific orthodoxy. The Coyote was, however, a player in the flow of consciousness. As are the birds and the bees and the cats and the dogs and the mice and everything else we convert from wave to particle in our ocular-fed brains.

There is a great deal of opposing research between physics and metaphysics. Between hard and soft science. I think Stewart Hameroff nailed it in context when he wrote that "science and spirituality are two sides of a quantum coin."

We are common men here. That is my position. We will speak to perception, not to mathematics. I believe one is as valid as the other. It's reasonable to assume that the Coyote did not equate its way to the Spirit Circle. The Coyote was called to serve from another dimension. I'm not saying someone in the Trinity manifested the Coyote. It's simpler than that. Let's just call the Coyote a *light-beam rider*.

In his *Summa Theologiae*, Thomas Aquinas felt there was a common standard between angels and photons. To do the work of God, an angel should have limited or no mass and travel at the speed of light. That would be seven- and one-half times around the earth every second. Certainly, fast enough to handle people's market demands for divine intervention.

So, these photon messengers get it done. I was honored in a reception line on the top floor of the Century Plaza Hotel in Los Angeles. The companies were Occidental/Transamerica. The C-Suite from both organizations was in the line or in the room. I had bested a company record and was being fawned over accordingly. For no apparent reason, I left the reception, took the elevator down to my room, picked up the phone, and called my dad. When he answered the phone, he was emotionally moved by my call . . . "Your grandmother just died," he said.

My grandmother was Armosa LaCasse. As a child, she raised me. We were together most of the time. My parents were working, and grandma was my light and example. We played cards. She was French, so the language was a mixed bag. We laughed and walked and talked about life.

My dad felt my call was "uncanny." It probably was.

PART THREE

TO PARIS—AND BEYOND

40

There must be something pivotal to the energy of the universe. More than the Spirit Circle Coyote or my grandmother and me. A reason for Don Martin to walk on the bridge of a ship he's never seen, except with his dead brother a decade earlier. What are these waves and particles feeding our consciousness?

In real-time, Asian honey bees change the pitch—therefore the sound—of their wings when attacked by predators. The penetrating warning of a bee in trouble.

When hunting, pack animals change the pitch of their bark based on success or failure. A cat's cry for food is different from a cry for play. Trees support collective needs. Jumping spiders, when sleeping, have rapid eye movement. Think spider having a dream in REM. Like maybe he's chasing you with a fly swatter instead of the other way around.

Cats make positioning decisions in one six hundredths of a second. Dragonflies hunt in a pattern and intercept their prey. All other hunts are some versions of hiding, chasing, and killing. Except for the dragonfly that flies a pattern and intercepts on the wing. And in this 21st century, every military airpower in the world is trying to figure out how that happens. The question then becomes, is the dragonfly *who*, as opposed to *it* . . . ?

Creating mental entropy is a fundamental process of the abstract mind. Among the accomplished are existentialist thinkers.

There was a time in Paris that cradled the Café Society. It was 1932–1933 when groups of twenty-eight-year-old French Philosophy students were aggregating as *mon petit camarades* of Metaphysics over endless cups of coffee. Three to a table. All day and into the night. They were trying to understand German existential thinkers who were deciding that "real" is only the perception of "real," and trying to prove "real" was a waste of time.

Tight groups of students gazed into their coffee on the Rue du Montparnasse. Endlessly trying to establish a belief system *that science was experiencing, not finding.* That the cups of coffee were as valid as the Periodic Table. Eliminating secondary questions. All of it was perception.

The students at these tables became the benchmark of existentialist philosophy. Simone de Beauvoir with Jean-Paul Sartre. Albert Camus and Karl Jaspers. All studying the High German mazamas, Martin Heidegger, and Edmund Husserl. Philosophy students, under the pressure of a coming war, staffed up the metaphoric test kitchen for the common man to learn how to walk in the fourth dimension.

Finally, it was Heidegger's capital "B" that changed the paradigm. Heidegger decided to spell being with a capital B. (Being) as opposed to (being). That moment stylized and began the introspective study of consciousness. Now the students were Being with their coffee. Heidegger had transformed existential philosophy into its version of the periodic table.

Today that's a tough sell in the hard sciences community. Nobel laureates like Roger Penrose do not drink in the existentialist café. However, the fashionable attempts to understand the cosmos of Paris circa 1932, as fantastical as they were, still catch a nod from the likes of Penrose, but maybe not in the main library auditorium of the Sorbonne in Paris.

Penrose notwithstanding, and after the Coyote, I doubled down on the transcendental nature of conscious-mind makeup. I began to reflect on events that were *outside the wire.* Like my dad said, my call from Los Angeles was uncanny. My recurring dream about my son. And friends who were once outside the spectrum before we met. I began to read into the genera: *The God Delusion* by Richard Dawkins. *The Emperor's New Mind* by Roger Penrose. *War of the Worldviews* by Chopra and Mlodinow. *Living in a Mindful Universe* by Eben Alexander and Karen Newell. And the studies in cognitivism at the University of Virginia now the epicenter of near-death experience (NDE) research. I read all of Sheldrake—maybe several times.

I began talking with people who, in their perception, experienced the geometry of space and time. I quickly found myself off my lines, drifting away from my dock. I was experiencing my research. Instead of an academic third party, I was getting in the mix.

I was completely free. Finished school. Away from the business. Now, a public scholar is stuck in his findings. I decided to go to the 1932 headwaters of existential thought. I would go to Paris. Retrospectively, it was clear enough that Christine triggered my move away from business and into education, so we would go together. We would go to the Left Bank, sit on the street, drink off the menu, investigate the coffee, and see if Heidegger was right. Because, if he was, that meant I could have a sit-down with Hemingway, with Joan of Arc, Charlemagne, Charles de Gaulle, the Marquis de Lafayette, Jim Morrison, and Bonaparte, the man. My academic adventure into the fourth and fifth dimensions.

We packed and flew Coach. As we boarded, Christine mentioned we were newlyweds, and the cabin service crew moved us to First Class with champagne. I leaned in and said, "What the hell was that? We're not married!"

She smiled and said, "Okay, you sit in Coach and leave me the champagne"—the platform marker of our relationship and the tone for the trip.

Paris was unexpectedly bigger than life. We walked into the Musée d'Orsay, and Christine began to cry. Standing three feet away from the real thing. The original thing. That's the thing. It's magic. In the Musée de l'Armée at Les Invalides, I stood before The General's uniform. It was Charles de Gaulle. Then I turned to find *Marengo*, the famous war horse of Napoleon, and that was that. We had arrived in Paris.

The next morning, we walked out of our hotel and into VE Day in Europe. A big deal in Paris. The streets were crowded. The cars and buses were stacked. We grabbed a couple of tarts from the Comme à Lisbonne café and made our way to the Paris Metro, stepping off at the Arc de Triomphe.

"We'll start in the middle," I said.

As we arrived, there were Kepi caps all around—that flat pillbox-looking thing worn by the French military. Old men. Leftover men. Some had white fabric big-eared caps. Must have been in the French Foreign Legion. We decided to take the stairs to the top. From there, we could see the length of the Champ Élysées. The city was staging the biggest parade of the year. A commemorative of when all the Allied Generals raced to be the first to liberate France and take a triumphant walk down this boulevard. And we had a top-down view of the whole affair.

Except, immediately after we went up—the last ones to go up—the Arc de Triomphe was closed. Two Americans standing alone atop the Arc de Triomphe watching the Victory in Europe VE-Day Parade. The problem, of course, was that wasn't supposed to be. The Arc was closed. And the cops and the Army and the Metro police were beyond curious. We were quickly found and escorted to the base. Christine raised her camera. We were standing among more French generals than are dead in the Museum. Christine wanted to photograph the adventure. The French Army was having none of that, and a Metro cop took her by the arm and gingerly danced her into the street.

I followed, laughing. "First Class," I shouted. "She sits in First Class!"

41

My life in Paris was rejecting a retrospective of itself. I walked the Seine along the Left Bank. Mingled with street merchants. Drank the coffee I imagined. Stared at the Gallery of Kings on the façade of Notre Dame and chatted with Christine after she spent the day between high-fashion shops on the Champs Élysées. For me, Paris was thinking fast and slow at the same time.

I was looking for the beyond of my life. Nothing in my past business career seemed to carry forward. I was standing at the beginning of me. Before we left Seattle, I had established correspondence with faculty at the Sorbonne. On the appointed day, I was to present myself at a side door leading into the student store. So, I did. A comparatively young man approached me, extended his hand, and inquired, "Doctor LaCasse?"

It makes no difference how many times you write, type, or dream of being on the top rung of the academy; when it comes to you out loud for the first time, you can feel it course through your entire body. Only one other time in my life had I had the same sensation. That was when Lana Kurtzer, probably the most famous bush pilot trainer of all time, stepped out onto the float of Taylorcraft N96266 and then onto the dock as he turned and said, "Okay, John, take her around."

As we left the student store and walked into the original courtyard of the University of Paris Sorbonne, I was, at once, in the Renaissance—in the five confirmations of the existence of God. I was walking with Thomas Aquinas.

As we got comfortable and Aquinas and I wafted our way through the courtyard, I said, "Ya know, Aquinas, none of your 13th-century prime mover, grand designer, first-cause bullshit holds up in modern physics. It can't be supported mathematically."

Aquinas smiled. We kept walking. The young man who greeted me in the student store seemed flummoxed by my bilateral behavior in a unilateral presence. He's got to believe I'm crazy. I'm sure he's thinking, *How does the University of Paris invite a visiting faculty member who carries on imaginary conversations with himself?* I would look to Aquinas and then my greeter. Finally, I said to this indeed perfect undergraduate student, "If you could hear at 38,000 Hz, you'd probably know what's going on."

In his uneasiness, he asked me who hears that high.

"Your cat," I told him.

He looked straight ahead for several steps then he asked me if I would like to purchase a sweatshirt from the student store.

Then Aquinas turned to me and said, *"Pope Innocent III just convened the Fourth Council of the Lateran for the very purpose of keeping bishops, abbots, priors, and Christians out of the taverns. Otherwise, I would invite you for a drink.*

I thank him. I tell him that when he comes to Seattle, he can stay with us on the *Sundog.* He asks, *How do you live in the clouds 22 degrees off the sun?*

I tell him we have much to discuss, and *we* agree to meet again.

I had come to Paris through the same apparition of my French grandmother, Armosa. In these opening moments, I realized why people were telling me about their transcendent experiences. They knew I would understand.

42

I finally realized that coming to Paris and walking with Aquinas represented the final breakpoint between *me* of mercantile transactions and *me* of phenomenology and perception. I was now the product of my own evolution. The reinvention of myself was fixed in place and riding on my shoulders. Walking headlong into the courtyard of the Renaissance was the tipping point.

I noticed Aquinas looked like James Spader on *Boston Legal*. The same kind of understated Machiavellian control. If I was to play off this guy, I would need to be like William Shatner and roll like a bad steely in a pinball machine.

While Christine continued her mercantile march between the Place de la Concorde and the Arc de Triomphe along the Avenue des Champs-Élysées, I decided to practice becoming a *light beam rider*. The most famous bookstore in the world is Shakespeare and Company, conveniently at Kilometer Zero on the Left Bank in Paris. I figured that if I sat long enough in the hangout of James Joyce, T.S. Eliot, and Ernest Hemingway, some of my new fourth- and fifth-dimension panache would gather momentum. Mixing it up with Aquinas was not going to be any light-duty deal.

43

I stopped for coffee by the river on my way to Shakespeare and Company. Paris is unique in its cultural savoir-faire. Two, Four, and Six-topper tables are not timed by maître d' hotels. Patrons can relax—should relax. History abides by its tradition. Now, ninety years of coffee for two at a table for three.

There were three women at the checkout counter when I entered the store. In my most American bourgeois style, I addressed the woman in the middle with, "Where did Hemingway sit?"

She was quick and replied, "everywhere!"

With that, I decided to jump the redundant shark with, "I'm having a meet-up with Aquinas and need some boost."

Then, punctuated with the body language of Juliette Binoche, came, "Follow me."

She rounded the counter with one hand attached to the corner and directed me to follow. We walked through the left side of the main room, down a narrow hall, turned right between the stacks, and stood silent. There was this alone theatre seat in brown leather upholstery. Stacks all around. She stood to one side, extended her hand to the chair, and said, "he read there, and when drunk, he slept there."

It made no difference if she was bullshitting me or not, she instantly knew what I was about, and she made it happen. I was about to be sitting in Hemingway's chair!

As she left, she turned and asked, "Do you need a book, or do you just want to burp and fart in his chair?"

Her smile was piercing. She was translucent. I knew I had Simone de Beauvoir just for the moment.

I asked for something worthwhile and said, "Surprise me."

She came back with *The Count of Monte Cristo* by Alexandre Dumas. I knew in an instant she was omnipotent and probably there when I got thrown out of high school. I was being set up by Aquinas, and he was handing me the playbook.

44

After days of returning to Hemingway's chair and—through guilt—buying book after book from the Shakespeare and Company stacks, I was awarded a special Shakespeare and Company carry bag emblazoned with the Shakespeare Kilometer Zero logo. I was their ubiquitous American customer. From the store, the river bank, and Hemingway's chair, I read Heidegger's *Basic Problems of Phenomenology*. Then his landmark *Being and Time*. I followed those two with Husserl's *Ideas*. Then, *The Phenomenology of Perception* by Maurice Merleau-Ponty. There were many more, including an anthology of ancient writings relating to Pythagorean philosophy.

I was finally ready to mix it up with Aquinas. BUT,

I should have known that would happen all around me. One of those classic Aquinas spectrum kinds of deals. I was outside the bookstore at noon. International pedestrians crisscrossing to lunch on every compass angle. I was looking at the river from a concrete wall adjacent to the bookstore. About fifteen feet high, there was a crack in the concrete, causing a light beam to fall off a bottle stuck in the wall.

I was holding *Ideas* by Husserl. The refraction sun angle from the water surface was answering the bottle. Photons dancing among the glistening wave for moments, one to the other, then off to infinity. My eyes were kind of watery. I was looking and not looking at the same time—falling into a lucid state but not completely asleep.

There he was! Aquinas was in the spectrum. Twenty-two degrees off the sun angle in the splash and exhaust spray of a French canal barge making its way up the river. He raised his hands to his mouth and shouted, *"Is this what you were calling a Sundog? That angle business where you live?"*

I raise my hands in kind and shout back, "Close, but no cigar!"

The canal barge passes and Saint Thomas Aquinas is sitting next to me on the wall. I try for a leg up now. I look straight at him and ask: "In your omnipotent presence, did you watch *Boston Legal?*"

He smiled and said, *"I know where this is going, John. And I know you think I look like James Spader. The problem is, you don't look like William Shatner."*

He stands up. Shakes droplets off his robe. Rattles his Rosary. Then says, *"Why don't we walk over to Place Saint-Michel and get some coffee. I think you and I should begin this relationship close to the symbolic conflict between good and evil. You don't look like Shatner—but Lucifer, maybe."*

45

The Place Saint-Michel is a public square bordering the Latin Quarter but still on the Left Bank of the river Seine. It was Baron Haussmann's idea in 1853 when Paris was restructured for pedestrian convenience. Now, it's an enormous in-your-face classic fountain sculpture of the Archangel—sword raised—about to lop off Lucifer's head. In our immediate case, the perfect backdrop for Aquinas to have a cosmic tactical advantage.

What he forgot was that Gabriel Davoudi, the original designer, wanted the head-lopper to be Napoleon Bonaparte. That didn't play well with Napoleon III, who was behind the whole remodel of Paris idea. The compromise became Saint-Michel the Archangel instead of Napoleon. So, although I was to sit with Aquinas under Saint-Michel, 21st-century physics suggests that time holds all information to infinity—never to change—past, present, and future. So, my buddy Aquinas was up against an omnipotent run-time error in his 13th-century brain, and I still had Bonaparte in my corner.

We found a sidewalk café on the traffic edge and took a table for two. The French waiter in black pants and white waist wrap brought two coffees as ordered. He asked, "Pardon Monsieur," if I was expecting someone as he placed the second cup across from me.

I smiled and said, "Were you around in 1950 when Jimmy Stewart and Josephine Hill played with Harvey, the invisible rabbit?"

"Non," he replies.

"No worries," I say, "that's whom I'm expecting."

The waiter smiled and addressed another table. Aquinas leans in and says, *"You must be kidding!"*

I laugh and open the conversation. "Among the reasons I'm happy you showed up, Aquinas, is the similarity in how your life played out and how my life is going today."

Aquinas responds with, *"Because you walked away from an exceptionally successful business, then managed to piss-off everybody in your arena, and then spent a quarter of your life recovering in school?"*

"You got it," I say. "The way I see it, when you began your monastic life at Monte Cassino and then jumped ship into Aristotelian metaphysics, you and I were on a symbolic parallel path in our own block of time. You had to figure out who you were then, and now, so do I."

"That's a tall order, John. And you already know the answers, or you wouldn't have set me up for this meeting under Michael the Archangel, knowing you have Napoleon in your pocket."

"God damn," I said, "you are exceptional!"

So, I push for more. "When you and I left the Sorbonne the other day, you would have invited me for a drink if it weren't for Pope Innocent III having opened the Fourth Council of the Lateran to keep bishops, abbots, priors, and Christians out of the taverns. Does that mean you and I are going to cross the lines between the 13th and 21st centuries?"

His response solidified why his curiosity has him on top of his game. He looks into his coffee, crinkles up his nose, squints, and says, *"Well, we will, at least in the case of how you live in the 22-degree sun refraction at a place called* Sundog.*"*

46

"As we talk, Aquinas, we will both be introducing conversation vernacular across the centuries. I guess we can figure that out as we go. I have questions that relate to your omnipresence. You will have questions relating to carrying forward spirituality since the Renaissance. Or did your anthropological realism stick over time?

"From a secular science perspective, your dualism did well. As for revealed authority, we will get to that. I'm not qualified to call for the question; however, together, we will find answers to many things. My street language may work against me in your interpretation of my sophistication. Not to worry. I am accustomed to freedom of speech in public spaces."

"Thank you, John. I guess that's Dr. John, as I am Dr. Thomas as well."

"John and Aquinas work fine for me. With you as the protagonist of Renaissance orthodoxy and me the finder of transcendental academic style, we make a hell of a pair."

We both smile.

"As to your earlier question, *Sundog* is my house. It's a boat—in Renaissance-size frame, a sailing ship, but we do not take it to war. We do sail it in the ocean along the west coast of the Americas, North and South. But here, it gets complicated. *Sundog* is a place, but as a nod to science, Sundog is two places at once. Not an accurate assessment in science but a great deal of philosophical fun. Along with being my boat, it is also a slice of the spectrum that shows in atmospheric ice that appears at twenty-two degrees of angle of the sun. That is because of the refraction angle through ice crystals. Two places at once is sort of a thing these days.

"But, Aquinas, before we talk more about Sundogs, I have a question of enormous importance to me personally."

Aquinas rests his chin in his right hand, and we begin.

"Are my sons ok and happy? You know they died."

"Yes, I know that," Aquinas says.

"That's a circumstance you and I do not have in common."

"Yes, I know that also," he says.

Aquinas takes it forward. *"John, your friend Elizabeth told you that the death of your boys was not about you, so the situation you suggest has no parallel with anyone else.*

"Death is a singular thing. The only real thing that happened between you and your boys was your semen to sow. The rest was up to them, and for a period, their mother, but their death was their destiny in its entirety."

"Well, if you believe that, Aquinas, you are going to buy your own fucking coffee!"

"No, think about it, John. Did you have any control over their death?"

"No."

"So, why do you think you had an impact or control in their life?"

"I AM the father! I speak with authority."

"Oh, that's good," Aquinas says. *"This is the issue we see in Heaven—among fathers of children—as an abstraction of how important parents are. Once a child enters the cosmos, it's the kid and God. The parents are simply placeholders."*

"I think we are getting off-topic, Aquinas. You are feeding me dogmatic nonsense from above the clouds, and you have never been a parent. You sit around in structured environments and recite the 21st-century version of the party line. And if you do that with the proper enthroning, you get a fresh robe, with *two hots and a flop* and the gaze of the Holy See. That does not make you an authority."

"First of all, John, managing the universe is not about parent-child relationships. Get off your horse about how important you are. We have a very big job managing all of creation."

"Relax, Aquinas! From what I read in your *Summa* and *The Physics of Angels*, you did a nice job of nailing down the operational side of the seraphim. So, more from the *First Cause* side of your argument is not necessary.

"From where I sit, Aquinas, you are an angel operator, just like every soldier who operates outside the wire. You report to your Head Military Figure in Charge (HMFIC!) And in your case, that seems to be God. You do not make policy."

"*Okay, I'll take that, but you have just made my argument about parents, children, and God. No outside entity makes policy! So, your two dead boys are in God's hands.*"

"And?"

"*And that's my answer.*

"*And I think that's going to be all my answers as we work through your anger and frustration about who you were, and are, in the cosmos.*"

"Waiter—*oh, server* . . . We . . . and I need some more coffee when you have time."

"Oui, monsieur. Will there be yet another?"

"Um, might be. I think my friend is going to need some support."

47

"You know, John, telling these people at Place Saint Michel that I need support is like the Saxons looking across the field at Charlemagne and saying, 'I don't think he has enough horses.'

"As far as you're concerned, I am the manifestation of hegemony. Keep that in mind!

"I certainly enjoyed watching you sitting in Hemingway's chair. Day after day, hoping for a connection to at least one of his five-toed cats. But you got me instead. Do you know why that happened?"

"No."

"Hemingway was considering coming down, you know. Yeah, he and I had a meeting. I told him, I said, 'Hemingway, I think you and LaCasse have the same problems. You guys are good at two things—drinking and writing.'

"I asked, 'What good comes from a meeting between Hemingway and LaCasse except, maybe, you walk to the bar and drink yourselves through dozens of hunting and fishing stories?' Worse, you both like cats!

"I mean, it would be world-class back-slapping and toasting."

I laughed. Then Aquinas laughed, and we both kept laughing. I was sitting at a sidewalk café in Paris, laughing with *San Tommaso d'Aquino / Doctor Angelicus*. I was in a transcendental state of unimaginable luck. I knew he was right. I would need to toe a few marks before I could get a live autograph on the title page of *The Old Man and the Sea*.

Then Aquinas leaned back in his chair, lowered his chin, laced his fingers across his chest, and asked, "Do you remember the Bahamas? That time when you were in the long black car?"

Aquinas watched me get cold—almost shivering. "Yes," I said. *"They were going to shoot you, you know."*

48

Now I'm watching Aquinas with great interest.

"That was one of my most interesting days," he says. "Sun Tzu, Mohammad, Abraham, and I were having lunch. There is this sort of hissing puff noise, and in walks Lucifer. He has a remarkable presence, you know! Tall, angular face, black suit, total command. He looks down at me and says, 'I think we have a problem in the Bahamas.'" "How so?" I ask.

'One of your guys is about to be executed by men from the Lansky organization. I think it's a mistake. I've already approved this rendition with the Lansky cartel, so I can't change my mind with any amount of credibility. I just didn't do enough research.'

Aquinas calls for the question. *"So, what's the problem?"* And the devil makes his case.

'This guy LaCasse recently stood against the Lansky organization. He's barely old enough to shave. With that kind of visceral instinct, I think he may have long-term potential. But I need a reason to call this off. I'm thinking; I tell Lansky that I just bought him from you guys, and I want to protect my investment. Maybe I can get this stopped.'

"So, Sun Tzu, Mohammad, Abraham, and I are going to sell LaCasse so you can save him from being executed by a drug cartel? Do I get that right?"

'Yes,' says Lucifer. "And then what?" I say.

"Lucifer thinks and responds, 'We can work that out.'"

Now, in the 21st century, over fresh coffee, within sight of Notre Dame Cathedral, I lean into Saint Thomas Aquinas—nose to nose.

"So, you sold my soul to the Devil as an investment favor to Lucifer!?"

"That's right."

"So, I spend the rest of my life as a bargaining chip between good and evil?"

"That's right. We figured, based on what Lucifer told us, you were volatile, so even though the Devil owned your soul, you would be hard to control."

"You, Sun Tzu, Mohammad, and Abraham decided this was some kind of tactical move?"

"That's right."

"So, I have a question. How is it that your gang and Lucifer all hang out in the same place?"

"Oh, you mean the Heaven, Hell, Purgatory stuff. That's all baloney. We can't figure out how it ever got started. All deities stand in parallel. We are in the Cosmos League. Just different teams. Everyone gets to play. We figured you would eventually come up in free agency. The Devil would cut you from his roster because you'd be a constant problem, and we would have a shot at getting you back."

"So, the Solar System is some kind of game board?"

"Right again," says Aquinas.

"Well, that explains why you guys like to have lunch with Sun Tzu."

49

Aquinas just put me in *Deus ex machina*. The unexpected and implausible. As a child of the universe, I am being traded as a commodity. The Cosmos is a multi-dimension game board. Space-time geometry drives decisions that become fixed in position forever. The formula for past, present, and future are identical. My life as a child, as a young man, and as an adult are part of a leverage game between good and evil. Between four old men having lunch and some snappy guy in a black suit with ties to organized crime.

And yet, I am thrilled with the whole affair. For decades I've been watched like a Matador in the ring. These guys have me standing in the Plaza de Toros de las Ventas watching for the third act to see if there is Suerte de Matar! Endlessly testing my mettle. Do I kill the bull? Do I spike the ball? Do I make a "Walk on" home run? Do I get a First Down? These guys play all the games at once. The field, the yard, the track, the arena—all the same. The ultimate game of Sapien Strain.

Aquinas is smiling now. He knows I understand. He knows I'm up for the game. He knows I was always up for the game. He sold me to the dark side, and then for sport, he tossed me a flashlight with no batteries. I should hate him, but I don't. I lean back in. We start again.

"So, Aquinas, what's your take on why I cold-cocked the football player in the lunchroom at Loyola?"

"*The key there, John, is why Simone de Beauvoir selected* The Count of Monte Cristo *for you at Shakespeare and Company. That was a kind of symbolic codices doppelganger of who you were to become. We were looking for how you would use leverage in your life. How you would find a tactical advantage."*

I was instantly aware of how Aquinas and Company play in a causality paradox. They can go back in time. Modify events. Time is a block of time. They play in five dimensions. So yesterday, today, and tomorrow hold no advantage one over the other except in a causality paradox where they can tweak your past to mess with your future. They must have a hell of a lot of fun, these guys.

Aquinas continues, *"You knew, as you were trapped under the lockers, you were without help. So, we were curious if and how you would position yourself to retaliate. To our absolute delight, you teamed with unstylish nerds: Radio Club, Science Club, Chess Club, and so on. You intuitively understood that a brain trust curious about space-time geometry could take down a 15th-century style athlete whose focus is running with an inflated ball. We needed to see in you the deduction and reduction. It worked."*

50

Having one's life turn into a mix between lab experiments and sport is indeterminate at best. But, until today, I never knew the difference. From my current sidewalk coffee perspective, every decision I made was contrived by a gaggle of old men playing with my future. I thought the "Free Agency" thing was funny. How can a person become unmanageable for the Devil? On its face, it's a contradiction in terms.

So, I reach back into our conversational bag.

"Aquinas, I bet you guys were having a hell of a time trying to keep my plane together over Mount Rainier!"

"Well, yes and no." Aquinas catches himself in his binary answer—expounds . . . and burps on his chin. *"Oops,"* he squeaks under his breath.

We both laugh at the human Aquinas. I tell him, "Ya know, Aquinas, when you make these visits, there isn't a requisite to be adaptively authentic. No need to demonstrate your creds with a hiatal hernia."

Then, from under a sheepish smile, Doctor Angelicus says, *"Well, John, for me, internalizing chemical elements as a human doesn't always work."*

I smile and remark that I can't believe we are having a conversation across the full spectrum of existence.

We keep going.

"I can just imagine the table-stakes argument over how to pull the mass out of a photon. Or the duality of the speed of light in the causality paradox. Forward for one observer is backward for another. Do you folks get involved in 21st-century physics?"

"No, we transcend that stuff. We have God. All you have are Einstein and Penrose."

Much laughing aloud. "Ok . . . touché . . . so how did your exceptional lunch crowd stop the oil cooler on my airplane engine from blowing a seal over Mount Rainier?"

"We didn't. We do not have control over a mechanical process. We only have access to wave frequency in Quantum Mechanics. Once there is a collapse of the wave function, a binary decision is automatic—you are dead or alive—out of our control, in fact, out of everyone's control. We can only operate in the spectrum section where you can be both dead and alive at the same time. Once the wave collapses and the particle lands, it's game over. The decision is made, like it or not.

"And the remarkable thing: Science and Religion look for the same science or belief-based answer and come up empty. Nobody on earth seems to know what drives subatomic decisions."

"You're kidding!"

"No, we seraphim must stay on the quasi-philosophical side of Quantum Mechanics, or it's out of our hands."

"Wow, that says a lot about how man is just a sack of atoms in interstellar space."

"I guess so . . ."

"So, let's say the engine seal parted over the mountain. Was there nothing you could have done?"

"Only in a transcendental way."

"Like how?"

"Well, we could have elevated your 'sack of atoms,' as you describe it, out of the cockpit and put you on the shore of the Skagit River fishing."

"Or, maybe, if Lucifer was at the table, maybe in the middle of a gunfight in a convenience store parking lot."

"Yeah, right! Wow! How many of those kinds of calls do you make?"

"Well, in terms of quantifiable accident frequency among humans, 1.35 +/- million per year or about 4000 per day."

"Holy shit!"

Aquinas smiles.

"So, in cosmic reality, your control decisions are isolated to real-time consciousness. You guys are only reactive in the buzz, so to say."

"That's right. We got to be quick if we think we will lose your wave frequency."

"That's a really big job, Aquinas!"

"Yes, it is."

"So, in your seraphim reality, you didn't need to sell me to Lucifer. You could have just transcended me up and put me on the beach in Nassau or Paradise Island."

"That's right."

"But your situation was complicated by the deal already on the table with Meyer Lansky."

"We were a disinterested third party because Lucifer was trying to back-wind what was already in position."

"So, you guys do have a kind of Hoyle protocol, even when you equally share the Hammer of Thor."

"You watch too many movies, John, but that's right."

"Well, that's starting to make Einstein and Penrose look better and better."

Aquinas yawns . . . and scratches his head. *"So, John, why aren't you asking about the second day? The day when the oil cooler did blow, and you almost crashed on landing?"*

"First of all, Aquinas, I did not almost crash on landing. I was on glide slope all the way in. But, more importantly, I was alone. The connection between parent and child trumps all the cards. I lost my sons anyway, you know that, but at least it wasn't in a fiery crash into the side of a mountain."

Aquinas positions his chin with his right hand. I'm focusing on a white marble façade. The emotions at the table are a peculiarity of nature. Both of us are momentarily characterized by an aura around us. We are quiet, and we are bright.

51

It finally began to hit me—the matter-of-fact casual nature of these conversations. I'm involved in open dialog with a deity from the 13th century. I'm looking at a memory and influence sapien subatomic system associated with lunch meeting contemporaries who influence major world belief systems. We are having coffee on the street in Paris within sight of how education matured, modern medicine was founded, societies unfolded, emperors dominated, religions proliferated, and governments spun in their ideologies. And we are talking about how this guy sold my soul to the Devil. Then played me like a sport fisherman over the transom. Now he seems to be angling with the net to ease me back into his boat.

What I'm initially getting out of this is an insight into my reactive life. Because I was being played, I ran my life like a rat in a maze. Like a steely in a pinball machine. My life was an endless train of bank shots off the Aquinas rail. Whenever I was close, he would slide another quarter under the cushion and lay down another game. Then he would have lunch with his buds and discuss my progress.

I think I'll try some Metaphysics on this guy.

"Aquinas, do you remember me on the ladder hanging drapes when I was with JCPenney? Did you also notice how I stopped writing the story before I got off the ladder?"

"Yes, I do remember."

"And, Aquinas, we both know that the spread between the hanging drapes event and my writing about hanging drapes is sixty years—right?"

"Yes, that's right."

"So, Aquinas, what happens to your perception of me when I stop writing?"

"I go off and do other things. Your events sequences are imprinted in time."

"So, okay, Aquinas—follow me here. Now we have two sequence events that are the same but don't match and are sixty years apart. You observe me in one sequence and read me in the other. Is that right?"

"Yes, that is correct."

"How do you and your buds handle unmatched sequencing?"

"That situation becomes null and discarded."

"It seems, Aquinas, we may have come upon a kind of situation singularity."

"What do you mean?"

"Well, what if I had come down off the ladder and, with my post-teenager erect cock crawled in bed with that woman and had my way with her all afternoon? You would know that sixty years ago, but today, I modify the sequence on paper. You don't know it today."

"Well, no, and yes."

"No and Yes." Hmmm . . . Okay, try this—then. Does that mean that I can write you in or out of a story, and my decision modifies reality in space-time geometry? That if I stop writing a story sequence, so stops your involvement?"

"In a way, yes."

"You are being kind of vague, Aquinas."

"So, Aquinas, let's nail this down so you can stop feeding me binary answers. Does that mean that with 21st-century pen and paper, I can toss you, Aquinas, Lucifer, Abraham, Mohammad, and Sun Tzu under the omnipotent bus, and you are stuck there?"

"Ahhhh . . . yes."

"Well, you cheeky bugger, how many people figure that out?"

"I'm not authorized to say, John. But you have just changed the game board by about fifteen orders of magnitude."

"How much are fifteen orders of magnitude?"

"Well, let's say a DNA string to the size of planet earth."

"Oh my, Aquinas! I think you better chalk your stick. I think this time I just put my own quarter under the cushion."

We order another round of coffee.

52

"Well, Aquinas, this is going to get interesting. First, I want to thank you for staying in the game and keeping me at the table. I further want to thank you for the *Summa and the Scala Naturae*. Thank you for being the guy who finally put Aristotelian philosophy in perspective. The guy who taught us *Seraphim, Cherubim, and Thrones*, because in the 21st century, the entire television-watching world learned all about you and didn't know who you were. I admire that kind of modesty. You are on top of your game, Aquinas, and now that the board is upped in orders of magnitude, I feel better about you and me having a little smack-down.

"I know who you are, Aquinas, because, for eight hundred years, you have had your cue and stick on the sapien table. And for six decades, you have had me in an ecclesiastical hammer lock while you continued to slide your quarter under the cushion. And for those foisting games, I want you to be clear.

"I am not little Willie Brown or Son House. I did not walk out of a Mississippi juke joint and walk to the intersection of Highways 49 and 61 to have the Devil tune my guitar so I could play whatever I wanted to play. Those boys sold their souls to the Devil and ended up with a Hellhound on their trail.

"No, Aquinas. You sold me to the Devil as a favor to the Devil himself. And you put your version of a hellhound on my trail. I understand you saved my life in the back seat of that long black car. I could feel the iron in my back, and the call was close. And I understand that I lived to play another day. For thirty years, you and your tribe watched the hellhound chase me, and, in some ways, I love you for that. For seventeen more years, I hid in school, studying the existential physics of life's biggest questions. And I love you for that.

"So now, Aquinas, now that we both can slide our quarters under the cushion, chock your cue, Tommaso d'Aquino / Doctor Angelicus, because on this day, at this table, you are the Shotgun Shack, and I am the coming storm!"

There is a refocusing of the eyes.

"John, do you remember when you applied to The George Washington University after being bounced out of the University of Maryland for challenging a faculty member's competence—repeatedly—and they finally got you out on a technicality?"

"Yes."

"Do you remember where you went—the conversation with the recruiter at The George Washington University at Foggy Bottom?"

"Sort of."

"Well, let me refresh your memory. First of all, the recruiter could not believe U. Maryland off-ed you with a 3.8 GPA. Then he read further into the file, paused, and asked, 'Do you understand who has the power here, John?' You remember that, right?"

"Yes."

"Okay, John, let's make the same GW assumption. You can take your gathering storm, my man, and stick it where the sun don't shine!"

"You haven't changed, John. You still don't get who has the power.

"I pulled your fat out of the fire long ago, keeping you alive by making a foisting bargain with my buddy Lucifer. Not everyone is so lucky, John! Keep that in mind."

Aquinas was spinning his Rosary as his knee vibrated under the table. Now there were two French café managers and one professional waiter standing next to the table trying to decide if I was a psychotic vagrant and if they should be calling the Paris Préfecture de Police.

53

Two Préfecture cops show up and politely but firmly ask me for my identification. I present a United States Passport. As we speak, one of them keeps looking at Aquinas's side of the table—at the cup of coffee. In English, they ask to inquire about my business in France. I tell them I am doing research at the Sorbonne University of Paris; that I am an academic Doctor Ph.D., and MBA, with an interest in transcendental thought in transactional transactions, or "TtTT, as we say in America."

They just stood there—motionless. I could tell they weren't sure if I was bullshitting them, but one thing I was sure: Aquinas was laughing his ass off across the table. The cop kept looking at Aquinas's coffee. Every time Aquinas laughed, the coffee would jiggle. Finally, the officer went to his knees and looked under the table. Nothing.

The second officer asked me if I might be also working at the Piazza Georges Pompidou Center as a street performer? I tell him I'm not. He looks at the jiggling coffee. I look across the table and tell Aquinas to *shut-the-fuck-up*. The cop reaches for his zip ties.

The café manager steps forward.

« Monsieur LaCasse est notre client du restaurant dit le directeur à l'allure importante. »

A préfère guest of the sidewalk café.

Yes, indeed!

"So, Aquinas, there is no escaping that our joint presence gathers attention in its unique singularity. How about we walk down the river promenade where my conversational tone with you won't trigger psychotic madman bells among the pedestrians?"

"Good idea."

With a wink, I thank the restaurant /café staff for saving me from three hots and a cot at *Préfecture de police*. I offer a large tip (American-style), which is gracefully declined (French-style), and Aquinas and I begin our walk along the river Seine. There is a certain amount of passerby curiosity as I stride back into God's illusion with his A-lister theologian.

"So, Aquinas, before we started mixing it up back at the café, we established that our lives in the earth frame were similar. You took positions against accepted doctrines, and I took the same kind of positions against the traditions of my peers. We both decided to fly in the face of orthodoxy. Why did we do that, from your perspective?"

"*You first must establish perspective, John. Some people believe God is a creature. Others believe God is an elaborate illusion brought on by an advanced species. The evolution of your modern science hasn't done that mix much good because, in this century, you guys are giving Nobel Prizes to researchers who believe everything is a hologram. That you and I, as well as the river, Notre Dame, and your favorite bookstore, are refracted from a flat plane center point accelerated by light.*

"*And what's even more bizarre, if one of these hologram-seeking scientists implies that man comes from God, they lose credibility. Lose University* tenure. Are branded as unstable religious quacks. Those of us at the head table shake our heads. We laugh all the way to the sex movie Lucifer shows every Friday night in the northern quintessence of earth aether. Sometimes he mixes it up with the Northern Lights, so people see elaborate visions of angels. Ha! Angels, all right.

"So, my rhetorical question to your question, John, is, how is coming from God any odder than you and I walking along a river that doesn't exist, except it might exist billions of times unless observed in the refracted light of a singularity flat plain of a holographic image? And, of course, we don't exist either unless we are looking at each other. It seems to me wrapping the whole package into a God would save a great deal of time and energy."

"Okay, Aquinas, I get that, but how do I sell you and the head table gang going to Lucifer's sex movies on Friday night to believers in the majesty of the Trinity?"

55

"Aquinas, your story reminds me of something Deepak Chopra wrote in *The Book of Truths*.

The most grievous failure of spirituality occurs in the face of evil. Idealistic and loving people who would never harm another person find themselves drawn into the maelstrom of war. Faiths that preach the existence of one God mount campaigns to kill infidels. Religions of love devolve into partisan hatred of heretics and those who threaten the faith. Even if you think you hold the ultimate truth in your hands, there is no guarantee that you will escape from evil. More violence has occurred in the name of religion than for any other reason. Hence the bitter aphorism: God handed down the truth, and the Devil said, "Let me organize it."

"What Chopra wrote, and what you're telling me, is we are awash in confusion about solid information in the universe. And the disturbing part is you don't seem to know any more than we do."

Aquinas snaps back, *"Who is the 'We' in that context?"*

I answer. "I would say it's every *sentient conscience system* with an abstract mind."

Aquinas clarifies, *"What about systems that demonstrate emotions without language?"*

I go all in. "Cats, dogs, elephants, all primates and organic substrates, and, some people say, trees."

"Okay, John, you're right. For example, if we take the Pythagorean Universe indicating nature is a harmonious whole—top down—we find harmonic frequencies with no explanations.

"I tried for years to equate the Pythagorean system to infinite happiness, but no God materialized. Just harmony. It's the same recurring problem in your interview with Dr. Eben Alexander, MD, when he was on the Harvard University Brigham and Women's faculty.

For a week, while in a coma, he found himself in the 5th dimension company of golden orbs and sacred acoustics, but no God. You famously wrote that he had gone through a 'T-symmetry' time reversal and was in a fifth dimension sit-down with Pythagoras, the man, and he didn't know it."

"Thanks for the compliment, Aquinas, but ya know, that isn't so far-fetched in the abstract mind. Last spring, I was sitting at a house party with this guy. We're having pizza and beer. He was a hell of a nice fellow. People kept staring at us, young girls circling us. I get up to refresh our beer. A young woman I knew got my attention. 'How do you know him?' she whispers into her hands. I had no idea who he was. I still don't know."

"Oh, John, you are my silly spiritual case study. Sometimes my omnipotence pays off. The guy you were with was the lead singer from the American rock band Portugal The Man. Fresh off winning a Grammy for Best Pop Musical Group at the 60th Grammy Awards."

"No shit! Amazing!"

"So, you see, John, with Dr. Eben Alexander, and now you, the hand of Pythagoras scrolls the spheres of the universe for an answer and is never satisfied."

"So, Aquinas, there is no God? Is that the deal? God is a G.O.D. acronym for something like *Divinity on Call*. God is a marketing idea—a committee invention that Lucifer produced, and it jumped to the top of the charts by mistake. Now you head table guys are stuck with it.

The God Concept.

"It sounds like a Devil kind of a deal to me. Lucifer produces this Friday night idea. Builds a sell-your-soul-to-the-Devil features and benefits package, slides it into the market right under your noses, then pulls the weenie out of the bun so you cannot find the Source Code.

"No wonder man is in delirium—always chasing an idea down a rabbit hole. There is no leadership from the top. You, Aquinas, along with

Abraham, Mohammed, Sun Tzu, and Lucifer, have gotten me in Paris to tell me that you guys are on an endless Snipe Hunt trying to find God!?!"

"No, John. You missed my earlier signal on perspective. *YOU are on the Snipe Hunt, and until you figure out who you are, you will never figure out who we are.*"

56

Along the river promenade in Paris, students from the Sorbonne meet, drink, study, and make love. The romance of the walk is dramatic and uplifting to one's heart. The reality is there are no restrooms, not exactly. Aquinas knows I need to pee. He, of course, doesn't.

"There are some advantages to being dead," he says.

Finally, I address the rock wall, within sight of a graphic sign admonishing people away from such activity. I empty my bladder.

"Is this your example of American exceptionalism?" comes from Aquinas. *"Do what you want anywhere you want?"*

"Give it a rest, Aquinas. The spring high water takes it all downstream anyway. If the municipality was that concerned, there would be relief stations along the river.

"Do you see the woman on the bench by the tree, Aquinas? If we stand here long enough, she will pee right through the slats—no problem."

"Jesus, Mary and Joseph, you are such a Neanderthal."

"Oh, I see, Aquinas. *'Jesus, Mary, and Joseph.'* How about *'Father, Son, and Holy Ghost?'*

"Do you think we've happened upon the Source Code, Aquinas?! All I had to do was pee on the river wall, and you come out of your hegemonic secret box?"

Aquinas looks straight ahead. We keep walking.

"John, why did you end relationships with such drama?"

"Oh, that's a good one, Aquinas. You are sitting in Monte Cassino for nine years. Your family was delighted that you would become their village abbot. You get your nose under the Greek and Arabic tent of Arabian-Aristotelian science. Your parents have you abducted on your way to Paris—for being seduced by such scientific rationalism. Then you stand against your colleagues and wedge yourself between Augustinian tradition and Papal criticism, get discredited worldwide, and end up being canonized a saint. Hell no, Aquinas. No drama there!

"I swear to whatever god is available, Aquinas, you are the biggest polemicist in history."

57

"John, have you ever thought about a phrase that becomes an aphorism?"
"No."
"Have you ever thought of people in terms of your combined relationship?"
"No."
"Okay, John, let's examine these four words: Since I met you. They are strangely specific words, John. And few words are capable of such specifics—while remaining fluid. Those words sum up the story of the nature of our reality—yours and mine.

"In both our cases, John, we were stuck in discontent. And, in both our cases, that had nothing to do with the Devil.

"You spent your life reacting. I spent my life reacting.

"We both made decisions on those four words—Since I met you.

"That way, we were free to breech the relationship and run. We operated in free agency full time.

"So, now, John, today I'm dead and lost to history. I get that. However, based on what I just said, am I dead?"

"Well, Aquinas, the cop at the restaurant figured I was crazy, and I'm not. And he was looking under the table for you, but you weren't there. So, I guess you're alive and just missing some of *your atomic structure*."

"Okay, so you and I are alive in various formats—but alive. Yes?"
"Yes, but aren't we sort of side-stepping the God issue, Aquinas?"
"No, we're not. We are addressing that very issue.
"Whether we exist in multiple formats in the order of time comes later. So, pay attention.

"What you are calling the 'Source Code,' John, is, in fact, the aether (also called ether) of the universe. The code makes up in electromagnetic waves (e.g., light and X-rays). God is not a handsome bearded man in brown sandals or a fashionable, flowing-blue-gowns woman levitating while laced in a white cloud. God is how we use the aether of the universe.

"God is the God hypothesis that has no explanatory power.

"So, you see, since I met you, you have been stonewalling our conversations with quantitative expectations. Looking for the initial condition. The source codes. The system. That's how I operated also in the 13th century, I mean. And as we are disappointed, we reject people. The 'Since I met you' syndrome, let's call it. The example is: Since I met you, I've come up empty-handed, in my opinion (IMO). That's what we trained ourselves to think; if we didn't get the answers we expected, we acted accordingly.

"You and I were stuck in the revolving door—I think that's what you call it—a belief system. No explanatory power equals no value. And, of course, explanatory power is the antithesis of God.

"Let me phrase this in a way you can understand before we move on.

"God doesn't care about quantifiable anything, especially power. God is always the gap hypothesis. All of gravity plays in this arena. God is the light beam rider—the concordance between space and time!

God is the energy of the universe."

"Yeah, that works."

58

"So, God is energy in the eye of Saint Thomas Aquinas. And God is everywhere in the eye of Baruch Spinoza. You, of course, know, Aquinas, that Spinoza was considered an Atheist. I understand that being Dutch, Spinoza would be considered secular, above all, but are you getting the similarity between you, the foremost medieval Scholastic, and Spinoza, who, in ethics, didn't believe in doing the right thing because God was in charge? You both are giving it up to God as you talk across both sides of the fence.

"It's like you guys all have the same fallback position, and the only way out is to have Alexander the Great slice his sword through your Gordian Knot. And, as you, I'm sure, will recall, my dear scholastic, it was you who nailed down the canon of parsimony when saying, *'It is superfluous to suppose that what can be accounted for by a few principles has been produced by many.'*

"Aquinas, I find it intractably wonderful that two of the universally recognized milestone philosophers are stuck with Ockham's Razor while chasing their intellectually fluffy willow-in-the-wind tails."

"*My dear John, against Cicero in the Roman forum, you would do well; however, against God in the universe, you are vacant and dull.*"

"See, there it is again, Aquinas. Your same argument. Pitch a belief system with no proof, and you automatically win by default. I am not the 'dull one' here, Aquinas!

"I am not the dull one."

59

"Okay, John, let us get out of who did what when arguments.

Let's take this into your 21st century. One hundred percent of your problems were, and are, due to your relationship with a conscience. Either your conscience or universal consciousness. And I know I'm correct, so save your rhetoric for the local tavern."

"Okay, Aquinas, I'll give you that. Let's go."

"All right.

"For centuries, man has tried to equate existence to mathematics, specifically geometry. Somehow there were answers to quantify. 'Proof,' as you call it.

"So, tell me, John, when you came down off the drapery ladder and found your way to the woman's naked body, which part of the geometric proof was driving your decision?"

"Holy shit, Aquinas, when you throw it down, you don't mess around!"

"So, John, my friend, you are now stuck right in the middle of your argument. All you decided was the reward was worth the risk. That it was somehow unsettling to mount your customer's wife, you did it anyway."

"Yeah, Aquinas! Just call it out. Say it straight. No point in skirting the issue. Just lay me out prostate on the steps of your sanctuary. The cold stone walls of your Holy Roman Church.

It's a matter of physics, you know. Not your mysterious hocus pocus.

"All boats have tipping points. It's a matter of physics."

60

"'Tipping points' is your answer? Physics is your justification?

"John, let me reacquaint you with the Third Law of Thermodynamics. When you begin to compromise your vision of yourself—of whom you thought you were, of what you may have become—your systems cool down, eventually to approach absolute zero. You become a closed system. In the lab, scientists look for stable entropy at this point. They look for a steady state of elements. Versions of quartz, albite, forsterite, diopside, and hematite.

"What that means in our conversation terms is your brain turns into a crystal. You are transforming your organic brain tuner into a rock.

"Now, you can do end-run confabulations of yourself at every marker. You are a dysfunctional illusion. You can avoid your 'system' because your afternoon tryst with your customer's wife killed your brain at absolute zero. The state where you cease to function as a preferred child of the universe. You have symbolically sold your newly formed cold soul to the other side. The vortex where you spin into a black bottomless crack, catching yourself with one elbow as you scrape off your fingernails, looking down at Dante's Inferno.

"This does not mean you stop functioning—oh, no. John, have you ever watched The Walking Dead? The TV show where Norman Reedus runs around shooting Zombies in the head with a crossbow? Well, guess what? You are now SAG-AFTRA-qualified on the set of The Walking Dead. You are a Zombie. Your brain is at absolute zero. You sold yourself out to a lower order.

"John, there are no Beings in the universe better-equipped to do circular arguments justifying failure than man. As a species, man is flawed.

"On the other hand, as a conversational companion, you are clinically interesting.

Do keep in mind the order of time, John. You are getting old and rickety. I, on the other hand, am infinite in space-time geometry.

"Any questions there, Johnny?"

61

"You know, Aquinas, as you and I tiff and wrangle, I'm reminded of something my friend Kelly Swensen said, *'It's not when one door closes another door opens . . . it's when you open one door, and another door opens.'*

"Let's change the theoretical framework of our conversation and move from jumping in bed with a strange woman (obviously, you have limited experience) to tradition and succession among men.

"As a young man, I spent a great deal of time with my dad in the mountains of Montana. We operated like "Hunter-Gatherers." We ate what we killed. Deer and elk, mostly. I was twenty years old before I tasted domestic beef or pork on our home table. Our family ate meat taken from the upland game. We made our bread, processed the meat, rendered the fat, collected open-range salads, and kept warm with small fires.

"We made money panning for gold and living day in and out with the forest primeval. We had a house in town, where my mother made certain I became exposed to art and science, but we lived in the woods.

"My father taught me how to quietly track in the forest like an Indian. How to work a ridge line stalking downwind. He showed me how to make traps from sticks and logs. I've carried a pocket knife for decades—I have a *Benchmade folder* in my pocket right now.

"So, here's my question:

"You and Aristotle held that man is positioned ontologically at the juncture of two universes—*the corporal and the spiritual.*

"Therefore . . .

"Are hunter-gatherers, e.g. hunters, corporal or spiritual?"

"John, there is ample evidence in prehistoric art that death by any means is spiritual.

Your question, in context, is regarding a belief system. This is what we know. Hunters who thank God for a kill will enter a transcendental state of spiritualism. That is roundly spiritual. In the eyes of his peers, a hunter who doesn't thank God for a kill is a thankless free rider. That hunter will not be invited back to the pack (man or animal).

"Traditional hunters feel a reciprocal agreement exists between the hunter and the hunted. Some of this is associated with ritual—drink the blood or eat the heart to capture the strength of the animal or man.

"There is a transcendental attachment—even to a dead animal. On separate occasions, you and your dad remained in the snow and ice overnight with your dead animal. You put your life in the body of your kill. And, for months, remembered the animal—the circumstance—and remained thankful at your table for a lifeless companion that you shot dead. That is not corporal. That is spiritual."

"Okay, Aquinas, using your context of *God as the energy of the universe*, am I mounting an attack against God by shooting an elk? By killing the elk under a sanctioned conservation program underwritten by the State. By using my elk "Tag" to shoot the animal. Is there anything in Chaos Theory (Quantum Entanglement) that says the dying elk resonates with God?"

"So, John, let's think of the question in the context of your friend Kelly's aphorism.

When you place the dead-hold reticle of your Vortex scope on the elk's heart and squeeze off a Win Mag 300/180-grain bullet—out the muzzle at 3000 feet per second—does the elk have a new door option?

"Is that your question—maybe your fear?"

62

"Okay, Aquinas, you have successfully snagged the question. Will a door open for the elk?

"I think these scholars describe the conscious state of the elk as I'm aiming the rifle.

a. Gottfried Leibniz . . . felt the world is composed of atoms of energy that are psychic . . .

b. Arthur Schopenhauer asserted that the inner nature of all things is Will. Gustav Theodor Fechner . . . contended that even trees are sentient and conscious.

c. Josiah Royce . . . adopted a theory that each species of animal is a single conscious individual—incorporating into itself the individual souls of each of its members.

d. Britannica, T. Editors of Encyclopaedia. "panpsychism." *Encyclopedia Britannica*, August 20, 2020. https://www.britannica.com/topic/panpsychism.

"So, Aquinas, Leibniz, Schopenhauer, Fechner, and Royce are not chopped liver! I would call their positions a universal conscience-mind consensus.

"There is this thing in Quantum Mechanics called superposition. I think that supports the next cosmic door opening for the elk. Kelly Swensen, a woman who traffics in advanced geometries, agrees. The doors are in constant rotation—in superposition. The elk is alive and dead at the same time.

"For example, visualize a pool table with you about to make the break. Every ball in the break must be able to be in every position on the table. Every ball is part of a probability of position. Regardless of where they end up, at the break, they have every position option available. But it doesn't stop there. Going forward in the game, the same situation applies. On every shot (no pun intended, my dear elk), every position is available in probability. The thing never stops. When you and I end the game and rack the balls, all the probabilities remain. The table is in a constant state of superposition for any ball into infinity. All you must do is chalk your cue stick and take a shot. At that moment, God grabs his microphone and notifies each ball it's welcome anywhere on the board. Then Kelly chimes in with her 'slip-stick' . . . 'Based on the angle of your shot, *the probability of the cue ball rolling to a stop within an inch of the corner pocket is very high.*' Then you and I sit leaning on our cue sticks and exclaim, '*Well, I'll be damned, the cue ball stopped before it dropped in the pocket.*' And we fully believe that is because of your shot on the break.

"Or was it because the time formula for past, present, and future are all the same, and God knew where the cue ball was going all along? The shot and the ball are in a predisposed block of time.

"Inside our question, the elk simply moves into superposition because that elk has been everywhere into infinity. The elk was there but he wasn't there. My shot rang out and the bullet exploded out of my barrel. Did I hit the elk, did I miss the elk, or did I shoot six hundred billion times into an Esher diagram? As the elk goes through the revolving door, the elk doesn't care one way or the other because God has him everywhere all the time.

"Doors to infinity—forever."

"Everything is everywhere."

"*So, John, was that your right triangle version of God saving the elk?*"

"No, Aquinas, it was my version of why you and I don't play pool. The balls know they're going everywhere all the time."

63

"*John, this revolving door elk notwithstanding, you seem to exist in an egotistical sublime regardless of who or what I might represent in holy orders. You fly in the face of my table mates. Men who understand the dangerous business of philosophy. All vilified and romanced in the glittering salons of education. You do not seem to care about anything, like you are immune to the dark prosaic of life. You seem to be living without a goal.*"

"Well, if it shows, Aquinas, then here's the story:

"When I went back to school, for the second time, I was in some last-ditch effort to recover who I was as a child of the universe instead of a foot soldier for commerce. We both know I was unhappy, regardless of my business success.

"On my first undergraduate try in sociology at the University of Montana, I quickly realized that I was a mole in a coven of witches. People working spells in tandem on witless students. As an undergraduate, I studied under Leslie Fiedler. He had me floating in a bath of water so I could graduate to the witch's cradle. A multi-axis swing designed to confuse brain symmetry. That way, I could think in other dimensions. Fiedler used me as a demonstration that a person, when in this transient state, could regulate body temperature. It bored the shit out of me. In my estimation, I was getting credits to be a shill in a sideshow. So, I played pool and drank beer until the registrar showed me the door.

"My next try at school was when I had gray hair. Big difference. But I kept getting tossed out. Not much had changed. The faculty was still laced with incompetence (not all, for sure), except I had a hell of a lot of life experience. And, as you know, I don't lie down easily.

"So, in an odd academic dichotomy, you and I may well be talking today because Leslie Fiedler had me floating in the water and swinging in a multi-axis cradle. Maybe higher education is a coven of witches, after all. And, of course, surprise, surprise; I became a teacher. I am a proud member of the American Association of University Professors (AAUP). I belong to several academic honor societies. And being listed in the publication Marquis Who's Who®, Warren Buffett's favorite midnight reader. He finds biographies fascinating.

"With a full basket of life experience, I signed on as Associate Faculty at The Forbes School of Business, now housed at the University of Arizona. While there, I was selected as Business Faculty Member of the Year.

"Once again, I was on top of my game with nothing holding me down.

"So, fearless bastard that I was, I decided to change my syllabus. My students would learn how to be tactical.

"Aquinas, you mentioned I seem to be *living without a goal.* It's not that. People have goals because they can't manage their life. So, life coaches tell them to have a plan and achieve goals. Jesus, I can't imagine anything more useless. If you need a goal, change jobs. And that's what I told my students. 'Get your eyes on the horizon!'

"The whole thing broke open when a student asked in class *how to buy a car without good credit.* I simply reacted with, *'Buy the fucking dealership!'*

And it was game on . . ."

64

"Oh my, John! I can just imagine the 12 Olympian Gods sending up an order for fresh horses and chariots. And getting back a hot anvil with the hammer and a note reading, 'Figure it out, people. Happy to send down some wheel spokes as necessary!'

"So, what did you tell the students about the car vs. dealership process?"

"Well, Aquinas, as you and I know, it's all a matter of perception. The student in question was a woman. So, I had a built-in problem with automobile knowledge. She had zero background in cars. The men in the class were laughing. I said, 'Kathleen, get strapped; we are going in at lock and load.' All the boys thought we were about to learn how to jack a car off the showroom floor at midnight.

"So, we began. I let Kathleen (Katy) use my Ralph Lauren Gent's briefcase. Inside the case, I put my business bible, on loan to me by my mentor, Jennifer Sullivan, *The Sign of the Seahorse. A Tale of Greed and High Adventure in Two Acts.*

"The class split up into segments. I had students vetting hedge fund portfolios for transportation inventory. Also, aggregators like Auto Nation.

"We had Katy practice:

(Act One)

How to walk into the dealership in casual business attire (slacks/blouse).

Do not look at any cars on the showroom floor, and do not ask for help.

Only look at the window sashes and floor tile. It is important to look at the ceiling.

Then walk outside with a tape and walk off the front lot footage.

When approached, say, 'I am looking into auto dealerships that might fit in a hedge fund portfolio.'

After that, every answer is 'I'm sorry. I cannot disclose that information.

'However, if your management would like a call, I can pass that request along.'

I tell Katy there will be milling around as men look at her from a distance. None of them count. Make a move to leave—start walking away. A new guy will appear. He counts. Ask for his business card. He will ask for yours. Say you're sorry, but no business card. You are part of a business class that is researching hedge fund portfolios. Ask for his card. He smiles and gives you his card. You smile and say, 'You never know; a fund could be *curious*.' Never say *interested*.

Leave the dealership.

(Act Two)

"Back in class, several funds have been contacted with mixed results. We picked the best response, and we have established a fee for the lead. The fee is three new cars for a charity auction. One of the cars will be passed to Katy as IRS rules apply.

"We call the name on the card and say, 'Do you remember . . . well, there is an interest. Katy gives her name to the dealership and thanks her contact for his courtesy.

"We reinforce the benefits of fees going to a 501(c)3 not-for-profit corporation.

"The hedge fund takes it from there.

"The students want to know what happens if they renege on the deal.

"I say, 'We have people who handle that.'"

Aquinas rolls his liturgical stole around his shoulders and asks,

"John, should I hear your confession?"

65

"No confession is required, Aquinas. I do not believe in absolution anyway. Even from the guys in the original apostolic age. You will notice I was named after St. John the Apostle, who was the last guy to leave the building in 70 AD. So, there is this expected tradition that I hang around after dinner.

"So, John, as we sat in the sidewalk café at Place St. Michel, and as we now walk along the river Seine—and I'm going to use your phrase here—you seem to 'bounce off issues like a steely in a pinball machine'—like you are afraid of them. And if we get close to grounded meaning, you deflect again. What will happen to you if we get to who you are? If we break through your mental body armor? I have lots of time, John. However, you are not the only guy who, when it comes to self-evaluation, can't hit his ass with both hands."

"Aquinas, what is this trash talk from the concise purveyor of essential truths?"

"Oh, you know, me and my table buds have strategic techniques for dealing with intransigent opposition. We sort of jump out of our terrestrial context. A way of letting you know that I am fully capable of taking a pee against the river wall or laying down conversational smoke to obscure the field, but at this moment, why would I need to become such a lowbrow pedestrian unless I'm trying to hide behind some ground glass image of who I am? And from my perspective, John, that's precisely what you are doing."

"You're overreaching, Aquinas. I don't have a problem with who I am."

"Oh, okay. Then I have a few areas I would like to cover.
"Why did you come to Paris?"

66

"Well, Aquinas, you better get in a Four-point harness because this is not going to be easy."

"Yeah, right! Like I haven't heard this kind of stuff before, John!?!"

"Being hegemonic isn't becoming, Aquinas; I'm trying to get to your question."

"You're right, John. I apologize. Carry on . . ."

"When I was a student under Leslie Fielder, floating in the water and levitating out of a witch's cradle, I passed it off as theatrics. But that's when I started binge drinking—trying to avoid what was happening. I went for sixty years trying to shake that off. What's worse, you sold my soul to the Devil in the middle of all this!"

"This better be good, John!"

"The net effect was, I was good at everything and happy with nothing. I was like the internet. My capacity was everywhere, and my value was nowhere."

"What does that have to do with my question about you coming to Paris?"

"Okay, pay attention, Aquinas; you are going to need to connect a few dots here. When I was studying for my MBA at Benedictine University, I would walk to the St. Procopius Abbey associated with the university in Lisle, Illinois. That is essentially *Chicago Land* in local parlance. I would walk to the front of the Abbey and just stand there. I didn't know why. But when I was in the shadow of St. Procopius Abbey, I had the same feeling I tried to drink my way out of at the University of Montana. I was there, but I wasn't there.

"I returned to Seattle and began doing research at the Suzzallo and Allen Libraries on the University of Washington campus. The Graduate Reading Room at Suzzallo has a distinctive look of Oxford and Cambridge colleges and the architecture of the St. Procopius Abbey at Benedictine University.

"Something was going on with me that was associated with the shadow of Gothic architecture. In the Suzzallo, I would have to leave the Graduate Reading Room and walk down the grand staircase to the foyer. I felt uneasy. Sometimes, physical stress in my jaw and neck and tongue. But, once again, didn't know why.

"Then, on an unrelated trip, I was in Paris—sitting in Sainte Chapelle, which is a 13th-century icon among the greatest Gothic architectural masterpieces on earth. It was designed to house Christ's crown of thorns, then in the possession of King Louis IX, who got it after it was pawned to a Vatican bank. That's the story, anyway. You would know better than me."

Aquinas begins smiling and moving his fingers together like Captain Francis Queeg in *The Caine Mutiny*. I continue . . .

"I'm listening to Vivaldi's *Four Seasons,* played by a French String Quartet. As I'm sitting, taken with the music, the same St. Procopius Abbey unease comes over me, and my mother shows up. Except, she is dead. Has been dead for several years. She came to me the same way you did. Sort of vibrating in sound and light. But it was Mom, all right. And she was looking straight at me.

"All the usual stuff applied. She was happy. She was mystical. She was ignoring gravity. It was like we were sort of floating around on the front porch of the old main house in Missoula.

"Comfortable and at ease.

"So, to your question, that experience was the hook that put me in Paris multiple times looking for answers."

67

"First, John, I'm going to give it to you that your perception of my selling your soul to the Devil didn't help your circumstance. I get that. You were never the Devil's man. You were like an errant truant in his camp. Never willing to completely comply. Had you started there, it would have been different. But you didn't. You came in the frame late after you were already standing for good in the Bahamas land grab by organized crime. So, in your case, the Devil didn't get the full package. You ended up in this bizarre yin-yang pondering your every circumstance.

"And to paraphrase your earlier exclaim, John, 'Surprise Surprise,' that's why I came down instead of Hemingway. To help you unravel your life. That's why I'm here."

"So, Aquinas, did we have to go through all this preliminary sidewalk drama before you brought that up?"

"I had to be sure of your fundamental stats. Sort of like a doctor checking the homeostasis in a blood sample."

"Oh good, Aquinas. I'm glad I am clinically interesting in the cosmos!"

"So, anyway, John, let's keep going with your story."

"Well, these feelings I have seem to come when I'm around Gothic architecture—or the images take place in Gothic architecture. After Jeff died, I stopped having the dream about him falling through high-tension wires. Then, when his brother John died, I end up in an immediate conscious clarity. I'm in a sepia-tone hue. There are Romanesque-Gothic frames where my boys are playing as children on stairs between arches.

I'm running to catch them, but I can't. They are laughing and tumbling and running in play. Then they disappear through the arches. I am left alone on the stairs inside the frame. I step out of the frame, and it disappears. My life rides on the back of an enigma. I am in and out of circumstances impossible to reconcile. I am living in a Penrose triangle.

"In circumstance after circumstance, I am riding outside the wire. Away from our usual dimensions. I can't figure out why or how."

"John, I, and my table mates Mohammad, Abraham, Lucifer, and Sun Tzu, think you're ready for an answer. Lucifer is going to cut you loose. Free from your restraint. But I'm going to let him tell you. So, let's go back to the bookstore and sit on the river wall."

We head for Shakespeare and Company at Kilometer Zero on the river.

"Aquinas, I'm getting the same Gothic architecture feeling right now."

"I know, John. But it's not about Gothic architecture. That seems to be an anomaly. Like a candle flame in meditation. A center of focus but not the center ring. What you receive is outside the chakra. What we notice getting through to you is a frequency harmonic. You can be in a superposition with someone you think about, regardless of distance."

"Aquinas, does the Devil know all this stuff?"

"Yes, and he is about to arrive."

68

Aquinas and I stood together on the river wall. The French Canal Barge approached as before. The water vapor mist rose off the water by the barge transom. Sun shone through and excited the water drops in refraction. And there he was. He walked up the light beam, and we were together. Aquinas stood erect and said smartly, *"Thank you for coming, sir."*

I thought that was odd until I realized that this guy was the Devil. At least several orders of magnitude more powerful than Aquinas. The Devil looked nonbinary. He could flash any gender in a moment. He was dressed in western contemporary business attire. Black shoes. No tie. Black trim hair. No shaggy rough nap or surface. This guy was tweaked.

The Devil addressed me and opened with, *"John, ever so long ago, I bought you away from Aquinas because I thought letting Lansky's men kill you was a bad idea. I still believe that was a good decision. It was interesting that at that moment, both Aquinas and I thought we could control you regardless of who owned you as a bargaining chip. That did not happen. Instead, you constantly flew against the glass. You were like a wild Hawk in a glass cage. But it got worse. Eventually, you found the chink in our armor.*

"Here's what happened:

"We use a pulsing 100,000hz frequency to manage people who have sold their soul to the Devil or, in your case, are sold to the Devil. That works down to 38,000hz, which keeps us clandestine, except for the upper auditory frequency of certain animals. Domestic cats, for example. Cats know who we are. So do crows.

"*In this way, we can control the auditory cortex for wave discrimination tasks (such as frequency discrimination) . . . and all of this becomes the relative timing of responses made by a set of brain neurons. In fact, your neurons.*

"*The problem that developed in your case is that you started isolating a segment of the frequency we use for control and began using it personally to communicate outside our purview in the Fifth Dimension.*

"*And there wasn't a damn thing we could do about it. Pardon my French. To my knowledge, it's never happened before. And my advice to you is to be discreet. Try and walk in our shoes if you can. What you managed to do allows you to subvert the time formula for past, present, and future. We do not take that lightly. Keep that in mind.*

"*So, John, I am releasing you out of this foisted Devil's bargain. You are free from this moment forward. But I admonish you to watch your step. You have obvious developed talent, but your time-in-grade doesn't even jiggle the needle. At some point, I will see you again.*"

Aquinas vectored to one side. Lucifer passed and asked, "*Will you be at lunch Friday?*"

Aquinas answered, "*I think we need to wing it.*"

They both smiled.

"Wow, Aquinas, I've always felt there is a monumental difference between being openly looked at and quietly seen. Lucifer just told me, '*We see you.*' Does that make sense to you, Aquinas?"

"*Yes, it does, John. Everyone at our table saw this coming. We just needed Lucifer to trigger the deal. We fully understand your dilemma. You seem to have your foot in both doors. Your vision is working in three dimensions, and your brain is working in five dimensions. To us, you became a living version of a hypersphere. That almost makes you a commodity once again. Be careful the Devil doesn't try to buy you back. He dresses nice, but sometimes he's a little Machiavellian. Don't ever tell him I said that, or he would, with great precision, kick my ass. We must remember he is, after all, the Devil.*

"*So, John, we might have unraveled your being conflicted over relationships and transactions. About how you handled risk. About how you reacted rather than observing. You were lucky, considering you were quick. In business, that got you called 'The Shark.' In education, that got you tossed out of multiple universities but made you a hero among students. Which among these defines you?*"

"It's the students. Students have a valid curiosity. They are not gerrymandering for market share. Students are refreshing for people with seasoned scars like me."

"*But, John, I keep waiting for you to mention your family. What about the people who supported you through all this?*"

"Aquinas, if you were paying attention earlier, you will remember I was raised in mountains among animals. I follow the way of quiet walking. Notice pack animals when converging and running together. It just happens. The lead dog doesn't turn over his shoulder and bark, 'I saw you take down that deer at Three Medicine Camp.' They simply converge and run together—they know how to react. If you lie down with a cat, you better not have any intentions beyond love and play. Always remember, if your 8-pound cat weighed 110 pounds, you would be lunch.

"Family is respected in silence and supported in steel. Besides, I don't notice you saying much about your father. The man who had you abducted by road agents on your way to Paris and placed in isolation for years because you weren't living up to his expectations. Must have been a hell of a guy."

"Is that called 'rubbing it in,' John?"

"Whatever tweaks your stole, Aquinas."

"What the hell is that supposed to mean? You were nicer when you worked for the Devil!"

70

"Life is a merciless process, Aquinas. I am playing in five dimensions and am simply regarded as a rogue player who can be dangerous. If you would get out of your dogmatic bias and stop referring to me as a Zombie because you keep seeing me on top of my drapery customer, I would appreciate it.

"But were you?"

"You will recall, I did not write the answer into that script, Aquinas. So now you can spin in the yin-yang of this binary sex show. There is little doubt you guys at the table have great power; however, in America, we won a revolutionary war by dressing like the forest and hiding among trees. I am happy—in fact, lucky—to be your protégé, Aquinas, but around 40000hz, I hear like a dog and see like a cat. So, let's put this in perspective, Aquinas. For you to see as I do, your eyes would need to be the size of tennis balls.

"Getting back to this 'chink' I found in your and Lucifer's armor. Are you curious?"

"Yes, for you see, John, once we pass into the golden orb of the seraphim, we relinquish certain creativity for happiness. You still have that quality."

"Okay, Aquinas, then let's you and I work through this, one situation at a time.

"One summer evening, I was sitting with Shiah Sarkowsky in my truck. He and I got together from time to time to discuss college and career choices. Shiah had directed us to his favorite ice cream parlor on Upper Queen Anne Hill in Seattle. As we sat, he mentioned I should start a podcast. I didn't know what that meant. He made it sound simple. So, I investigated the mechanics of podcasting. We took it forward with Spotify as "Tension" on August 11, 2019. Today, we play in forty-one countries. Ross Stewart Andrew, a longtime friend and colleague, happened to listen to our broadcast while in Scotland. He was taken with the frequency quality of my voice and arranged for us to become a studio. Now we record from the Ross Stewart Andrew Studio in Seattle.

"The principal of a new social media app 'Wisdom' heard our podcast and recruited me to Wisdom because of our content and my voice.

"I opened on Wisdom, and immediately a woman called my open line to say, 'There was just something about your voice.' We had a conversation, and when I closed that line, I knew I hadn't been speaking with a random caller. After she called, another woman called to say she waited for me every podcast—just waited to hear my voice.

"Are you getting where this is going, Aquinas?"

Yes, we are going straight down your Narcissistic rabbit hole. John, about John, on John."

71

"Aquinas, your lack of 21st-century exposure has you stuck in the Seraphim Syndrome. But I appreciate and enjoy your myopic capacity, and I further enjoy comic improv. Especially jingles like *John, about John, on John*.

"They make me think I'm Elton John playing 'Rocket Man.'

"All I was trying to do was establish a base point marker for when I unwittingly tapped into your control frequency. It's remarkable how harmonics go together. For example, what follows is a set of Pacific Northwest cloud harmonics that describe you as a *Pythagorean glass oscillation developing as a fiery devil queller*.

'There once was a man from Grants Pass. His balls were made out of glass. When they tinkled together, they played 'Stormy Weather,' and fire shot out of his ass.'

"Aquinas, I think you know Grants Pass is in Oregon, right?

"Now, shall we walk down Boulevard Saint-Germain and see if we can pick up any new ideas from coffeehouses?"

"*Well, my dear John, you primitive feudal jackass, I love you like a brother. Let's hit some coffeehouses so you can tell me about Rena, the woman you saw in the Southern sky.*"

"How do you know that?"

Aquinas winked.

72

"Well, Aquinas, we are back to the harmonics of the universe. Let's take a pass on Saint-Germain and use a vendor at Jardin du Luxembourg. I figure if it worked for Napoleon and Josephine, it should work for us. Maybe we can go for a banana split. They are the best here, you know. So odd, a banana split in the Luxembourg Garden. Have you ever had one—a banana split?"

"*No, but I'll take your word, John. This is a good decision. It's beautiful here. Your Napoleon reference is funny in context. When I was walking around Paris, it would take Napoleon six more centuries to show up.*"

"I forgot, Aquinas, you are a Time Lord. Have you ever heard of Doctor Who?"

"*No.*"

"Well, anyway, you asked about Rena."

"*Yes.*"

"There was this woman named Rena a long time ago—maybe sixty years ago. She and I were taken with each other—the magnetism of youth, I guess. Rena was a waitress at the café called the Minute Kitchen in Missoula. It was a hangout for university students. We were among them.

"After a weekend shift, Rena and I became officially connected in the back seat of my buddy, Sam McClay,'s two-tone grey Ford. It was like most of these events, I suppose, but it wasn't. There was a feeling there that never went away. Never could get a handle on how I felt about Rena. It was just different. We never hooked up again. Went on with our lives.

"Now we can *fast-forward*—that's 21st-century lingo, Aquinas—to last year. That was when Merrilee Sweeney contacted me. She was my first open-line caller on the Wisdom app. She was the first woman who called because of a connection to auditory frequency. Something about how I sounded.

"Merrilee and I talked off and on for weeks, each time getting closer. Eventually family entered the conversation. Her mother's name was Josephine.

"Then, to my astonishment, Merrilee spontaneously sends me a picture of her mother. Just sent it. No prompt. I was unstrung when I saw it. A picture of the Rena I remembered. The same features, same hair, same angles in her cheeks. Merrilee's mother, Josephine, was a visual doppelganger for Rena.

"The following morning, I was looking south out my living room window. It was about 5:30—early. I was looking into a group of clouds making up over the city. I was asking God—don't laugh, Aquinas—to help me with Rena. *Was Rena in that picture of Josephine?* And, once again, in a refractory aberration just like you, and Lucifer off the river, and my mother in the music of Sainte-Chapelle, there she was—Rena in the clouds. Looking right at me.

"I've done enough reading to suspect the paranormal connection I am having with Rena is possible. The protagonists of hard and soft science exist in formulaic physics and metaphysics fudge factors, so for me, what I see is what I get.

"Merrilee and I continued to talk, almost every day, for months. We began to realize that there was a superposition between us. The signs go beyond coincidence. One day, I asked if she remembered Earth Wind & Fire. She was stunned. She knew them not only by sound but also by lyrics in 'The Way of the World.' In conversation, we realized she was walking alone along a ridge line in Laguna Niguel, California, as I was walking the beach on the northern tip of Orcas Island in the American San Juan Islands. While I walked along the water, I picked up a piece of Jasper, the rock of the rock band Earth Wind & Fire.

"On another occasion, we realized we both had 'Big Medicine'—Sacred Amulets of the White Buffalo from Montana. She showed hers, and I showed mine.

"After that, we noticed we both had amulets of Crows.

"Then Merrilee told me that she was abandoned by her father. In her disappointment and anger, she let me know I was not that man, but in her next sentence, she said, 'You are the father I never had.'

"The following morning, at 5:30—early again—I'm looking out my living room window. Rena caught my attention in the Southern sky.

"She smiled, and I cried.

"So, my question, Aquinas: Am I stuck in a three-way trichotomy between Merrilee, Josephine, and Rena? I suspect Rena in the Southern sky is Rena in the back of Sam McClay's Ford. I know Merrilee, and I do not enjoy a normal relationship. Her mother, Josephine, seems to be watching her. I just hijacked your control frequency, and now I'm resonating with a former tryst in the back of Sam's car. Stack on that a woman in this century who experiences a cosmic connection between us."

"*See, that's the problem, John. You are operating on a fractional frequency. A slice of this and a slice of that . . . I agree that what you and Rena in the Southern sky have been experiencing is real. What I need to check is, what are the* Coriolis *effect vectors out your living room window at 5:30* A.M.*?*

"Are you serious, Aquinas?"

73

"Well, I guess if I'm going to place a rifle shot at 1300 yards, the *Coriolis* effect of the earth would be important. But what does that have to do with Rena in the Southern sky?"

"*Remember, John, when you were talking about the revolving windows of opportunity for the elk?*"

"Yes."

"*In a conscious state where your image in the sky is dependent on various physical processes, we check to understand if the image exists and if there is something that is likely to be the image. And it will be the* Coriolis *effect of the earth that continues to rotate the windows of opportunity—Rena being only one of the trillions of options.*"

"Aquinas, is this the kind of smoke you lay down when you are trying to vector someone away from their position?"

"*No, John, it's just that other slice of frequency you don't have. So, I'm being courteous as opposed to inventing a confabulation for your benefit.*"

"*What I'm going to do, John, is a kind of double-blind test of the aberration. If I can position you in an unplanned circumstance away from your usual comings and goings, and while there, we can find a sign that develops on cue, your story becomes believable at the table.*"

"So, what do you have in mind?"

"*Well, someplace quiet. I'm thinking of the Picpus Cemetery here in Paris. Let's have you standing at the iron fence looking at the memorial monument of the Marquis de Lafayette, the French hero of the American Revolution. He was a protégé of your man George Washington. We always liked him.*"

"Will you provide the colors and a United States Army band? Or do I go a cappella with 'La Marseillaise'?"

"No, John, no band."

"Shit!"

"But you can certainly sing if you want to."

"So, Aquinas, when do you want to do this?"

"How about tomorrow morning—say about 10:30 A.M.?"

"That works for me."

Aquinas and I part company for the day, but I know enough about our relationship to believe he will be at the cemetery as described. When Aquinas left me, he didn't just disappear. Instead, he dissolved into a state between low and high entropy. From the acute definition in his molecular system to smoothing toward infinity and eventually chaos, I took this theatrical disappearance as a signal from Aquinas about the physics of the universe. Like we are in the state of transition from high to low entropy and, eventually, we will fade to black. Pretty scary stuff.

As I'm walking back to the hotel, I encounter long strings of people in white lab jackets with signs chanting loudly in French. It turns out three of the Left Bank hospitals went on strike for more pay. The American Hospital of Paris, Hôtel-Dieu Hospital, and University Hospital's Pitié-Salpêtrière.

I stepped to the curb to grab a cup of coffee as these people marched by. Doctors, nurses, and operating staff. While watching, I began to reflect on the strangeness of the last few hours. I have a meet-up with St. Thomas Aquinas on the river Seine across the street from Shakespeare and Company. After a conversation, he decides to invite Lucifer the Devil to come down and release me from a previous contract. Aquinas knows I want to talk about Rena in the Southern sky, and so he baits me into that queue. Now we are going to go visit the Marquis de Lafayette at a local cemetery where he's going to do hocus-pocus to decide if I'm psychotic. And now, I'm sitting here with a cup of coffee, watching the entire medical staff of three hospitals march down the street with pots and pans demanding more money.

I squint to look both ways as they march by. Maybe I can see Napoleon standing behind a canon at the end of the street.

74

"Okay, Aquinas, I'm here. 10:30 A.M., just like you asked.

"Yes, John, **we see you**."

"What is this 'we' business?"

"Well, we decided that all of us—Abraham, Mohammed, Sun Tzu, and Lucifer would look in on this experiment with you and me."

"How did you arrive at that?"

"Well, your story about Rena in the clouds is more convincing than the usual stuff we hear, especially considering your background, and your time in grade with Merrilee Sweeney answers preliminary questions that would usually come up. So, in your collective case, we feel we have something in you that becomes a potential value proposition among the Seraphim."

"John, speaking for myself as Sun Tzu and The Art of War, I feel there's a great deal to be learned tactically based on your testing for signs over the past months. I believe Mohammed agrees."

"That's right, Sun Tzu. I do agree. Because I originated in Mecca, Arabia, and established the religion of Islam, my similar miracles have been subject to Muslim devotion and reflection dating to the first millennium. So, I have the chops—to use your phrase—to join my fellows in our appraisal of your activities in the fifth dimension. And I think Abraham also agrees."

"Yes, I do, Mohammed. You and I come from different belief systems but similar circumstances. I came along a little later as the first of the Hebrew patriarchs; however, I had great influence according to the biblical book of Genesis. It was God who called upon me to find a new nation in an *undesignated land, and almost three thousand years later, my activity remains the biggest land grab in history."*

"Oh, give it a rest, Abraham! Even if you got the land, your engineering skills are so shallow, urban planning is impossible."

"Hang on, everybody! In 610, it was I, Abraham, who was visited by the angel Gabriel and informed that I was the messenger of God."

"Yeah, right!"

"What do you think, Lucifer?"

"Well, as John and Aquinas work through the spin, at least neither of them claims to be the official pipeline to God. If anybody talks to God around here, it's me. It was I, Lucifer the Devil, who had the official smackdown with God . . . and we called it a draw. He got the house, and I got the foundation . . . I think Sun Tzu gets that. Right, Sun Tzu?"

"That's right, Lucifer, you and God split the card and gave us yin yang to the Way of the Tao. What do you think, Aquinas? You are very quiet."

"Well, have any of you been looking at John for the past several minutes?"

"No . . ."

"Abraham, look to the left. Over by the first station next to the gate. What do you see?"

"Holy Mother of God! I stand in disbelief! I've never seen the cosmic power of a light beam rider! Aquinas, is that John??"

"Yep . . ."

"What are you doing over there, John!?"

"I'm talking to Merrilee. What the f . . . are you guys doing?

75

I call for the question. "Have we had enough, or do you guys have some more tests in mind?"

Aquinas responds with *"No."*

There was a lingering harmonic effect where I was standing. I can only see Aquinas, but I knew everyone else was there. They were looking at the ground, the Devil being very focused on the overriding actuality—*what did John just do?* Nobody was willing to advance the question. After all, they are Seraphim and, in some cases, very powerful, so they don't embarrass themselves in front of such a minor league player who just gave a first-hand example of classical physics across the full spectrum.

I decide to let them off the hook.

"Gentlemen, about 440 BCE, Pythagoras was trying to thread the needle between mathematics and philosophy. He came upon the idea that there was *harmony* between angles and spheres. He also was gender-specific in schools. Unlike most thinkers of the time, as he established schools, he laced his faculty with women, treating both men and women as minor examples of numbers—Odd and Even. Odd numbers were men, and Even numbers were women.

"When I wrote *Fight for the Quantum*, I was studying Pythagoras. It occurred to me that this guy was idiosyncratic in thought experiments. He was a daydreamer. I thought if he sees a relationship between angles and spheres, could that relationship be rationally transferred to acoustics? After all, he saw women as even numbers. So, five hundred years before Christ, he was seeing women as commonsensical, that is, rational.

"I understood that in cosmology, an equation always prevails. All equations seek balance; therefore, the cosmos represents the rational root of its existence. Pythagoras viewed women as rational numbers. To Pythagoras, women represented a form wherein their number can also be simple fraction integers. Not in men—no simple fractions. Only complex symbols conjoined to numbers.

"So, only women had the circuitry to reduce stress from acoustic emission. Men would need to give the structure some ongoing chink-a-dare to justify the male self-assumption.

"While I'm aggregating these ideas, Merrilee identifies my voice frequency on Wisdom, a social media app. Within the first moments, we knew it was 'Game On.' She was followed in rapid succession by two other women—Kelly Swensen and Jacqueline Way.

"Now I was connected to a Trinity of women supporting Pythagorean Theory.

"This connection placed everything ad hoc to the magnitude of the big picture. These three women and I could play in infinite acoustics.

"I had come full circle. Getting away from exceeding the limits of restraint in business and using research from seventeen years in the academy, I was finally walking into the light.

"And a half hour ago, Merrilee decided to jack my aura 700 nanometers into the EM Spectrum."

76

As his Seraphim table mates retire back to heaven, Aquinas remarks on Marquis de Lafayette: *"It just occurred to me, John, that when Lafayette came from France to join George Washington, he was only twenty years old. With zero experience in just about everything except cafés and bars, he was appointed a Major General in the Continental Army. Then he manages to chase British Commander Lord Cornwallis across Virginia and pick up a British surrender at Yorktown. The war was over. He was hailed as the 'Hero of Two Worlds.' Is that the game you are playing here, John—keeping your foot in both doors?"*

"Aquinas, are you implying I have zero experience?"

"Well, in relative terms, it's like Lucifer said, 'You don't even move the needle.'"

"Yeah, Aquinas, but we kicked your ass with those 700 nanometers into the EM Spectrum!"

"Yes, you did. John, tell me about these other women in your acoustic queue."

"I will. Let's walk."

"Okay."

"There is a woman in Canada who came in on a sublunary EM frequency when she heard me speak. She was researching changes in the 432hz heart frequency range. She called herself Jacqueline. Jacqueline Way from British Columbia, Canada.

"Her idea was that random acts of kindness change the human heart frequency for the better. She called her organization 365Give. She brought her story to TED Talks and drew one of the largest audiences in TED Talk history.

"Her interest in heart frequency and our corporate technical capacity lent itself to equipment for sample group quantitative testing. You see, when I wasn't fishing for Seraphim, my partners and I were talking to contract officers at the United States Department of Defense. We were SAM CAGE Code federal contractors. Very interesting secret stuff. In some cases, top secret. Even today, I'm an advisor to a new kinetic energy company's board of directors. I suppose you already know all this stuff, Aquinas, but I got to speculate that the games we play beat the hell out of your 13th Century Arrows and Slings.

"Anyway, Jacqueline and I became conversation regulars, and, just like with Merrilee, it became all about recognizing our frequencies on the margins. And how we experienced a kind of *morphic resonance* in unison. That's a phenomenon researched by Rupert Sheldrake—that nature is habitual as opposed to being governed by 'laws.' Unlike Jacqueline, he postulated his position on TED Talks and was banned. Until tens of thousands of his followers complained.

"Jacqueline and I were coming up with astoundingly similar reference points.

Eventually, that led us to her Owl and my Hawk. Now we had birds in the frequency mix that were revered because they could presage events, especially the Athene nocturia in Greece. Jacqueline tells me she has an Owl chatting her up from a tree behind her house. And I admit to spending months with an injured *accipitriform*. That's Hawk in street language. I start stacking '*living with my Hawk*' stories in our conversations.

"The hawk and I would look at each other for hours, trading eye signals and neck rotations. I would exercise her (never did know the gender) by tying a fishing line around one leg and letting the hawk fly away to be reeled back in when we had enough. The hawk and I lived together, ate together, perched together. When the flying exercise patterns were dynamic enough to satisfy my concern, I took the hawk to a mountain ridgeline in the Mission Range of Western Montana and let her go. She flew high, then circled, then did a low pass over my head. I waved her off. She did a wingover looking back, and I cried. Finally, she took for the horizon. I don't remember how long I stood there. My hand was bleeding. Her talons sliced through as she rotated off my fingers. It didn't matter. And it changed me forever.

"Then, Jacqueline's mystery Owl gets sick, *and along comes this shaman.*"

77

Vancouver, British Columbia, is the largest city in Western Canada. The city supports a global mix of culture, education, and commerce. Vancouver is a major Pacific Port, utilizing 16,000 hectares of water with hundreds of kilometers of shoreline. But to Jacqueline Way's Owl and John LaCasse's conversation with Aquinas, its importance rests in its intersecting the traditional lands of Salish Coast First Nations.

"So, you see, Aquinas, what was about to happen was me watching Jacqueline and her Owl show me the river of life. Were you there, Aquinas, when the coyote walked into the spirit circle at Moses Lake?"

"No, but you should be happy to know your Moses Lake Coyote story is among the most famous of all Seraphim stories."

"Well then, you will enjoy this because here we go again.

"Indigenous communities have evolved and refined their practices over several thousand years. They understand mythologies and traditional knowledge. They view everything as interconnected, thereby coupled through natural ecosystems. They look at planet Earth as alive and having a soul. Jacqueline's Owl is in that system with everything else.

"So, Jacqueline told me about the Owl. How he sits in the tree and looks at her—just looks at her. *It's riveting,* she says. She knows, and I know, the Owl in mythology can foreshadow events. So, what's going on behind her house? The Owl is famous for its presage of death. Is someone going to die? Jacqueline doesn't bring it up.

"This goes on for days. The Owl begins to get visually smaller. Like sinking into itself. Then, one evening, the Owl begins to hoot—but low and slow. The hoot frequency Jacqueline describes as dire and frightening. Her entire family seemed called to the back of their house to watch the Owl. Eventually, the Owl became quiet but looked at everyone with increased intensity.

"Jacqueline recalls that around 11:30 P.M., everyone went to bed.

"Every morning, Jacqueline gets up early to exercise and meditate. So, it's barely light at her Vancouver latitude. She gets up off the floor, mat in hand. She places the mat on a chair, walks to the kitchen, and starts some coffee. She wanders to a window as she waits for her coffee. As she addresses the window, she is looking at a man, not in Native regalia but with a commanding Native presence, standing about thirty feet off the front of the house. She has no feel for why the hell—except she does. She opens the door, and the Salish Man says:

'I have come for Uwila.' Jacqueline walks toward the man. And he asks for Uwila.

"As she relates the story, I can tell both she and the Native man are in complete unison over what's going on. When they walk around to the back of the house and toward the tree where the Owl was perched, they saw the Owl's body as relaxed. He kind of did a fluff, and then he fell out of the tree. Dead on the ground.

"Jacqueline is standing in amazement. The Native man says, 'Uwila has honored you by dying in your house. Well, *at* your house.' And he smiled.

"She asked, 'What should we do?'

"And with all the command of a deity, the Native man says, 'We will make him ready, and you will keep his honor.'

"Then she watched the man with the precision of a taxidermist dress out the owl, placing its head, wings, and tail in front of Jacqueline. 'You will keep these,' he said. 'They will be good for you and your family.'

"Aquinas, Christine and I are core members of the Burke Museum on the University of Washington campus. We have worked on a T-rex, carefully removing sandstone. My father was an amateur taxidermist. I know how this stuff is supposed to play out. This man was seamless with the Owl he called Uwila. His dress cuts, as Jacqueline described, were in another dimension. The entire affair was as it should be. The Owl called to the tribe to say he was dying. Jacqueline and her family were kind and respectful. The tribe sent their man. Jacqueline has the icon of Uwila.

"Once again, we witness the comingling frequency among Beings."

"So, John, the coyote walks into the Spirit Circle at just the right moment. Merrilee has unimaginable EM power. Jacqueline has Uwila, the Owl, deciding to die in her yard and signals the Salish Shaman accordingly.—what else you got?

78

"What I have is a walking-talking Euclidean thought experiment: Kelly Swensen.

"One morning early, I was about to begin my conversation on social media when a call came in on the platform. I'm not ready, but I pick it up. I hear a woman's voice say that she waits for my program every morning. That she just wanted to say that—to tell me that. I'm flummoxed but grateful. I am about to open the show with a conversation about Jim Holt's book *When Einstein Walked with Gödel* at Princeton, so I keep this woman on the air with me and begin . . . well, holy shit, when she spoke, it was like I was rocketing around in the aspect's infinite dimensional systems. I was thinking maybe she made a mistake and thought I was at the Max Planck Institute.

"After the program, I get a call from Martin-Jon Garcia in Chicago. He does a morning program Tao Te Ching (Tow). He was developing a *Follow the Tow* iPhone app for us pedestrians. He heard Kelly and me earlier. Garcia tells me *she is the real deal and to pay attention*. I shoot back with my academic best 'No shit, Sherlock!'

"Martin-Jon Garcia and I became friends and are to this day.

"So, Aquinas, I decide to follow the advice of Garcia, and Kelly becomes a daily event. That decision developed into morning walks with her in the Arizona desert. I don't want to overblow a presumption, but the walks took on the character of Einstein and Gödel walks across campus. As she walks, she is sending me Euclidean interpretations of desert flowers. One day I call for the question, 'Why did you call?'

"'Because you listen,' says Kelly Swensen.

"Kelly and I are becoming our version of empirical aesthetics. We drift along on the parabolic geometry of desert flowers.

"Kelly is difficult to describe in our conversation context, Aquinas, but she is the fifth dimension of unimaginable scope and capacity. She is in the Trinity. At least when she is not accusing me of selective amnesia for missing a morning walk in the Arizona desert.

79

"You spin a worthwhile story, John. These women are in your 'even number' binary oppositions. How you view the state of the human state. Among the Seraphim, we find a more balanced approach. Men are at least allowed in. But your 'trinity' is highly leveraged toward women, like one hundred percent. And, yet, every time you support a position, you use men. You don't see that as a confirmation bias? A kind of attitude polarization, maybe?

"Aquinas, society doesn't give me options. When I discuss my relationship with these women as being in dimensions outside the wire, some constructionist lab rat tells me I am operating in an 'illusory' correlation.

"So, I am now operating on the advice of famous Ashram thinkers in Mumbai. 'If you're having a bad day, John, Fuck-Em. Go home and get some sleep. There are no elegant roots today anyway.'

"I always enjoy closing my eyes and visualizing an Ashram bobblehead guru raising his hands in grace and saying, 'If you're having a bad day,' and so on. It just makes me smile.

"Holy Moses, John. How did you become so culturally irreverent!?"

"Simple enough, Aquinas. I came on this storied life wearing Herman Melville's 'White Jacket.'

"In the middle of the story, I had to *be cheery with my lads* for Captain Ahab until I became my own harpooner striking the whale. I will never get that blood out of my snout.

But to your question, men exploit women without regard for their strength and capacity. Among the top 100 luminaries for Metaphysics,

Epistemology, Ethics, Politics, and Aesthetics, there is one woman and ninety-nine men. That, my dear fellow, is confirmation bias.

"*Okay, John, point made. I think we should go back to the Sorbonne, where we first met, and get you positioned to become a fractional frequency light beam rider.*"

"Are you telling me, Aquinas, that there is a category for me in the Seraphim?"

"*Yes, a category of One. You are the only subject we are aware of who managed to hijack our control frequency. So, you are the number one Fractional Frequency Light Beam Rider. (FFLBR).*"

"Is that pronounced flubber, Aquinas?"

"*Ha-ha, John, no. It's way more sophisticated than that. In fact, in this year-end Seraphim package, we plan to have you included as a 'Bonus Poster Calendar.'*"

"Oh, that's cool, Aquinas. Do you plan to have my bare ass on a psychiatrist's couch in silk?"

"*No, John! We could never get that past committee.*"

"You're serious?"

"*Of course, I'm serious. I think the only Yes vote would be Lucifer. He likes that kind of stuff.*"

"*For the love of Mike!* Gerrymandering corruption in the Seraphim! Who knew?"

"*John, I haven't heard the, For the Love of Mike since 1918.*"

"I figured, Aquinas. Just another Gotcha from the *FFLBR.*"

As Aquinas and I arrive at the university's courtyard, Aquinas opens with, "John, as you and I are forever interlocutors, I would like to establish one rule of engagement, especially considering my history with the University of Paris/Sorbonne faculty. My fellows included Alexander of Hales, St. Bonaventure, and Albertus Magnus, among others. They would expect me to make good choices. So, maybe you could temper your answers toward more thought."

"What is that supposed to mean?"

"Well, for example, if I were to say Levi Strauss, you might say, 'I don't know why you would buy those. The 501 shrink-to-fit Jean is unpredictable, and they remain stiff for months.'

"Is that correct, John? Would you just jump in and say that?"

"Yeah, I probably would."

"Conversely, if you were to say Levi Strauss, I would most likely say, 'I think Strauss did as much for social science as anyone. Especially in the intellectual circle around Jean-Paul Sartre's café society existential pioneers like Heidegger, Husserl, and Merleau-Ponty.'

"You see, John, every circumstance is different. In that conversation, we better know whether the talk is around a Bavarian immigrant who arrived in San Francisco in 1850 during the Gold Rush or a Belgium-born French social anthropologist and leading exponent of structuralism.

"Also, John, I feel the trinity of important cosmic women you engage with—Kelly, Merrilee, and Jacqueline—would appreciate a little less hubris on your part. Especially coming from a first-order Throne."

"What are you going to do, Aquinas, get me in the cast with Emilia Clarke and Sophie Turner—maybe as a stand-in for Kit Harington?"

"No, John. You ARE a first-order Throne."

"And that is why, Aquinas?"

"John, look out on the Rue de La Sorbonne. What do you see? Did you notice the siren a while ago—an ambulance skidding to a stop?"

"I guess. Lots of action on the street today, Aquinas."

"John, do you see the pedestrian being worked on by the French ambulance EMTs?"

"Ummm . . . yes."

"That's you, John. The man on his back on Rue de La Sorbonne is you. You had a heart attack as we walked over here, and the EMTs can't bring you back around. You are about to be officially dead."

"What the Fuck are you saying, Aquinas!?"

"You're dead, John. D-E-A-D."

"Aquinas, for Christ's sake, we've been talking the whole way over here."

"John, I was trying to make a point, and I thought our conversation was going well. Why break the pentameter? Let's just keep talking."

"That's it, Aquinas? I just drop over dead, and we keep talking?"

"Yes, that's what happened, all right, John. You just dropped over dead."

"What the Fuck, Aquinas. Did it not occur to you to tell me I was dead?"

"Well, you weren't dead right away, John. It took about twelve minutes for you to make the break. I know you understand Dualism, here in the land of René Descartes, my friend. Your conscious Being did a sort of seamless transition."

"But why, Aquinas? Why now? Why here?"

"John, I've been doing this for almost nine hundred years. I don't always remember to pick up all my messages. I'm guessing the committee did a fast analysis of your profile. Probably decided to get you in under the wire. You know, before you set yourself up to be banned from Heaven, just like you kept getting tossed out of college."

"What about Christine? My family! My friends! What about them?"

"As I'm watching the EMTs rifle your wallet and pockets, you have something—a card. An international membership in the Neptune Society—yes?"

"That's right."

"So, you know, then, it's all handled. All contacts will be made. Neptune Society will scoop you up. Cook you to size and deliver you in a small box to Seattle."

"Holy shit, Aquinas. Let's sit down."

After a few minutes . . .

"I have an idea, John. Why don't we walk over to Shakespeare and Company on the river? Lots of good photon refraction there. Maybe I can get a heads-up from the committee."

As we walk, I am reflecting on being dead. So, I ask, "What's next, Aquinas?"

"Well, John, once I get clearance, you will check in and receive a quick scan of your back and shoulders for wings. You must understand these are just Throne wings. No associated power comes with it."

"What the hell good is that, Aquinas? Just a bunch of feathers flopping around on my back?"

"Just listen. Practice listening for a while.

"Well, John, we're here."

"No, we're not. The bookstore is way up the street, past the café."

"I know, John. I want to show you something."

"Okay."

"Look at the wall across from Shakespeare and Company."

"Okay."

"Now, I want you to think about being on the wall in front of the bookstore. Just think about it right there—please—NOWHERE ELSE!"

So, I close my eyes, I guess anyway, and focus on that wall. And, "OMG Aquinas. I'm right there—on the wall. Just like that. On the wall!"

"Indeed! So, you see, John, it won't be just feathers flopping around on your back."

I smile and reach a hand to my shoulder. Nothing yet . . . hmmm.

Aquinas spots a barge . . .

"Here comes a French Canal Barge," he says. I don't know why he keeps saying the whole thing—French Canal Barge.

Then he says, *"Let's see if I can hook someone."*

Hook someone, I'm thinking; it is probably time for Aquinas to go home.

As the barge swings to our point on the river, all the conditions reappear and apply. Mist and smoke. Refracted light and beams off the water. Now it seemed almost routine. The obvious power. The light refraction. The reality of unbridled speed. There he was. On the beam, just like before. He walks up the beam.

Aquinas makes a sort of yes sir pirouette and vectors left.

And Lucifer says, *"Hi John, you might remember, I said we'd meet again."*

I glance at Aquinas and say,

"Yes Sir!"

THE END OF BOOK ONE

REFERENCES

George, L.J. (1997). Why the need for Indian welfare act? *Journal of Multi-Cultural Social Work*, (5), 165-175.

United Nations (UN) Economic and Social Council. Indigenous Peoples and Boarding Schools: A Comparative Study Permanent Forum on Indigenous Peoples and Boarding Schools. (2010, April 19-30). *Declaration of Rights of Indigenous Peoples,* (2010:E/C.19),. http;www.un.org/esa/socdev/unpfi/documents/E.C.19.2010.6%20EN.pdf

ACKNOWLEDGMENTS

Being grateful to friends and family for providing the real-life platform for this book seems a little thin. I mean, considering the exceptional quality of input. However, it's a starting point. Many authors have detailed discussions with experts in their field. Scientists who drizzle over existential algorithms for direction. And these people are acknowledged with thanks. But, in the early years of my various careers, not much led to constructionist algorithms. What did happen was men and women would nudge me along my path. They were like broom sweepers in Curling. They made the ice of life just a little faster.

The best tactical positioning statement I ever heard was from Pam Martin—a 40-year career Lead Cabin Service person on heavy jets. She had two drunks in the first-class front-row Boeing 747 from Seattle to Tokyo. They called for more drinks. "Gentlemen, one of my jobs in the case of an emergency is to get passengers off the aircraft. If you guys are drunk, I'm not going to bother."

I remember one morning when Bob Martin brought his son Don into the office. Bob was a key customer and friend. A Vice President of Weyerhaeuser and a Renaissance man on any yacht.

Bob stood there with his son and said, "I want you to make something out of this kid."

I put him to work selling boats. He was terrible. But that's where it stopped because he was good at everything else. New yacht christenings became magic because of Don. I became a better pool shot because of Don. And I learned the real meaning of Copland's *Fanfare for the Common Man*.

Eventually, Don became a Big Ocean-Big Ship Captain and an attorney. Ended up running all Jones Act operations for ConocoPhillips. Yep, "make something out of this kid," Bob said. Umm—, the bigger probability he made something of me.

One day this guy walks into McGinnis Yacht Sales. The salesman who had the up thought he looked like a flake. So, I stepped in. I was new and got the slag from the seasoned brokers. The guy wanted a starter boat and bought the first boat we saw. A 54' motor sailor.

Then he bought a 46' Chris-Craft. Then he bought an 80' Grebe Flush Deck Motor Yacht. Then he bought a 60' commercial boat and kept it at Fishermen's Terminal in Seattle. Then he bought a 183-foot multiple-deck research ship which became the platform for adventure movies on Discovery Television. He would have me meet him at Boeing Field in his Lear. We would fly to almost South America, and he would buy another boat. Put a captain aboard and meet the new boat in Alaska.

Monday morning, I'm still asleep in our master stateroom. It was early. This Hughes jet helicopter comes in low and slow. I get this downdraft *Whomp, Whomp, Whomping, next* to my boat. My phone rings. "Want to go up the Inside Passage this morning?" I drive to Boeing Field. We head for Canada. At Campbell River, British Columbia, we need fuel. The field is closed for low visibility—thick fog. But we need fuel. We get on the radio and call YBL Campbell River. The tower understands the problem. We are on the shoreline hovering at street light altitude.

YBL Campbell River starts our approach vectors.

"Come off the water and up Highway 19A."

"Roger that."

"See Gas & Go just north of Jubilee Parkway."

"Roger that."

"Follow Jubilee Parkway West and see U-Haul Store."

"Roger that."

"Cross Inland Island Highway going west."

"Roger that."

"Go 2,000 feet along Jubilee Parkway—See the Tower."

"Roger That."

We get fuel. Canadian Customs kisses our paper, and we continued to Alaska on the deck at +/- 500 feet altitude. We landed the helicopter on his boat. A small crowd is gathering. As we are spooling down, he says, *You're the owner. I'm the pilot.* Then steps out from behind the collective, and as he walks through the people toward the bar, he looks back with a smile: "I'm just the pilot. He's the owner."

I knew the answers, but what the hell, Ron? What about a cold beer?

Ron was building one new Motel every 72 hours across the United States.

Ron Rivett, Super-8 Motels

I had a small office in the AGC Building on Lake Union, Seattle. A shared space. I just opened my shop for business, and money was tight. My office was on the third floor. Herman Sarkowsky's office was on the entire ninth floor. He is coming down from nine in the elevator, and I get on at three. Herman asks How I'm doing. As I listened to his next comments, whatever I said was lost in the wind. "I'm building the new AT&T Gateway Center downtown, so I'm leaving the AGC Building. Would you like my office space?"

Well, that was silly. I can barely handle a file cabinet, and Sarkowsky is offering me the ninth floor?

I declined his offer, and he says, *I give you the option,* and he walks into the AGC lobby.

The AT&T Gateway Center goes up—is among the tallest buildings on the West Coast and a Seattle landmark. Herman moves out of the AGC building. I sit on the AGC third floor with a box lunch and a shared secretary.

One day the AGC Building Manager walks into my space.

"I understand you have an option on the Ninth Floor?"

I sold my option to a law firm. With the money, I opened a new street-level office on Westlake Avenue and spun deals all over the world.

Herman put me in his Citation 10 to San Diego for a look at Light Horse, a 100-foot Flush deck motor yacht. It was a million dollars. He liked the boat. We are standing on the dock waiting for the ride back to the airplane. Herman reaches into his coat pocket and pulls out his checkbook. "What are you in for, John?"

"$100,000," I say.

He writes the check and hands it to me. Our ride is idling at the curb.

Frank Orrico owns seventeen shopping centers. He walks into my office imagining a fifty-foot idea.

We talk. I take the idea to a graphic artist. Frank comes back. "Is that it?" I ask. "Yes."

We start building him a fifty-foot pilot house sedan. Frank knows Bill Boeing.

We start building Bill, a fifty-foot pilot house sedan.

The story ends up a double truck in the Sunday *Seattle Times*. Makes my mother cry.

A guy reads the Orrico and Boeing story and calls. "Will you build me a seventy-five-foot Cockpit Motor Yacht?" "Humm . . . yep."

I met Brian Bourgoin when he was diving for treasure in the Caribbean. He was on top of his game. He still is. He knew a guy setting up for an expedition. Brian shoehorned me into the deal. I brokered the ship. That became contracts that must remain secret—it's a world-class treasure, after all. Brian kept my heart in Montana, as he is a hunting regular in the Big Sky State, and his family owns property around Sula, north of Missoula. He brings me rocks when he comes back to Washington. Anyone who watched *Yellowstone* on television knows Brian in actuality.

Jim Chrysler flies floats. So do I. So did Lana Kurtzer.

In the Pacific Northwest yacht business, float planes are like cabs in the city. Kurtzer taught me how to fly floats. Chrysler taught me how to stay alive on floats. Both these pilots are in the "Fly the Biggest Piece Back" category. Both A&E Mechanics. Both Check Pilots. Both mix humor with experience. . . .

Kurt (Kurtzer) used to have me do mandatory flight maneuvers over his girlfriend's house. That way she would know they were going dancing that evening. Kurt was tall. Barely fit in the airplane, so he would fold himself up and nap. I wondered about that. "Oh no, I know what you're doing. I can feel it—smell it—just don't puke on my pants."

A guy stuck his plane in a tree in Alaska. Jim (Chrysler) got a hop north. Pulled the airplane out of the tree and flew it back to Seattle.

One morning a family was anxious about a scenic flight around Puget Sound. Jim was busy. I was up getting ready for a check ride. They arrive. I'm on a T-Craft float pumping out standing water. The family mingles. One of them is in a chair. They roll him down the dock. Jim is sort of caped over the guy. Helping as required. I squinted my eyes. Shaded them from the morning sun. The guy in the chair was Stephen Hawking. His handler wanted the best pilot available anywhere—well, of course.

My boys and I met up with Hawking that evening and spoke at length through his equipment. It was amazing!

Jim Chrysler coming around the Space Needle on approach to Lake Union made the 2022 Picture of the Year for *The Seattle Times*. He's got to be the best bush pilot in North America. Stephen Hawking thought so.

In many categories of pioneers in big yachts, I am the last man standing. To those men and women who gave me the platform.—Thank You—RIP

When Christine sent me back to school, my entire life changed. I became a student of the biggest ideas in the universe. Her capacity to love me, despite me, provided the foundation for the most interesting ride in the universe. And that is a large slice of this story . . .

There are people in my life who endure my idiosyncratic vestments.

Christine Burgoyne is first among equals. A woman of extraordinary breadth and scope who is not from this world because if she were, she would have left me behind long ago.

Jennifer Sullivan, my gift from God. The woman who helped my dying son drink from a straw and pee in the street.

Ross Stewart Andrew, for killing the Fifth Horseman in the Apocalypse.

Pat Rhodes, Herman Sarkowsky, Steve Sarkowsky, and Shiah Sarkowsky, for being in my corner against jaw-dropping odds.

Bill Boeing for teaching me how to drink a $20,000 glass of wine.

Mike Marchand, Ruth Jackson, Ellen Fitzgerald, David Frappier, Sandy Chapman, Jim Nigg, Dan Vanlaar, Christina McDonald, Robert DeCicco, Joann Feher, Mike Burgess, Rosie Roppel, Connie Hall, Tom Feher, Chelsea Burgoyne, Phil Stanley, Shiah Sarkowsky, Morgan Barry, Laura Loomis, Bill Johnson, Charles Loomis, Tere Paine, Anita Machina, Debbie Dechine, Robin Chapman, Sharon Kirks, Allison Feher, Michael Machina, Martin-Jon Garcia, and Libby Kelleher Carr, for perspective.

Doctors Baldwin, Biehl, Bolen, Fellows, Horan, Ingraham, Kuppusamy, Smith, and Stone, for keeping me alive.

My parents, Marie J. LaCasse and John B. LaCasse, and my grandmother Armosa LaCasse, whose unconditional love gave me self-confidence, broad understanding, and experience both in nature and culture.

ABOUT THE AUTHOR

John LaCasse is a board advisor at Constructis Roadway Energy, host of the *Tension* podcast, and author of *Fight for the Quantum* and *After Your Children Die*. He enjoys membership in The American Association of University Professors, academic honorariums in Kappa Delta Pi, and Golden Key, with a biographical profile in MARQUIS Who's Who®. He lives in Seattle with his life partner, Christine Burgoyne.

Barbara Kindness began her writing career in 2nd grade when she was the weather reporter for her class newspaper. Future endeavors included a 15+ year career at the U.S. Information Agency, Microsoft's Encarta Reference Suite, as Media Liaison for World Champion and Olympic Silver Medal figure skater Rosalynn Sumners, and with various freelance assignments for other authors, including actor Hugh O'Brian.

www.ingramcontent.com/pod-product-compliance
Lightning Source LLC
Chambersburg PA
CBHW010929180426
43194CB00045B/2838